"A well-articulated and very posit[...] happen when we return to the f[...] valid, principles upon which this [...]

—*U.S. Congressman Ron Paul, Texas, Republican*

"If you care about this country and its potential, read this book! Have conversations you have never had, feel hope that you have never felt, and then GET POLITICAL!"

—*Kara Anastasio, Democratic Candidate, U.S. House of Representatives, 7th District, Ohio*

"The need to bring government back to the people calls for a new revolution—one of decentralization. Democracy is maintained when decision making and accountability are at the local level, which is the most efficient and most economical way of governing. We CAN Restore America by a return to government by the people."

—*David Miller, Iowa State Senator, Republican*

"Remembering what America was yesterday strengthens the foundation we stand on today. Cleveland and Noyes have recaptured the passion and vision of our Founding Fathers; retracing politics back to morality, civility, and a government for the people."

—*Gary E. Johnson, Governor of the State of New Mexico*

"What a joy to discover a new breed of politician who wants to expand our freedoms, enliven communities AND save our environment! Clyde Cleveland and Ed Noyes give us a striking vision of what is possible in politics—and in our lives. Iowa could easily become the state to emulate. Hallelujah!"

—*Jennifer Read Hawthorne, Co-author,*
Chicken Soup for the Woman's Soul

"Intelligent, articulate, compassionate, insightful, spiritual, ecological, inclusive, promoting sovereignty and freedom, built on a foundation of love. A far cry from the top down federal government that is the best money can buy."

—*Jeff Hutner, Writer, Producer and Director,*
Practical Visionaries: A Documentary
Celebrating Genius in Service to Life

"Clyde Cleveland and Edward Noyes have drawn a clear map to political freedom and economic prosperity. This book makes me want to move to Iowa."

—*G. Edward Griffin, Documentary File*
Producer and Author of The Creature from Jekyl
Island: A Second Look at the Federal Reserve

"Cleveland and Noyes have a vision for America that must be heard and carefully considered. This book lays out a game plan that will restore our environment and change our country forever."

—*David A. Kidd, President of Earth Share, Founder of American Free Tree Program (12 million trees planted by volunteers), 2002 Independent Candidate for Ohio House District 52, and Author of* Growing America, The Story of a Grassroots Activist *(available October 2002)*

"I have known Clyde Cleveland for 18 years. His passion for his work is infectious and his brilliance will transform the Iowa economy. This book describes the authors' vision to make Iowa the role model for how to govern the people for the people."

—*John Douillard, D.C., Ph.D., LifeSpa; Author of* Body, Mind, and Sport *and* The Three-Season Diet; *former Director of Player Development for the New Jersey Nets*

"Cleveland and Noyes have real solutions, and anybody can understand them. They are brilliant, and they write in plain language, with passion—for our country, our world and all of our lives."

—*Lynn Waters, CEO, Global Verde, LLC*

"This is, simply put, one of the most inspiring books I have ever read. We must not only read it, but also learn from it and act upon that knowledge. It is our responsibility as citizens of this great country to help RESTORE our constitutional, libertarian principles based on natural law. Spread this message. Most importantly, elect citizens to office who will preserve, protect, and defend our Constitution—and our God-given (not government-given) liberties."

—*Robert Ewing, Vice Chairman, Ohio Natural Law Party*

"The ship of state is floundering under the weight of big government and a storm of oppression. This book is the procedural manual for getting our state (and our country) back on course. The prescriptions are simple, powerful, and effective because they are based on natural law."

—*John Freeberg, Developer of Abundance*
Eco-Village, Jefferson County, Iowa

"With individual dreams of personal freedom, health, and prosperity, courageous people take the road less traveled to Iowa. Their good ideas and wholesome respect for work can rebuild our rural economy, not from government handouts, but with targeted global enterprise. With Cleveland and Noyes in Des Moines, far-sightedness will find welcome here."

—*Lynn McKeever, J.D., Executive Coach, and Business*
Owner, Lynn McKeever & Company, Grinnell, Iowa

ReStoring *the* heart *of* America

A RETURN TO GOVERNMENT BY *THE* PEOPLE

by Clyde J. Cleveland

and Edward F. Noyes, J.D.

Better Books

Restoring the Heart of America—A Return to Government by the People

Editor: Kristine Ellis
Cover Design: Jody Majeres
Layout and Production: Kris Anderson

Cleveland, Clyde J. and Noyes, Edward F. –
    Restoring the Heart of America: A Return to Government by the People / Clyde J. Cleveland and Edward F. Noyes, J. D.

p. cm.

Includes bibliographic references and index.

ISBN 1-886656-09-6

Library of Congress Catalog
Card Number: (I'll supply this)

1. Politics   2. Iowa
3. Public office   4. Political parties   I. Title

Publisher: Better Books, LLC. Fairfield, IA 52556

Printed and bound in the United States of America

06 05 04 03 02   10 9 8 7 6 5 4 3 2 1

"Look at the entire world. Which countries contain the most peaceful, the most moral, and the happiest people? Those people are found in the countries where the law least interferes with private affairs; where government is least felt; where the individual has the greatest scope, and free opinion the greatest influence; where administrative powers are fewest and simplest; where taxes are lightest and most nearly equal, and popular discontent the least excited and the least justifiable; where individuals and groups most actively assume their responsibilities, and, consequently, where the morals of admittedly imperfect human beings are constantly improving; where trade, assemblies, and associations are the least restricted; where labor, capital, and populations suffer the fewest forced displacements; where mankind most nearly follows its own natural inclinations; where the inventions of men are most nearly in harmony with the laws of God; in short, the happiest, most moral, and most peaceful people are those who most nearly follow this principle: Although mankind is not perfect, still, all hope rests upon the free and voluntary actions of persons within the limits of right; law or force is to be used for nothing except the administration of universal justice."

—*Frederic Bastiat*, The Law (*June 1850*)

About the Authors

Clyde J. Cleveland is a successful entrepreneur with a passion for restoring our natural resources and securing individual freedom. His enterprises have brought more than $27 million of venture capital to Iowa, directly and indirectly creating thousands of jobs. Clyde co-founded the Fairfield, Iowa, "Evening a Month for America" constitutional study group in 1999. This program, dedicated to educating the community on the founding principles of the nation, led to his decision to run for governor.

After nearly 17 years of working within criminal justice, **Edward F. Noyes, J.D.,** has a deep-seated commitment to reforming the system so that it is genuinely effective as well as a reflection of spiritual principles. Ed opened his private practice in Fairfield, Iowa, in 1985, and now specializes in the areas of criminal defense, family law, and civil causes of action. In 1995, Ed produced one of the first local cable access programs in Iowa, "Community Empowerment, Rediscovering Our Unlimited Resources." The program reflects Ed's faith in communities and the vision of the Founding Fathers.

Constitutional scholar **Richard Campagna, J.D.,** is a multidisciplinary professional with a long and distinguished record in public and community service. He is an attorney, psychological counselor, college instructor, linguist, and international businessman. He holds several degrees, is fluent in six languages, and is an accomplished legal, literary, and medical interpreter. Richard's belief in Libertarian principles and staunch support for our constitution and the common law have never wavered.

Table of Contents

Chapter 17. Guns and Peace:
Restoring a Natural Right 239
Clyde J. Cleveland and Edward F. Noyes, J.D.

Chapter 18. Health Care:
Promoting Preventative Care 251
Clyde J. Cleveland and Edward F. Noyes, J.D.

Chapter 19. Monetary System:
Reverting to Real Value 259
Clyde J. Cleveland and Edward F. Noyes, J.D.

Foreword

We have a bold vision for our state.

- Imagine Iowa with a prosperous economy, a reasonable property tax, and no state income tax.

- Envision thriving communities that draw young families in search of small farms and a rural lifestyle for their children.

- Picture a business climate that spurs entrepreneurs to rate Iowa as an ideal place for new business.

- Think of our state being energy self-sufficient, dependent primarily on renewable energy sources, with beautiful parks and clean rivers and lakes that draw visitors from across the country.

- Imagine Iowa governed by people who recognize individual liberties above all else.

This is the Iowa we can create—with your help.

Clyde Cleveland and Ed Noyes are running for governor and attorney general of Iowa to begin turning this vision into reality. It will require true reform but it can be done. And once we achieve it here in Iowa, the rest of the country will look to us to lead the reform of the nation.

Central to our vision of reform is the belief that restoring the fundamental governing principles of individual liberties will lead to prosperity. But there is no time to lose. Not only are the two major political parties taking the state down a path of destruction, our way of life is under assault by a national government and corporate game plan that does not include most Iowans.

I don't know about you, but I'm tired of seeing negative articles in the national press about Iowa. Articles like the one in the *New York Times* in which Elizabeth Becker wrote: "Huge government subsidies encourage large-scale farmers to cultivate their lands to the hilt. That has meant more intense applications of fertilizers, pesticides and herbicides... The situation is particularly acute in Iowa... As a result, there have been 152 fish kills in Iowa over the past six years—leaving 5.7 million fish floating dead in rivers and lakes—and temporarily closing half the state's beaches last year." ("Big Farms Making a Mess of U.S. Waters, Cities Say," Feb. 10, 2002)

Or maybe you read about the PricewaterhouseCoopers 2002 "Money Tree" study. Every year the company does a study on venture capital investments, state by state. This statistic is an excellent indicator of the overall vitality of a state's economic vitality. In recent years, Iowa ranked 50th out of 50 states in venture capital invested. You can't get any lower than that, right? Think again. Iowa now accounts for 0.005 percent of the country's venture capital, putting us in 51st place! We've been passed by Puerto Rico!

So what is our current crop of politicians doing about this sad situation? Every two years the Cato Institute, a respected Washington, D.C., think tank, evaluates the economic policies of all 50 governors, comparing their fundamental policies on economic growth. The 2000 report lists two As, a few Bs, a lot of Cs, a handful of Ds, and 3 Fs. Well, guess where Iowa's current governor fell in this evaluation? A big F.

Does that mean the Democrats are responsible and the Republicans would fix things? Hardly. The Republicans control the legislature, and they had the governorship for decades.

Clearly, it is time for a change.

A thought-provoking editorial in the *Des Moines Register* (November 2001) by columnist David Yepsen aptly summarized what it would take to grow Iowa's economy. He said we need to:

- mobilize investment capital,

- nurture technology-based companies, and

- increase the vitality of Iowa's environment for starting new companies.

I found that editorial appealing and relevant because, in 1986, Clyde received a national award for his work in all three areas. Not only did he raise $22 million in investment capital that was invested primarily in Iowa-based, start-up companies—creating thousands of jobs—but those companies were environmentally friendly! For that he was named "America's First Socially Conscious Venture Capitalist" by Conscious Investors Ltd., an international investors organization.

Imagine having a governor who has actual experience in creating exactly the kind of jobs and entrepreneurial environment we have always longed for in Iowa!

When I first met Clyde, it didn't take long for me to recognize his leadership qualities and personal commitment to his ideals. A professional speaker and successful businessman, Clyde is totally enthusiastic about restoring the fundamental governing principles of our country. He also has a lifelong dedication to restoring our natural resources.

Clyde and Ed kicked off their campaigns on November 5, 2001. The response from the media was extraordinary. They immediately saw what I had seen—*candidates who could win an upset victory over the major parties*. During the week following their announcements to run for office, Clyde and Ed toured the state and received more media coverage than any other Iowa third-party candidate has received in a year of campaigning. I knew then that we were on the way.

An article by Jeff Ignacious in the *River City Reader* was indicative of people's receptiveness. Ignacious wrote: "Clyde Cleveland just might be a Ventura-like wild card in what's expected to be a hotly contested race for Iowa governor in 2002. Incumbent Tom Vilsack, a Democrat, is considered vulnerable…If he can get his name and ideas to the public, Cleveland could sneak, Ventura-like, into the governor's office." ("Shooting for the Top, Libertarian Gubernatorial Candidate Clyde Cleveland Is Smart and Polished. And He Has a Fighting Chance," Dec. 5, 2001)

When the political writers believe your candidate can win, you know you are striking a chord!

I hope you now understand why I am so excited about this campaign. If you too can imagine a better Iowa, take the time to read this book. Learn how we can restore the fundamental principles of government that made our country and our state so prosperous and free. Read about workable solutions to the tough problems the two major political parties just can't seem to handle.

I believe that once you read about the philosophical underpinnings of our approach to government and our incredibly innovative and creative ideas for making Iowa one of the most desirable places to live in our nation, you will want to be part of this campaign.

Mark Nelson
Chairman, Iowa Libertarian Party
May 2002

Introduction

When the great thinkers of the New World came together in the 1700s to create the United States of America, they envisioned a nation in which citizens had the absolute maximum amount of individual freedom. Their goal was based on their understanding of God's law as well as on their knowledge of government. They knew that the societies in which individual freedom was paramount were the societies in which the people were the happiest, most prosperous, and most evolved.

Criticizing our nation's Founders has become commonplace in today's America, but no one can argue with one simple fact: never in the history of the world was a country created with so much freedom. And for more than 200 years, that freedom has drawn refugees from throughout the world who come here in search of a better way of life.

We have much to be grateful for as U.S. citizens in the 21st century. We also have much to fear. Our government has strayed from the fundamental principles of freedom that served as the basis for the Declaration of Independence and the U.S. Constitution. No longer is it a government for, or of, the people.

We believe that many of the more perceptive Founders knew that their first attempt at government would not last, and that future generations would have to re-form the republic, using the knowledge gained from experience. It is with that intention—to return to the principles of natural law and restore our liberty, prosperity, and unalienable rights—that we have launched our campaigns for office.

This book explains our vision for restoring government to the people. You can also visit www.clevelandforgovernor.org to learn more about our campaigns.

The first section of *Restoring the Heart of America* explains our individual commitment to our course of action; the second section describes our philosophy, and the third section, our solutions for critical issues facing our state and nation. The last section of the book is all about you, explaining what you as an individual can do to ensure a victory for our team.

As you will see, we co-authored many of the chapters. Those that pertain to our individual areas of expertise carry our individual bylines. In addition, we asked Richard Campagna, Clyde's running mate and candidate for lieutenant governor, to explain how Iowa lost its sovereignty (Chapter 6). A constitutional scholar with a J.D. from Columbia Law School, Rich is eminently qualified to speak to this issue.

We hope you will think seriously about the information in this book and on our web site. We also hope that once you have thought about it, you will act on what you have learned. If our country is going to be saved, it will be saved by starting right here in America's heartland. The time is right, and the process is under way. But we cannot do it without you.

Our goal, after all, is to return government to *you*.

Acknowledgements

There are many people who have helped with this project, some worked with me directly on the book, some just gave me inspiration, and others kept our campaigns going so both Ed and I would have time to write: Kevin Litten, Mark Nelson, Rich Moroney, and all the Libertarian executive committee members of Iowa; Jim Lark of the national Libertarian Party; David Ballou; Lynn McKeever; Mark Hanson; Connie Huebner; Rae Bales; Karla Christianson; Joe Seehusen; Deborah Williamson; Jason Gross; Candice and Jeff Schneider; Bob Dekema; Susanna Felder; Art Atkinson; Heather Clark; Charlie Morenus; Kris Ellis; Warren Wechsler; Jody Majeres; Frank Ramsey; Chip Hoyt; Jason Switzer; Doug Marguia; Tony Camero; Arnold Mathias; Wayne and Pam Slowick; Jerrie Noyes; Regan Engle; Jay Marcus; Roger and Nancy Leahy; Rick Grote; Paul Damon; Wayne and Shirley Jones; J.D. Miller; James Bonner; Tom Hoyt; Don Burgmaier; John Harvey; Keating; James Lindner; Louis Engelhart; Jennifer Hawthorne; Richard Boddie; William Prouty; Dorian Punj; Larry and Ali Lioy; Ben and Sylvia Olson; William and Brenda Turner; and Nathan Otto.

I would also like to thank Gerry Gear, Kingsley Brooks and the other members of the Natural Law Party's executive committee for their early endorsement and support. Ed Moses of the Reform Party supplied me with valuable information on key issues. Ericka and Rich Dana of the Green Party were a big help with the energy chapter.

I would also like to thank all my associates on the ticket with me—Rich Campagna, Fritz Groszkruger, and Ed Noyes. Ed is going to be a great attorney general and he has been wonderful to work with as a co-author. Ed has been an incredible inspiration and source of knowledge from the first day we started discussing the issues in our constitutional study class three years ago. Rich's qualifications will make him the most effective lieutenant governor the state of Iowa has ever seen. Fritz, a true family farmer, is exactly what we need in a secretary of agriculture.

My father, Clyde S. Cleveland, taught me to think for myself from the age of two. I will never be able to express my gratitude for his lessons. My mother, Margaret Cleveland, who passed away a few years ago, would have been our biggest promoter. She gave me the ability to think through my heart, the greatest gift of all. Both parents were World War II Vets and extremely patriotic lovers of liberty.

My four children and brand-new grandson inspire me every day of my life in so many ways. I am doing all of this for them and their children. Finally, I wish to acknowledge my wife, Debbie, who has put up with me and my unique way of operating for 32 years!

Clyde Cleveland

My acknowledgements must be both human and divine. Without the Creator having endowed within us our inalienable nature, our eternal quest for freedom and truth would not exist.

I must acknowledge all those who have served the cause of liberty throughout history, including those brave souls who had the courage and insight to declare that this continent was to serve as an example for all others.

I give thanks to the Native Americans, who preserved this land in its pristine condition through their reverence of nature and commitment to the seventh generation. I pray that your efforts not be in vain.

To those humble ones who, facing the judgment of the law, came to me needing help, I say thank you for helping to remove judgment from my heart.

To my parents, Allen and Patricia Noyes, who, through their actions, showed me what was worthy of serving, I give you my deepest gratitude and respect.

I want to acknowledge Clyde Cleveland, a genuine, modern-day patriot, who not only allowed his commitment to freedom to manifest, but encouraged myself and others to demonstrate our commitment.

I must acknowledge my beautiful wife, Jerrie, who graces my life with her unconditional love, wisdom, and support.

To the fellow patriots who studied the Constitution each month with Clyde and me, I say, good job. May the fire of liberty which burned in our hearts spread throughout the land.

Finally, to those who read these words and feel the cause of freedom rising within, I acknowledge your spirit and ask that we may work together to lead this nation to the fulfillment of its highest destiny.

Edward Noyes

Section One:

"What I Can Do, I Should Do"

"All that is necessary for the triumph of evil is that good men do nothing."

—*Edmund Burke*

"I am only one, but I am one. I cannot do everything, but I can do something. And because I cannot do everything, I will not refuse to do the something that I can do. What I can do, I should do. And what I should do, by the grace of God, I will do."

—*Edward Everett Hale*

Chapter 1. Why I'm Running for Governor of Iowa

By Clyde J. Cleveland

In 1999, I had the opportunity to help organize a constitutional study program in Jefferson County, Iowa. The course, "An Evening a Month for America," started with a daylong seminar on the U.S. Constitution led by the president of the National Center for Constitutional Studies. After the presentation, we split into small groups that met every month to discuss reading materials and a monthly lesson.

This program literally changed the lives of those of us who participated. As we learned the principles of the freedom formula used by the Founders to frame the Constitution, we became inspired by their knowledge. More importantly, we imbibed the same spirit that led them to create a country that would be an example to the rest of the world.

As Ed and I sat with our friends discussing the principles that serve as the basis of our nation's Declaration of Independence and Constitution, we inevitably started asking ourselves, now what? We realized that most citizens don't have a clear understanding of these fundamental principles of freedom, because this knowledge has not been taught in our schools. We also realized that this knowledge was too important for us to sit idly by and let it be subverted. After many discussions regarding our duty to act, we finally made the decision to run for state office.

> "The principles on which we engaged, of which the charter of our independence is the record, were sanctioned by the laws of our being, and we but obeyed them in pursuing undeviatingly the course they called for."
>
> —*Thomas Jefferson, to Georgetown Republicans in 1809*

Our candidacies for governor and attorney general of Iowa were inspired by our heartfelt desire to finish the quest begun in the 1700s by those individuals who were divinely inspired to create a society based on freedom and individual sovereignty—a society built on the belief that it was humankind's natural right to exercise the free will given to each person by the Creator. Such a society, the Founders believed, would create the environment for achieving maximum human growth, an environment in which the human spirit could soar.

We believe that many of the Founders understood that achieving such an environment would take more than one attempt. As they may have suspected, the governing principles the Founders believed in so deeply have been eroded over time. We have launched our campaigns with the intention of enlivening these principles in the hearts and minds of the people. We recognize that this is the first step toward re-forming government.

"I will not refuse to do the something I can do" wrote 19th-century author and noted abolitionist Edward Everett Hale. That is the same conclusion Ed and I came to. The "something" we could do is to try and do whatever possible to re-instill the founding principles of our country.

That basic commitment is why we are running as Libertarians. We believe the fundamental principles of the Libertarian Party are the same fundamental principles that inspired the Founders.

The principles of the Libertarian Party are:

- The individual is born with free will and is sovereign.

- Each individual should be able to exercise his or her free will without restraint, as long as they do not limit or infringe upon the rights of others.

- The only excuse for the use of force would be self-defense.

- Society should be built upon the foundation of civil (noncoercive) organizations; government should be absolutely limited to only its essential function. This would involve the enforcement of laws that are very limited in number and whose sole purpose is to protect the fundamental natural rights of the citizens.

- The government that is best is the government that does the least.

I'm running for governor of Iowa to make fundamental changes in Iowa based on these principles. I believe that if we achieve the changes described in this book, we will spark a movement that will change the nation. The Midwest is often referred to as "America's heartland." We see the people of Iowa as the "heart" of the heartland.

The 18th-century French philosopher Charles Montesquieu was the first to make the connection between geographical conditions and the culture, temperament, and personality of the people who live in that particular area. He believed that the natural laws of a particular culture were directly tied to its geographical conditions. Iowa has deep, rich soil and a beautiful but simple landscape. Is this not a good description of our people?

Iowans are slow to anger, intuitive, friendly, courteous, averse to judging others, family oriented, rooted in the land, and deliberate in their decision making. I have been all over the country and I can truly say that Iowans have a depth and richness of character that is unmatched. This is the "heart" of the heartland and what sets the state apart

I believe that each of us carries within ourselves everything we need to know about how to live our lives. What is in our hearts is our blueprint for living. People in search of their individual truth need only to listen to their hearts.

Just so, as the heart of the heartland, the people of Iowa can reveal the blueprint for governing that is most in tune with our inner nature. If we do that, we will in effect be doing what the Founders described in the first paragraph of the Declaration of Independence: recreating a society based on "the laws of nature and of nature's God."

Ed and I know that speaking the truth is where our power is. Throughout our campaign, we will talk about Iowa's environmental, economic, and social problems, and the solutions we believe represent truth. We will not speak negatively of our opponents. We will however tell the truth about institutional corruption.

> "In a time of universal deceit, telling the truth is a revolutionary act."
>
> —*George Orwell*

Essentially, that is what Iowa faces—a pervasive institutional problem. Once an institution is past its prime, it no longer represents its original ideals. The institution becomes interested in maintaining power, and it does that by forming relationships with other institutions that in turn want to maintain their power.

This is what has happened to our major political parties. They maintain power by forming relationships with corporations, unions, professional associations, and other organizations. Amazingly, the same institutions usually support both major parties! That is why the Republican and Democratic parties become more alike all the time and why nothing of substance ever happens that is not guided by powerful special interests.

The following quote from U.S. Senator Zell Miller, a Democrat from Georgia, is remarkable for its candor: "Soft money—big money—from special interests to both parties controls things in a way that is nothing short of bribery. One of these days someone…is going to get through to the American people just how really messed up it has become. And when that happens, the American people are going to rise up like that football crowd in Cleveland and run both teams off the field." ("Zell Miller rips Washington bribery," by Jim Galloway, *Atlanta Journal-Constitution*, Jan. 15, 2002)

We all pay the price—literally—of the dysfunctional system Miller describes. In 1776, our country fought a revolution to gain its freedom from what was considered an oppressive government that had an excessive and unfair taxation. The level of taxation for the average colonial citizen in 1776 was 5 percent or less of what they earned. Today the average American family's tax bill—including all government taxes along with excise taxes and fees—is well over 50 percent of what they earn! This is the truth that is not being told to the American people.

Our tax money supposedly funds solutions to our national problems. But those problems are not being solved. In fact, in almost every instance, the problems become worse because of government involvement. For example, farm communities are suffering as a result of federal government policies that were created over the last 50 years to intentionally hasten the movement of the rural population to the cities (see Chapter 11). Iowans have been paying taxes to a government that has been trying to destroy our way of life. Does it make sense to continue to pay for our own destruction?

Our two-party political system and our entire government has become corrupt. We offer an alternative vision that is positive, inspiring and all-encompassing. And it is a completely different approach to politics than what you are accustomed to.

We know there is a better way. If the people of Iowa are willing to look at what our campaign has to offer, they will see that we have the solutions to the problems facing not just Iowa, but the nation. Our campaign is all about solving problems, returning your money and restoring your power. But we need to get the message out. People need to gain a clear understanding of the problems and our solutions. When they do, they will realize that we are the only party that can implement those solutions.

The next step is up to you. You will have to decide to get involved and help us win the election. If you do, Iowa will resonate truth, freedom, and love to the rest of the nation. You will have an Iowa you can be proud of, an Iowa that your children and grandchildren will not want to leave.

> "Life is at its noblest and its best when our effort cooperates with God's grace to produce the necessary loveliness."
>
> —*William Barclay*

"I looked ahead and saw the mountains there with rocks and forests on them, and from the mountains flashed all colors upward to the heavens. Then I was standing on the highest mountain of them all, and round about beneath me was the whole hoop of the world. And while I stood there I saw more than I can tell and I understood more than I saw; for I was seeing in a sacred manner the shapes of all things in the spirit, and the shape of all shapes as they must live together like one being. And I saw that the sacred hoop of my people was one of many hoops that made one circle, wide as daylight and as starlight, and in the center grew one mighty flowering tree to shelter all the children of one mother and one father. And I saw that it was holy."

—*John G. Neihardt,*
relaying Black Elk's Vision on Harney Peak,
Custer, South Dakota; Black Elk Speaks

Chapter 2. Why I'm Running for Attorney General of Iowa

by Edward F. Noyes, J.D.

As I rode my Harley across the sandhills of Nebraska on the way to Sturgis, South Dakota, in the summer of 2001, I was at peace with myself once again. I had traveled these same roads in my youth on another motorcycle journey, one that seemed to define my life and to be predestined. When I was seven years old, I had a vision of traveling on a motorcycle and experiencing freedom for the first time. That vision was fulfilled when, 12 years later, I experienced "the call of the West" and left home for the first time.

My family traveled to the Black Hills (known as the Paha Sapa to Lakota natives, who regard them as holy) almost every year. We worked hard all year in order to receive the blessings of a two-week vacation. My parents exemplified a work ethic based on obligation to family, God, and nation. Through witnessing their commitment, which they lived every day of their lives, and their faith in the "American way," I gained a firsthand understanding of the real strength of our nation.

For some reason, I have always been drawn to study the Native American way of life, perhaps for the same reason I've always kept my eye on national and world politics. Through my research on the Founders, I discovered that they too studied the people who lived here first, basing much of their model of government on the tribal organizations that existed for hundreds of years before Columbus arrived. Not coincidentally, the Founders also researched the tribe of Israel, originally led by Moses, as well as the Anglo-Saxons, to discern the essence of a political system that would most efficiently meet the needs of the people and simultaneously protect their God-given liberties. The yearly pilgrimage of the "freedom riders" which I joined to the natives' holy land seemed to symbolize our right to pursue happiness, based on principles of liberty and freedom.

Growing up on a small farm in Nebraska, I came to love my state and nation. In my youth, I could not discern the difference between the swelling of pride I felt when listening to the Cornhuskers winning football games and my innate love for my country. My love for God and my parents was clearly a part of it all as well. When I was chosen with my friend to raise the flag every day at the American Legion Building my sixth-grade class occupied, all was right with the world.

I remember canoeing down the Elkhorn River in Nebraska in my early teens with my best friend and discovering a massive drainage pipe dumping barely treated sewage into the river. We were both so upset with this defilement of our beloved river that we attempted to stop the flow into the river. We threw the largest rocks we could lift into the flow and watched the force of the water knock them out of the way. My first attempt at environmental cleanup had failed miserably.

Later in high school, when I read George Orwell's book *1984*, I was so shocked by the imagery that I made a personal commitment (the first commitment I remember ever making) that if I ever witnessed the phenomenon of Big Brother and Double Speak, I would do something about it. That commitment led me to realize that I was powerless unless I understood how the world actually worked. Over the past 30 years, I have devoted myself to this inquiry.

> "The [Colorado] legislature…postponed a bill
> requiring schools to teach patriotism…after
> Republicans and Democrats couldn't agree on
> how to define it."
>
> —USA *Today*, Feb. 8, 2002

College led me to not only study business, but to obtain a degree in wildlife biology and agricultural economics at the University of Nebraska. My love of nature was always with me. Law school subsequently appeared to me as inevitable and helped me to further understand the workings of the world.

No matter where I went during the Sturgis rally, I could not escape talk of politics. Can you imagine 500,000 freedom-loving motorcyclists enjoying life together within a 100-mile radius? Among them were my old college friends, who live in Rapid City and who complained of the government imposing its will on the people. I could not help but talk about what I had learned about the vision and principles of our country's Founders. I explained to my friends that over the past three years, I had participated in the "Evening a Month for

America" program, sponsored by the National Center for Constitutional Studies. Each month, we completed certain readings from *The Making of America* textbook and *The Five Thousand Year Leap,* by Cleon Skousen. Through these readings and the program study materials, we came to understand why our Constitution was created as it was and the intentions behind the Founders' masterful work. We were able to compare what was intended to what had eventually come to exist in our modern-day country. Despite my high school, college, and legal education, I had never before understood what was behind the creation of this nation.

> "You have rights antecedent to all earthly governments, rights that cannot be repealed or restrained by human laws, rights derived from the Great Legislator of the Universe."
>
> —*John Adams*

As I was leaving my friends to set up camp near Sturgis, I felt compelled to encourage them to do two things: (1) become educated about the essence and purpose of the Constitution, and (2) run for office if they intended to effect a change in their local politics. I wasn't aware at the time that I was also talking to myself. Later, after reflecting upon the way our legislators are presented with bills entirely drafted by special interest groups, I realized there ought to be someone, or some organization, that existed to protect the rights of the people themselves.

While in law school, I made the decision to not study criminal law any more than the required courses, believing I would clearly never practice in this area. My reasoning was obvious: I did not want to be involved with "criminals."

However, when I started my own practice in small-town Iowa, often the only work available was to provide the court-appointed, legal defense for people charged with a crime who could not afford to hire a private attorney. As I began to represent these people, who were obviously the most downtrodden and weakest members of our community, I came to realize how much I naturally cared about them. I came to see them as some of the most humble, good-hearted, and honest people I had ever met. People you might call "the salt of the earth."

I also discovered that many were innocent of the charges against them, or that they had been "overcharged." I felt the weight of my duty to represent these people, as well as the weight of the state with its power to accuse and judge others. I saw good men sent to prison, and their families humiliated, even though the pre-sentence investigation report acknowledged there had been no victim. I saw families left without breadwinners, as well as the effects of having their father labeled a criminal, leading to welfare and divorce. I, and everyone else involved in the system, saw men and women returning again and again to jail and prison, despite the Code of Iowa mandate that every sentence was "to provide maximum opportunity for the rehabilitation of the defendant, and for the protection of the community from further offenses by the defendant and others." I saw that rehabilitation of the defendant, restoration for the victim, or protection against further offenses was rarely an actual result of the system.

While providing legal counsel to a thousand inmates at a local prison, I saw firsthand the type of men and women being held behind bars for some reason or another. I was surprised to learn that some of these inmates were extremely bright and well versed in the law, despite their circumstances. Perhaps in order to save money and discourage inmate legal actions, Iowa had eliminated the law libraries from its prisons and replaced the inmates' right to legal materials with one lawyer, who was paid $1,000 per month for 20 hours of work. Serving in this position, I discovered that 90 percent of those in custody were no different than anyone you might meet at your job or anywhere else. (I couldn't help but think of the words of Jesus: "For all have sinned and come short of the glory of God.")

I came to understand that the decision on whether (and when) to grant parole to over 8,000 inmates is determined by a total of five parole board members. As a result, I learned that many very good and capable people sit in prison for years without ever having their parole status even considered. I also saw how difficult it was for inmates to stay connected to their families, or to feel supported by those on "the outside."

After having participated in the day-to-day world of criminal defense for over a decade, I resolved to devote myself to reforming the system, rather than being just another participant upholding the status quo. I had no idea how that commitment would manifest itself.

When I left my friend's house in Rapid City, I rode my motorcycle to the nearest car wash. As I was wiping the bike down, a stranger walked up to me and exclaimed, "We should be riding to Washington, D.C., to protest the loss of our rights, instead of being at this rally!" We spoke briefly about the status of our country and how we felt a loss of freedom from the weight of top-down government. As I pulled away, I had to wonder why he had felt compelled to approach a stranger in this way.

On the day I left the Black Hills, I traveled to Scenic, South Dakota, at the edge of the Badlands. There I met a distinguished gentleman rider who had run for state office in New Jersey. A young Native American approached us asking for help and sparked a lively discussion of the federal government's role in providing welfare for the natives of this country. We also spoke for several hours with two brothers who were running a barbecue stand for bikers venturing through that area. I finally asked one of the brothers what his political philosophy was. He stated that he was a "Liber—tarian." I had not used the word in speaking with him, and I could tell that he had never uttered the word before that moment.

Within a few days of my returning home to Iowa, Clyde Cleveland told me he was running for governor of Iowa as a Libertarian. He then asked me if I would run for attorney general on the same ticket. When I reflected upon the opportunity, I found myself facing a decision that contained little choice. I realized that the office has the capacity to directly impact what I have discovered to be most important in my life.

I am running for attorney general of Iowa because I am committed to:

- Restoring to the people a political system that cannot be controlled to the detriment of the people themselves.

- Returning to the local communities the ability to manage their own affairs, as envisioned by the Founding Fathers.

- Implementing a criminal justice system that is not only effective but is humane and achieves its stated objective of genuine rehabilitation.

- Bringing about lasting economic prosperity that also fulfills our responsibilities as caretakers of the earth and all who live here.

- Leaving behind a world that we can be proud of—for our children, our grandchildren, and future generations.

The final reason I am running for attorney general is because I was asked.

The man who presented this opportunity to me deserves to be the next governor of Iowa. His background, commitment, and depth of knowledge have not been seen in politics for a very long time. I give you my personal guarantee that if the people of Iowa elect him and the other outstanding candidates running on the independent, Libertarian ticket, we will present choices that, if embraced, will result in Iowa truly leading the nation towards its highest destiny. I have no doubt that by returning Iowa (the "heart" of America's heartland) to a bastion of freedom, the blessings of liberty will rain down upon the people and restore our land.

Section Two:

The Principles of Freedom

"A government big enough to supply everything you need is big enough to take everything you have...The course of history shows that as a government grows, liberty decreases."

—*Thomas Jefferson*

"When the power of love overcomes the love of power, the world will know peace."

—*Jimi Hendrix, 1942-1970,*
American musician, singer, songwriter

Chapter 3. Bottom-up versus Top-down

By Clyde J. Cleveland

In 1981, I founded a company called United Investment Groups, Inc. (UIG). Eventually, UIG employed 40 people and raised over $24 million, $22 million of which came into our Iowa office and funded several early-stage companies headquartered in Iowa.

The people who worked for UIG were devoted to a cause much bigger than a run-of-the-mill business enterprise. As UIG's mission statement avowed, our purpose was to fund companies that were creating solutions to all of our social and environmental problems. When people came to work at UIG, they felt they were coming to help save the planet.

In our quest to make our world a better place to live, we did some remarkable things and funded some great companies. Many of those companies are still in business today. Some have faded, but their highly educated employees remained in Iowa, some starting their own businesses and hiring their own employees. Given how the ripple effect of every new job creates even more jobs in the community, UIG resulted in thousands of new jobs in Iowa.

UIG also had an impact on the state's environment. Soil Technologies, a biotech company in Jefferson County, Iowa, makes a cover crop that uses algae to fix nitrogen and replenish the soil. Research funds from UIG helped Soil Technologies lengthen the shelf-life of this product from 24 hours to 48 days. This cover crop which is sold to farmers all over the world, has enormous ecological implications. Farmers reported a 95 percent reduction in chemical costs when using the product, as well as increased yields and improved quality.

Soil Technologies' cover crop is also used by 30 percent of the golf courses in this country, greatly reducing the amount of chemical fertilizers used on the fairways. This reduces pollution of nearby streams and rivers.

Over the years, UIG set up limited partnerships to fund several other environmental companies:

- United Wind Industries received $600,000. This partnership purchased windmills for a wind generation farm in Palm Desert, California.

- United Fibertech Ltd. was funded with $2.8 million, which was awarded to Tetratech Industries of Austin, Texas, for research and development. Tetratech had the technology to take any fibrous agricultural waste product, such as wheat straw, and create building materials for homes or offices. The end product was amazingly strong, pest resistant and fireproof. The ecological implications were enormous. Because the waste product the company was using would normally have been burned, increasing air pollution, the process had an immediate impact on air quality. Many buildings were built around the country using

Tetra board, including the office buildings my partner and I built in Fairfield, Iowa, in 1983. The company that bought the technology is now seeking funds to restart operations.

• Magnetics Research International (MRI) received approximately $3 million in venture capital from us. The company had a highly innovative technology to make electric motors more ecologically sound and energy efficient by using principles of magnetism. MRI was in operation for 10 years before selling its technology to a larger company.

• UIG raised $3.5 million for three additional companies as well—Global Integration Technologies, Inc.; Oasys, Inc.; and Minitech, Inc.—all of which provided research and development services for electronic innovations designed to increase productivity.

As a result of UIG's accomplishments, in 1986 I was invited to an international conference on socially conscious investing, hosted by Conscious Investors, Ltd., an international investors organization. At that event, I was named "America's First Socially Conscious Venture Capitalist."

I am quite proud of that award and of what we accomplished at UIG. I will never forget the people who worked with me there. Unfortunately, that work ended when the tax laws changed in 1986. The act eliminated research and development tax credits, along with many favorable rules for passing tax benefits through to limited partners, destroying many companies that depended on tax benefits to raise money for enterprises. UIG had invested substantially in a large offering that had taken more than a year to get approved by the

Securities and Exchange Commission. About three days after it was approved, the tax law changes were announced, effectively eliminating the offering. UIG simply could not recover.

Yes, the so-called federal Tax Simplification Act of 1986 put us out of business. Not to mention the fact that the act did not simplify the tax code; it actually made the code significantly more complex and indecipherable. (You can bet that the impact of a bill will always be just the opposite of what the name implies!)

The Cleveland for Governor campaign
is about changing the world.

I learned from my UIG experience that if you are going to do something, do something very big and do something very good at the same time. In other words, have your goal be to change the world! Working for anything less than that just isn't any fun. It doesn't get your juices flowing to do it any other way.

The goals of the Cleveland for Governor campaign are all about changing the world. We want Iowa to lead the nation to a better way of living. We believe that the solutions to all of our problems are available right now. But the systems of organization in this country hold us back from restoring both our individual freedom and our environment.

Our Founders had a vision of a country totally in tune with natural laws. They had studied Cicero and Locke and Montesquieu, all of whom spoke about natural law in great depth. The Founders were also great students of the Bible. To them, God's law and natural law were the same thing; natural law was God's will expressed. In the Declaration of Independence, the Founders termed it the "laws of nature and of nature's God."

I have found that discussing the fundamental principles drawn on by the Founders dissolves misconceptions about the past and provides a framework for understanding how we can transform our present-day society. Examples of how these principles work can be found at various points in history.

> "I know of no safe depository of the ultimate powers of society but the people themselves, and if we think them not enlightened enough to exercise control with a wholesome discretion, the remedy is not to take it from them, but to inform their discretion."
>
> —*Thomas Jefferson*

Consider the story behind Visa International, for instance. Dee Hock founded the company in 1968 with nothing but a list of principles which he had gleaned from a lifetime of observing nature. Were those principles successful? Within a few years, Hock's company was the largest commercial enterprise on the planet, with $1.25 trillion in annual revenues!

The amazing thing about Visa was that nobody could find the center of the company. As one observer said, "The center was like a noncoercive enabling organization that existed only for the purpose of assisting owner members to fulfill their activities with greater capacity, more effectively, and at less cost."

Hock described his company as a "chaordic organization," embracing both the chaos of competition and the order of cooperation. In his book, *The Birth of the Chaordic Age*, he lists the principles behind a chaordic organization as follows:

- It should be equitably owned by all participants.

- It must not attempt to impose uniformity.

- It should be open to all qualified participants.

- Power, function, and resources should be distributed to the maximum degree.

- Authority should be equitable and distributive within each governing entity.

- No interest should be able to dominate deliberations or control decisions, particularly management.

- To the maximum degree possible, everything should be voluntary.

- It should be nonassessable.

- It should introduce, not compel, change.

- It should be infinitely malleable yet extremely durable.

This list of Hock's is a very good list of libertarian principles. What's more, the observer's description of the company's center serving as an "enabling organization" is an accurate description of a libertarian perspective of government.

In addition to Hock's story, there are far earlier examples of the success in following the principles of natural law. Both the Anglo-Saxons and the early Israeli's people under Moses were bottom-up societies. The Anglo-Saxons were the dominant people in England, until the 11th century and included descendants of the Scythians, or Goths, who originally migrated from the region of the Black Sea. Some scholars believe that the Goths were remnants of one of the "lost" tribes of Israel and that the code of laws that they handed down from generation to generation was based on the same commandments that Moses received on Mount Sinai.

The governing principles followed by both the Anglo-Saxons and the Children of Israel—such as equal representation, inalienable rights of the individual, and local resolution of problems to the maximum extent possible—were almost identical to Hock's principles. As with his chaordic organization, the bottom-up model worked well for the early Israelis and Anglo-Saxons, and led to greater peace, prosperity, and freedom for their people.

Moses
Aaron   Joshua
Council of Seventy
(A Senate)
Elected Representatives
(A Congress)

600 Groups of 1,000 Families
6,000 Groups of 100 Families
12,000 Groups of 50 Families
60,000 Groups of 10 Families

More than 600,000 families, more than
3 million people with power to govern themselves.

Pyramid 1. Ancient Israeli Model of Government

We talk about those examples because three of our most knowledgeable Founders—John Adams, Thomas Jefferson, and Benjamin Franklin—all believed these civilizations were the most worthy of copying. In fact, they proposed that the first national seal for the United States of America reflect these two civilizations.

**ORIGINAL PROPOSAL FOR
THE AMERICAN SEAL**
(Artist's Version)

The Founders' vision of a bottom-up republic was thriving by the time French historian Alexis de Tocqueville came to America in the 1830s. He was astonished that "government was invisible." What he saw instead was a country in which local problems were solved by individuals, families, and a plethora of community and civic organizations.

By 1905, the United States was one of the richest industrial nations on the planet. With 5 percent of the world's land and 6 percent of its population, the country was producing almost half of everything produced in the world, including clothes, food, houses, transportation, communications, and luxuries. Most importantly, people were coming to the United States from all over the world to enjoy unprecedented freedom.

Pyramid 2: The Bottom-up Model of Government

Then things began to change, and the country started moving toward a top-down model of governing. It was so gradual that no one realized it was happening. In 1913, those who wanted to turn the power pyramid upside-down made significant gains. That year, the first income tax was passed and the Federal Reserve was created, essentially ceding the constitutional authority of Congress to create money to private individuals. Since 1913, the top-down government model has become predominant. Now most of the power is with the federal government instead of with the individual and the family.

Federal Government

State Government

County Government

City Government

Townships/
Civic Organizations

Individuals &
Families

Pyramid 3. The Top-down Model of Government

As a result of this shift to top-down, command-and-control, force-based government, Americans have less freedom every day. There is never a time when power relinquishes itself; it just grows and grows until the people wake up and realize what has happened to them. We are confident that Americans want their freedom back and want this process reversed. We believe it is time to flip that pyramid back to its proper configuration (Pyramid 2), with the power once again held by the individual and the family. It is the solution to all of our problems. Drug abuse, crime, poverty, welfare, inadequate health care, underfunded retirement, and all of the other social problems we face are always more effectively dealt with on the local level

We are not right wing, nor are we left wing. We are UP wing.

Once people understand the details of the fundamental principles we want to restore in Iowa, the standard debates of the Republicans and Democrats—and all of the contentious arguments over issues—just melt away. These are natural laws and universal principles that have worked for thousands of years. In our hearts, the citizens of Iowa and of the nation still believe in a bottom-up society. We have simply allowed our institutions to grow too powerful.

To me, this campaign is a spiritual quest. I hope every person in Iowa will make it a spiritual quest as well. We are in the midst of a worldwide battle—on and below the surface—between forces that believe in top-down, command-and-control management of society and those who believe in the principles of bottom-up management, freedom, and individual sovereignty.

"Government is not reason. It is not eloquence. It is force, like fire: a dangerous servant and a terrible master."

—*George Washington*

The defining quality of top-down management will always be force. And when a society is dominated by force, fear is the emotion that predominates. The bottom-up model is based on individual sovereignty, with the fundamental governing unit being the family. What quality holds families together? Love.

Therefore, the essential unifying principle of the bottom-up system—and the predominate emotion—is love. Love on one side, fear on the other.

The Top 10 Characteristics of Bottom-up vs. Top-down Societies

Bottom-up	Top-down
Love	Fear
Freedom	Control
Noncoercion	Force
Local control	Centralized planning
Abundant creativity	Stifled creativity
Optimism	Despair
Strong families	Breakdown of families
Personal responsibility	Dependence
Universal opportunity	Concentrated power
Prosperity	Poverty

When I speak to high school kids, I tell them our campaign is about bringing love and light to the political process. I explain that we are not right wing or left wing. We are *up* wing. We are for returning to a bottom-up model of governance in this country. And that model is based on love and freedom—we want to *uplift* people not control them. Our children understand this message. They know intuitively that there is something rotten about our current government and our institutions. They are responding to our message with great enthusiasm and energy.

The only way we can defeat those who would attempt to control us—the elitists who believe they know how we should live, and all those powerful special interests who have consolidated their control over the political process—is by bringing in love. It is the most powerful force on earth. We do this by returning to a bottom-up model of governance. It is within our power to do that, and we must do it for the sake of our children and our grandchildren.

Jimi Hendrix said, "When the power of love overcomes the love of power, the world will know peace." I would add, when the power of love exceeds the love of power, we will have peace, prosperity, and freedom—and the most effective solutions to all of our environmental and social problems will occur spontaneously, and naturally, from the bottom up.

> "America is a bottom-up society, where new trends and ideas begin in cities and local communities...My colleagues and I have studied this great country by reading its newspapers. We have discovered that trends are generated from the bottom up."
>
> —*John Naisbitt*, Megatrends, *based on a 12-year study of 2 million local events*

"The two parties should be almost identical, so the American people can 'throw the rascals out' at any election without leading to any profound or extensive shifts in policy."

—*Carroll Quigley*, Tragedy and Hope

Chapter 4. The Great Deception

By Clyde J. Cleveland

So how does it happen? How can a society that has successfully operated in a bottom-up mode allow itself to morph into a society based on fear and force, rather than freedom and love?

The forces of top-down, command-and-control institutions have become extremely adept at masquerading as proponents of freedom and justice. Whether they come from the left or the right makes no difference in the end. Hitler was a fascist and Stalin was a communist, but what difference did the label mean to the people living under either regime? None. Totalitarianism is slavery, whether it comes from the right or the left. And whether Republicans or Democrats are in control in Iowa or at the federal level, we continue to lose our freedom at an ever-increasing pace.

In 1967, I was a freshman at Indiana State University. I had three priorities at the time: partying, partying, and partying. It was no surprise that I became Rush chairman of my fraternity. Remember "Otter" in the movie *Animal House?* That was me.

There was an event however that was about to change my priorities—the Vietnam War. During my second semester of school, I completed an extensive research paper on the roots of our country's involvement in this "conflict." It was the first time in my life that I realized the media were nothing but a huge propaganda machine. When I discovered that the American people were not being told the truth about our involvement in Vietnam, my perception of our institutions began to shift dramatically.

I switched my major from business to political science and became more and more immersed in the Left's view of government. In 1969, I joined the Socialist Party. I was convinced that the only way to save our environment, end oppressive wars, and create true justice for the little guy was to take control of the government, and by doing so, control the evil and unbelievably greedy capitalists.

It was a few years later that I began to realize that socialism was based on a misconception of human nature. And it was later still that I fully realized that collectivism in all its forms—socialism, communism, fascism—is nothing more than an incredibly deceptive scheme enabling some of the most powerful people on the planet to increase their power and wealth.

Does this mean that all those who believe in collectivist policies are knowingly part of a deception? Absolutely not. Very few people really understand the nature of what is happening when they vote for candidates who support policies that move us closer and closer to a purely socialist or fascist state. Remember, the many Germans voted for Adolph Hitler, who ran on a platform that sounded exactly like those of some of our modern-day American politicians. Hitler's proposals included strong anti-smoking laws as well as national registration of firearms. I believe that, in most cases, many candidates do not thoroughly realize the full picture of what they are doing.

The one feature of the socialist vision that I still agree with is a belief in a more evolved society. All of us have a natural desire to improve the world and to help our fellow humans achieve happiness. That sense of duty is a given and it drives us all. The utopia envisioned by socialists, however, can never come about through coercion, because a society based on force will never allow the full creative expression of the people. The path to achieving maximum prosperity for everyone, a totally restored environment, and a dramatic reduction in social problems is clearly *not* by following the path of collectivism.

Looking back over the last 40 years, it is truly amazing that despite the complete and utter failure of federal programs to eliminate poverty and drug abuse, improve education, restore our environment, reduce crime, and solve other social problems, most people still don't realize that this paradigm does not work. It is truly a testament to the power of the media, which continually support the fallacy that top-down government can be compassionate and solve problems it was never designed to solve. The truth is, all problems can be more effectively solved through noncoercive institutions.

> "Nature [has] implanted in our breasts a love of others, a sense of duty to them, a moral instinct in short, which prompts us irresistibly to feel and to succor their distresses."
>
> —*Thomas Jefferson*

Human beings have certain natural tendencies. We naturally want to improve ourselves and expand our territory of influence. Most humans are naturally inclined to help others, although this inclination is subordinate to our more basic desire to act in our own self-interest. We also have an innate need to express our free will. Throughout history, the predominant struggle has been the conflict between those who want to express their free will and those who want to expand their territory of influence by controlling others. The English historian Lord Acton once said, "Power corrupts and absolute power corrupts absolutely." Any student of human nature knows that the drug of power is the most addictive drug of all.

Our Founders knew that creating an environment conducive to maximum freedom required limiting the growth of government because governments are made up of people who have the natural inclination to increase their power. This clear understanding of government and human nature brought about the world's freest nation.

The inherent desire for power and control never sleeps. In the 1800s, the proponents of growing government found the perfect tactic as the theories of Marx, Engels and other collectivists began to sweep Europe. They appealed to that natural human desire to help others. Since then, the collectivists have perfected their ability to appeal to the compassionate hearts of the people—and in so doing, expanded their power—by presenting a never-ending array of social programs to help the poor, children, the disabled, and others. They gain the votes of the compassionate and, of course, those who come to depend on the programs. The extra bonus is the loyalty of all those who work for the new bureaucracies that are created to manage the new programs.

In her famous essay, "Why I'm Not a Conservative," author Ayn Rand described the insidious process which takes a society inch by unremarkable inch to socialism in this way: "The goal of the 'liberals'—as it emerges from the record of the past decades—was to smuggle this country into welfare statism by means of single, concrete, specific measures, enlarging the power of the government a step at a time, never permitting these steps to be summed up into principles, never permitting their direction to be identified or the basic issue to be named. Thus, statism was to come, not by vote or by violence, but by slow rot, by a long process of evasion and epistemological corruption, leading to a *fait accompli*."

Note that Rand refers to conservatives as part of the process. She understood that the two parties presented to the people in their "democratic" process provide only an illusion of choice. Either choice, they still get statism. And with statism comes increasing governmental power because as the government grows, so too must force and coercion increase in order to extract the necessary finances from the people to pay for the growing government.

The growth of force has to happen gradually so that the people do not wake up and realize what is happening. As Lord Chesterfield said, "Arbitrary power...must be introduced by slow degrees, and as it were, step by step, lest the people should see it approach."

What will it take for Americans to wake up? How many Wacos, Ruby Ridges, and outrageous search-and-seizures in the name of the war on drugs will we endure before we realize what is happening?

"At Waco, was there really an urgency to get
those people out of the compound at that
particular time?...At Ruby Ridge, there was
one guy in a cabin at the top of the mountain. Was it necessary for federal agents to go
up there and shoot a 14-year-old in the back
and shoot a woman with a child in her arms?
What kind of mentality does that?"

—*Clint Eastwood*

The concept of socialism is attractive, especially to young
people and those who have not been taught the fundamental
principles of natural law-based government. It seems logical
to the uninformed that instead of relying on a private charitable infrastructure, the government can take care of
everyone in need and be responsible for implementing altru-
ism throughout the country. A convincing case can also be
made that the government can be the most fair and equitable
controller of the nation's resources. And of course, the government is the only power that can keep people from
exercising those greedy tendencies not to share the wealth. It
is thought that through government-run education, everyone
can learn to be compassionate and caring, and that we all
have to sacrifice for the common good.

A majority of youth in a recent study thought the phrase
"From each according to his ability; to each according to his
need" was part of the Constitution. In fact, it is the underlying principle of Marxism. What children are not taught is

that everywhere this principle has been put into practice, it has failed. That is, it has failed to work without coercion.

When people have a choice, they are not inclined to sacrifice the fruits of their own labor for the achievement of a larger social goal. It is simply not natural behavior, and eventually force is required to maintain the system.

The monstrous social experiments in Russia, China, and other communist countries, which have resulted in the mass murder of tens of millions of human beings over the last century, could have been avoided if intellectuals and philosophers had not ignored the most fundamental natural principle of human behavior. Human beings, because of their survival instinct, will act in their own self-interest. Any institution, government, or business that ignores this fundamental fact of life is doomed to fail. Propaganda, mind control techniques, or brute force will all fail eventually.

Socialism cannot be implemented without force. That force always increases over time. There is no place in the process of the growth of government where the statists will stop the process. There has never been a government bureaucracy that has come forward and said, "You know, we have completed our task now and there is really no need for the taxpayers to continue to fund our department." Frederick Hayak wrote convincingly in his classic The Road to Serfdom that, once begun, the process of collectivism (in whatever form) always leads to a totalitarian government and serfdom for the vast majority of the people.

The question inevitably arises: If this is true, why would so many seemingly intelligent people fall for this philosophy? The answer is multifold, but most simply do not realize what they are doing. The compassionate nature of the message is so great, and the intellectual credentials of the proponents are so dazzling, that people fall hook, line, and sinker for the entire program. For the most part, they are extremely well-intentioned individuals. The message has been so well cloaked in terms of freedom and social justice that it is difficult for most people to distinguish between the principles of the Founders and the principles espoused by the collectivists. When you consider that the founding principles are no longer taught in our schools, then you can begin to see how this new and completely contradictory philosophy has gradually taken hold. Add to this the fact that the media are completely influenced and owned by those who are promoting this agenda, and you can begin to comprehend why so many would be deceived.

The group who clearly understand the big picture—the creation of a world dominated by a ruling elite, with one government ruling the entire planet—are near the top of the socialist hierarchy. No one describes this better than Edward L. Bernays, Freud's nephew, who is known as the father of "spin." In his book *Propaganda*, Bernays writes: "Those who manipulate the unseen mechanism of society constitute an invisible government which is the true ruling power of our country. We are governed, our minds molded, our tastes formed, our ideas suggested largely by men we have never heard of. This is a logical result of the way in which our democratic society is organized. Vast numbers of human beings must cooperate in this manner if they are to live together as a smoothly functioning society. In almost every act of our lives, whether in the sphere of politics or business, in our social conduct or our ethical thinking, we are dominated by the relatively small number of persons who understand the mental processes and social patterns of the masses. It is they who pull the wires that control the public mind."

These are the people who believe themselves to be the intended rulers. They are usually adherents of the philosophy that there is no divine intelligence; it is just us and it is up to the most intelligent humans to control the masses of igno-rant common people. These people have bought into the idea that it is altruistic for humanity to have the world run by the smartest among us. They will make the best decisions and care for the common people. Many of these people actually think that they will be in control and have ultimate power in this ideal order. But that is not the reality.

Above them is the highest level of the socialist hierarchy, and as I said before, these are some of the wealthiest people in the world. Those who benefit the most from socialism are those who ultimately control the entire program—men like Cecil Rhodes, the British diamond and gold mogul who founded the "Society of the Elect" in 1891. Their money has funded the socialist movement since midway through the 19th century. Without their money, the socialist move-ment—being fundamentally dehumanizing, destructive, and unnatural to human behavior—would have vanished from the face of the earth long ago.

Why would the wealthiest among us want to fund worldwide socialism and turn America into a socialist nation? The answer is simple. Since the 1800s, these wealthy families have been buying influence with the federal government. The Federal Reserve System, created in 1913, is a private corporation with no reserves. The owners of the commercial banks that own the Federal Reserve effectively control all the money loaned to the U.S. government. Think of the incredible influence that gives them over our politicians and entire political process. In effect, they have controlled the government for almost 90 years. So why not implement socialism, which makes the government, which they control, even bigger and more powerful. Understanding this whole scheme is impossible unless you constantly remember that "absolute power corrupts absolutely."

It is not possible to explain this entire story in this book. To learn more, read *The Creature from Jekyl Island: A Second Look at the Federal Reserve*, by G. Edward Griffin. This book offers the best and most comprehensive explanation of the situation, including the historical perspective.

The stumbling block to total global control is the U.S. Constitution. That incredible document, stating that all the power is derived from the people, is still the supreme law of our land. Their solution to that is straightforward: weaken the United States in every conceivable way and gradually transfer all the sovereignty of the United States to the United Nations.

There is nothing like the U.S. Constitution, founded on the principle of individual sovereignty, to worry about at the United Nations. The charter and founding documents are patterned after the constitution of the former Soviet Union, which allowed all constitutional "rights" to be abrogated by enforcement provisions. The Soviet constitution, for example, had a clear provision for freedom of religion. However, it also had a clause in it that allowed any provision in the constitution to be overridden by the Soviet penal code. Under the Soviet penal code, parents who tried to teach their children religion were subject to life imprisonment, and many Soviet citizens spent their lives in prison under this provision.

In other words, the UN charter, like the Soviet constitution, has no meaning. It is a fraud. The United Nations is the perfect government for collectivists. The people have no rights. It is truly a government of the governments, by the governments, and for the governments.

What happens to the darkness in a room when you turn on the light?

As I said, the funding of the socialist movement in the United States started a long time ago. The first major focus of the wealthy elite was education, with the idea of gradually "educating" our children to accept the state as the sovereign power, rather than this nasty and unworkable concept of "individual sovereignty."

Their position was clearly stated in the first newsletter of the General Education Board, which was funded with an initial grant of $1 million by John D. Rockefeller in 1902. This organization later became the Rockefeller Foundation, which funded the Teachers College at Columbia University, birthplace of the theories that have influenced our educational institutions for decades. All of the founders of Columbia's Teachers College, such as John Dewey, were adherents of Marxist theories. As the newsletter stated:

"In our dreams, we have limitless resources and the people yield themselves with perfect docility to our molding hands. We work our own good will upon a grateful and responsive rural folk. We will not try to make these people or any of their children into philosophers or men of learning, or men of science."

So much for the concept of education being about developing the full potential of each individual child. It appears that the goal is to create good little docile citizens, who do what they are told and serve their masters, the ruling elite.

On February 17, 1950, James Paul Warburg, the former president of the Council on Foreign Relations, told the U.S. Senate: "We shall have world government whether or not we like it. The only question is whether world government will be achieved by conquest or consent." (*Losing Your Illusions*, by Gordon Phillips). From my study of the proposed "world government," the desired system would be made up of a single currency, single central bank, single centrally financed government, single tax system, single political system, single world court of justice, single head (one individual leader), and single state religion. Each person would have a registered number, without which they would not be allowed to buy or sell. Anyone refusing to take part in this system would be "re-educated" or eliminated.

As Hayek foretold in the 1940s, socialism and collectivism in all its forms ultimately leads to brutal totalitarianism.

Is this really happening now in our country? Isn't this just a "conspiracy theory"? It all seems so unbelievable! Yet, Texas Congressman Ron Paul, a medical doctor and one of the few congressmen with the guts to stand up to the constant transfer of sovereignty to the United Nations, has reported that the World Trade Organization is now *demanding* that the United States change its tax laws. In his newsletter, he wrote, "It's hard to imagine a more blatant example of a loss of U.S.

sovereignty. Yet there is no outcry or indignation in Congress at this naked demand that we change our laws to satisfy the rest of the world. I've yet to see one national politician or media outlet even suggest the obvious, namely that our domestic laws are simply none of the world's business." (Jan. 21, 2002)

> "Good intentions will always be pleaded for every assumption of authority...There are men in all ages who mean to govern well, but they mean to govern. They promise to be good masters, but they mean to be masters."
>
> —*Noah Webster*

In *Losing your Illusions*, Gordon Phillips quotes a statement made by David Rockefeller at a 1991 Bilderberger meeting that really sums up the whole ball of wax. "We are grateful to the *Washington Post*, the *New York Times*, *Time* magazine, and other great publications whose directors have attended our meetings and respected their promise of discretion for almost forty years. It would have been impossible for us to develop our plan for the world if we had been subject to the bright lights of publicity during those years. But the world is now more sophisticated and prepared to march towards a world government. The super-national sovereignty of an intellectual elite and world bankers is surely preferable to the national auto-determination practiced in past centuries."

A very large percentage of the leaders of our media, government, major political parties, wealthy foundations, and largest corporations believe—or are under the influence of individuals who believe—that the world would be better off with them as a ruling elite. Even people who can't, or won't, believe what I've described must at least acknowledge that people in government, and those who influence government, do what they do not only to increase their power, but because they honestly believe that they are smarter than the rest of us and that they know best how we should live our lives.

We disagree.

We are here to inspire, motivate, and bring light and positivity to Iowa and the rest of the nation. We believe in freedom, we believe in the power of love, we believe in individual sovereignty, and we believe in the sanctity of the family. It is not our intent to frighten or discourage people by describing the full extent of collectivism. Rather, we believe it is extremely important for every person to know the truth. The concept of bottom-up versus top-down government cannot be fully understood without understanding the nature of the agenda of the top-down proponents. Those who believe in command and control are just too good at confusing people. They position their programs to appear as something other than what they are. They have used that most refined human tendency, compassion, and under the guise of democratic socialism, increased their power over others to create a seemingly overwhelming power structure.

We have to remember that those who seek to control others always want those they control to think that it is futile to fight back. We have to remember that the "the laws of nature and of nature's God" want us to be free. We are designed that way.

Think of the Star Wars Trilogy, in which the dark side of the Force increases its stranglehold over the free people of the galaxy by its overwhelming advantage in weaponry and numbers. And *Braveheart,* where Mel Gibson's William Wallace fights the seemingly unbeatable forces of the English king, valiantly rallying the forces of freedom.

We are in a battle between force and freedom, coercion and love, darkness and light. We will, with your help, bring in the light. It is a great opportunity to be involved in this effort!

"God has given to men all that is necessary for them to accomplish their destinies. He has provided a social form as well as a human form. And these social organs of persons are so constituted that they will develop themselves harmoniously in the clean air of liberty. Away, then, with quacks and organizers! Away with their rings, chains, hooks, and pincers! Away with their artificial systems! Away with the whims of governmental administrators, their socialized projects, their centralization, their tariffs, their government schools, their state religions, their free credit, their bank monopolies, their regulations, their restrictions, their equalization by taxation, and their pious moralizations!

"And now that the legislators and do-good-
ers have so futilely inflicted so many systems
upon society, may they finally end where
they should have begun: May they reject all
systems, and try liberty; for liberty is an
acknowledgment of faith in God and His
works."

—*Bastiat*, The Law

"The spirit of the times may alter, will alter. Our rulers will become corrupt, our people careless…From the conclusion of this war we shall be going downhill. It will not then be necessary to resort every moment to the people for support. They will be forgotten, therefore, and their rights disregarded. They will forget themselves, but in the sole faculty of making money, and will never think of uniting to effect a due respect for their rights. The shackles, therefore…will be made heavier and heavier, till our rights shall revive or expire in a convulsion."

—*Thomas Jefferson*, Notes on Virginia, *1781*

Chapter 5. A Paradigm Shift to Freedom

By Clyde J. Cleveland

The introductory quote for this chapter has to be one of the most perceptive insights ever written. Thomas Jefferson and the other Founders had an incredibly deep understanding of human nature. Drawing on their vast knowledge of history, government, and natural law, they set out to create a civilization that would offer the most freedom and opportunity possible. They were determined to provide an environment conducive to the full development of the individual, even though they realized from the beginning that the nature of some humans to expand their influence over others would begin eroding individual freedom.

The Founders did everything they could to limit the power of the newly formed central government, creating checks and balances between the branches of the federal government as well as federal, state, and local governments. Even so, they realized their safeguards would not be enough; eventually a future generation of Americans would be called upon to revive the fundamental principles upon which they based the founding documents. Jefferson and the others clearly foresaw that if this future generation did not answer the call, the freedoms they fought for would be lost.

Conditions right before the Revolutionary War are similar to those we face today. The Founders knew that to achieve freedom, they would have to stir the hearts of the people so they would support the effort to separate from the top-down, command-and-control regime of King George. So too do we have to stir the hearts of the people, awakening them to the fact that we no longer are governed by people who understand, or believe in, the fundamental principles that inspired our founding documents.

But how do we flip the power pyramid back to where it belongs, with the people in charge once again? With all the existing institutions fighting for power in this country, and here in Iowa, how do we make this happen? Fortunately, we have a model from the past to emulate.

In January 1776, about two-thirds of the delegates to the Continental Congress were not planning to vote for independence. Even as George Washington was in the field fighting the war for independence, most of the delegates were trying to figure out how to patch things up with England. In late January, Thomas Paine published *Common Sense*. The first printing sold out in one day. The second printing sold out in one day. It is believed that over 500,000 copies were sold over the next 11 months, in a country of less than 2 million people! The small pamphlet so powerfully and effectively articulated the case for liberty that a passion for independence swept the country. By July 4, 12 of the states' delegations voted for independence, New York abstained, and we had the unanimous decision required to declare independence from England.

A paradigm shift had occurred in a matter of a few months!

A paradigm shift is a significant change in an existing pattern or model. In this case, we are talking about a change in the structure of society. But what we are really talking about is a change in the hearts of the people, returning to a more comfortable and natural way of being. A change that appeals to the heart can happen quickly and effortlessly.

We believe that it is our nature as humans to cherish freedom. We are born with free will, and political and economic freedoms are an absolute necessity to develop our full potential. Also, functioning in accord with the "laws of nature, and of nature's God" is the key to restoring civil society and our environment. History has shown that by simply tapping into what is within our own nature, a paradigm shift can occur incredibly fast.

The theme of our campaign is "A Paradigm Shift to Freedom." We can create a paradigm shift in Iowa *and in the rest of the country*. Every human being, deep within his or her heart, yearns for freedom. It is our job to articulate our message so well that we can awaken that love of liberty in every Iowan. If we do that, we will win.

People have called us "Green Libertarians" because of our commitment to the environment, and we do believe the Green Party has many good ideas (see Chapter 13). The common ground between the parties is finding solutions to environmental problems that do not involve government coercion. Force is not in tune with the laws of nature and of nature's God, and we believe using government force to accomplish our goals will be counterproductive. We are hopeful that we can form a very effective coalition with the Green Party—as well as with third-party advocates, disaffected Republicans and Democrats, and apathetic citizens who usually don't vote. We will work with anyone to increase freedom and restore our environment!

The paradigm shift set in motion by *Common Sense* occurred quite rapidly because it was a shift in tune with human nature. The last century of institutional consolidation of power in our country can be overturned in a few months or years, as soon as enough people wake up. Each one of us is important.

One of the most important things we hope you gain from reading this book is that you, as an individual, are very powerful. You can bring together a small group of people who believe in bottom-up government and transform your community. By doing so, you will set an example for the community down the road. Soon your state is affected and eventually the whole country. That is the whole idea here. It all starts with you, the individual.

YOU ARE VERY POWERFUL!

> "I am only one; but still I am one. I cannot
> do everything, but I still can do something. I
> will not refuse to do the something I can do."
>
> —*Helen Keller*

As we travel around the state talking to people, we tell people that we have a huge advantage over our Democratic and Republican opponents—we are able to tell you exactly what we believe in because we are not influenced by the large institutional contributors funding the major parties. That also means that we will be in a position to follow through on our commitments without pressure from the special interest groups.

This point alone should give our campaign the momentum necessary to put our entire slate of candidates in office. The people of this state are desperate to give someone else a chance to govern, and now is the time.

All of our proposed solutions go back to the bottom-up versus top-down model. Every single thing we plan to do in office is designed to take power and money away from government and give it back to families and communities. This election may be the only time in your life when you will be voting for yourself!

Normally when you vote for politicians, you hope they will be good stewards of your money and use their power in the interests of the people. We are presenting you with a completely different situation; this is an opportunity to vote for people who want less power and less of your money.

I'm running for governor, but each of you individually should be your own governor. Each Iowan should govern his or her own life and community. The governor of the state should have limited money, power, and responsibility. For this to happen, everyone has to take responsibility for their actions and their communities. The policies of our administration will make it possible for every community in Iowa to have the resources and opportunities to solve their own problems and become empowered in every way imaginable.

You can read our solutions for specific issues in Section Three, but briefly, our major goals are to:

- create economic vitality and prosperity

- restore our environment

- create energy independence

- help Iowa's family farms become profitable and competitive.

- empower communities

- dramatically reduce Iowa's incarceration rate

We do not believe that depending on federal or state government is the way to achieve these goals, or for that matter, to solve most of the problems we pay our state and federal governments to solve for us. We want to *eliminate* poverty, drug abuse, crime, and other social woes by restructuring our governmental system to be in tune with the laws of nature. We believe it is a much more compassionate approach to eliminate human suffering than to institutionalize all forms of suffering, making them permanent fixtures of society.

Right now, 72 percent of our federal tax money that goes to federal welfare programs stays with the bureaucracy in Washington, D.C.! That is right, only 28 percent goes to the people that are supposed to get help (Martin Gross, *A Call for Revolution*). On the other hand, 75 percent to 80 percent of the money raised by private charities goes directly to the people they are helping. We could eliminate this tremendous waste of money by transferring all federal welfare dollars to state and local governments, and then allowing each state to develop its own way of working with private organizations.

It is the same thing with education. As presidential candidate Gary Bauer pointed out during his 2000 campaign, more than 75 percent of your tax money that goes to the federal government for education stays in Washington, D.C., to pay bureaucrats. I don't know any parent who thinks those bureaucrats are helping to educate their kids. The bureaucrats spend most of their time thinking about how to increase the size of their department, not teaching your children. It is a *total* waste of money.

Because local governments are closer to the people and more familiar with the unique conditions in their localities, they will always handle welfare and education much more efficiently than federal or state government.

Iowa's state government is too big and spends too much. The *wasted* money that goes to state and federal bureaucracies should be in private hands, being *invested* in:

- start-up businesses

- savings accounts which in turn provide loans to individuals and businesses for start-ups and expansions

- farm expansion

- private charities

- education

In other words, we need to shift money wasted at the state and federal levels to local governments and into the productive private sector. That is the only way to grow an economy, and it is the only way to achieve our goals and solve our social problems.

> "The less [government] the better. As far as your personal goals and what you actually want to do with your life, it should never have to do with the government. You should never depend on the government for your retirement, your financial security, for anything. If you do, you're screwed."
>
> —*Drew Carey*

"The budget should be balanced. Public debt should be reduced. The arrogance of officialdom should be tempered, and assistance to foreign lands should be curtailed, lest Rome become bankrupt."

—*Cicero*

"Those who ignore history are doomed to repeat it."

—*George Santayana*

Chapter 6. How Iowa Can Regain its Sovereignty

By Richard Campagna, J.D.

The Rome that Cicero describes in the opening quote sounds eerily similar to today's America, does it not? Are we doomed to repeat the cycle of Rome and other republics? If we ignore history as Santayana warns, we will assuredly experience the same fate.

Our Founders were well aware of these cycles in history, and they did everything possible to create a constitution that would allow our republic to last for many centuries. Our Constitution provides the framework for a republic with very limited powers given to the central government. But the protective chains the Founders embedded in the Constitution have been broken. In fact, they have been pulled wide open, and they need to be refastened.

The Constitution is the law of the land. The original framework still exists, but we need to grab the chains, pull them together again, and put a big padlock on them so that they can never be broken again. This will require education, time, energy, dedication, and a massive commitment by many

Americans working together. The question is, do we have the will to regain our freedom? Is it worth it?

Yes. Cicero also said, "What is so beneficial to the people as liberty, which we see not only to be greedily sought-after by men, but also by beasts, and to be preferred to all things."

As a constitutional scholar, I believe the tools are still in place to regain our freedom without going through a cataclysm as Thomas Jefferson predicted would be necessary, stating "our rights will expire or revive in a cataclysm."

Broken Chains

The commerce clause of the U.S. Constitution (Article I, Section 8) expressly authorizes the federal government to regulate interstate commerce. Since the landmark case of *Gibbons vs. Ogden* (1824), the U.S. Supreme Court has interpreted the commerce clause to mean that the national government has the exclusive authority to regulate commerce that substantially affects trade and commerce amongst the several states. This express grant of authority, which some refer to as the "positive" aspect of the commerce clause, implies a "negative" aspect of the clause—that the states *do not* have the authority to regulate interstate commerce. This negative aspect is often referred to by constitutional scholars as the "dormant" or "implied" commerce clause.

The dormant commerce clause is cited when state regulations are considered to impinge upon interstate commerce. Despite that, it is generally considered that the states should have unfettered authority to regulate commerce and other activities within their borders. And usually, even the most nonlibertarian of courts will balance the states' interest in regulating specific matters such as the length or weights of trucks traveling on their roads against the burden that these internal regulations place on interstate commerce.

Traditionally, Libertarians have been strongly opposed to the judicial interventionism emanating from ever-expansive interpretations of the commerce clause and the so-called supremacy clause in Article VI of the Constitution. Article VI provides that the Constitution, laws, and treaties of the federal government are the supreme law of the land. The supremacy clause is important in the ordering of state and federal relationships. When there is a direct conflict between a federal law and a state law, the state law is almost always rendered invalid. Because various powers are concurrent (within the joint purview of the federal government and the individual states), it is important to have a constitutional mechanism to determine which level of government is supposed to prevail in a particular situation.

When Congress chooses to act exclusively, it is said to have "pre-empted" an area. In this instance, a valid federal statute or administrative regulation takes precedence over its state counterpart on the same general subject. However, the U.S. Congress rarely makes clear its intent to pre-empt an entire subject area against state regulation. Thus, the courts must often determine whether Congress intended to exercise exclusive dominion over a specific area. This issue is often litigated in the context of the commerce and the welfare clauses.

Interplaying with the commerce clause and the supremacy clause is the all-important and often misunderstood and underutilized 10th Amendment. It defines the powers and limitations of the federal government and reserves *all* powers not granted to the federal government to the states. Each state has its own state constitution. Unless the state constitutional provisions conflict with the U.S. Constitution, or with a valid federal law, state constitutions are supreme within their respective state borders.

Over time, interpretations of these clauses have eroded traditional regulatory and police powers of the states to the point of emasculation. The 10th Amendment, in particular, has never been properly used or appreciated by constitutional scholars, who have other political agendas, to act as a counterweight to the supremacy clause.

One of the many exemplary emerging issues related to the commerce clause has to do with state attempts to regulate Internet transactions. Once termed the Information Highway, the Internet could be said to be today's super-highway, used to transport information and speech all over the globe. Is cyberspace activity therefore interstate commerce? Does the commerce clause restrict states from interfering with cyberspace activity?

According to at least one tribunal, the answer to both questions is yes! A particularly significant case (*American Library Association vs. Pataki,* 1997) involved a New York state statute that required libraries to filter the data their patrons could access over the Internet. The court based its decision on the commerce clause and held that the statute was unconstitutional. Its reasoning was that "the burdens on interstate commerce resulting from the statute clearly exceed any local benefit derived from it. The Internet is one of those areas of commerce that must be marked off as a national preserve to protect users from inconsistent legislation that, taken to its most extreme, could paralyze the development of the Internet altogether."

In summary, the traditional libertarian position on the commerce clause still stands, despite an apparent inconsistency with respect to the case cited above. Our federal republic was created by the joint action of the several states. Through a gradual erosion of the intent of the framers of the Constitution, the federal government now controls the domestic affairs of the states. The courts over the years have allowed the commerce clause, the welfare clause, and other dispositions of the Constitution to be interpreted in ways that the Founders clearly did not intend, most of which have been consistent with a "quasi-socialist" agenda.

The federal government has no authority to mandate policies relating to state education, welfare, natural resources, transportation, private business, housing, health care, drug use, and the like. The federal government should therefore divest itself of operations not authorized by the Constitution. Congress should extricate the federal government from enterprises which compete with private enterprise. The 10th Amendment must be respected and strengthened vis-á-vis the supremacy and commerce clauses. Given our fluid common law, and precedential judicial system, this could come about by simply providing a better civic education for our citizen litigants, attorneys, and judges.

Although the court in the American Library Association case was probably deciding wisely with respect to reliance upon the commerce clause to annul burdensome state regulations of the Internet in this case, it should have gone much further and suggested through elaborate dicta that one or more constitutional provisions in the Bill of Rights and else-where would likewise prohibit the federal government from regulating the Internet. Given that the Internet is now a global network, we Libertarians would urge national govern-ments around the world (including our own) to apply similar reasoning and would further urge any worldwide associations and agencies not to delve into this murky and potentially destructive legislative and administrative territory.

The example cited above regarding the Internet is an impor-tant illustration of how the Constitution can be used in a flexible and changing fashion to achieve a wide variety of solutions to societal problems. However, this case is some-what different from the general trend of wrongly divesting Iowa and the other 49 states of our sovereignty. If citizens, attorneys, and an "enlightened" judiciary would reassert our constitutional rights and common law protections under tort and contract law, urging more balanced interpretations of the Constitution and other statutes, the intent of the framers would once again become reality in the context of the new millennium.

In Iowa, for example, many citizens are aggrieved by the real and perceived effects of hog lots located next or near to their property. While elaborate legislative and administrative solu-tions have been proposed, this issue can be best handled through local courts, which would apply common law princi-ples of tort, contracts, and equity. Once again, utilizing the lowest level of government necessary, starting at the bottom and working upward, usually works best and provides the most protection for individual liberty.

Our judicial system is uniquely poised to allow our citizenry to reclaim our cherished civil and economic liberties through "bottom-up" government. The common law, our carefully crafted constitutions, and our innate instincts are all that we Americans require to resuscitate our eroded personal freedoms. I have little doubt that we will rise to the challenge.

"If the abuse be enormous, nature will rise up, and claiming her original rights, overturn a corrupt political system."

—*Samuel Johnson, Delegate to Constitutional Congress and U.S. Senator, Connecticut*

Chapter 7. Restoring the Integrity of the Political Process

By Edward F. Noyes, J.D.

When asked what I think is the most important reform that needs to take place in state and national political life, I say that we must reform the political process itself.

The majority of eligible voters in Iowa (and 80 percent of young voters) fail to consider their political opinion important enough to vote. I don't blame these people for their apathy. They intuitively know that the system itself has become so controlled and corrupted, and so distant from their own lives, that they have simply given up. To correct this reality, we must return to a political process that involves the people to the maximum degree and ensures that they are fully informed and educated, so that whatever decisions are ultimately made are based on the highest level of unbiased intelligence.

To understand the forces that exist to take away our freedoms through manipulation of the political process, I like to refer back to the presidential election of Thomas Jefferson in 1800. The Constitution had been enacted in 1787, just 13 years earlier. Jefferson's preference was to remain at his beloved Monticello and refrain from public office, but he agreed to accept the nomination for the presidency and was elected at this critical time in our country's history.

Before Jefferson's election, the editors of some of the major newspapers had been sentenced to prison for their criticism of the new federal government, under the guise of the Alien and Sedition Acts of 1798. In one of his first acts as president, Jefferson freed these men, as it was obvious to him that the constitutional guarantee of freedom of the press—which he had helped formulate—had been violated.

What can we learn from this little bit of history? And what can we do as a nation to re-establish the integrity of the process?

We must remember that, since time immemorial, there are always those who have desired to control the political process for their own benefit. These forces know that if they control the decision-making process, whatever they want can be easily accomplished.

One of the more recent examples occurred in 1996, when Ross Perot was denied the right to participate in the nationally televised presidential debates because the Presidential Debate Board decided he was "not a viable candidate." I knew then that we were in serious trouble in this country. Perot had received 19 percent of the popular vote in the 1992 presidential election, and yet it was determined that he was not viable. Not coincidentally, all of the members of that decision-making board were either Republicans or Democrats. Nor was it a coincidence that, by almost all accounts, Perot won every debate he was allowed to participate in that year.

What is important here is not whether you supported Perot; it is the fact that the process itself was so controlled (and controllable) by the status quo. Clearly, by controlling the debate, the powers that be can effectively control the outcome of the political process. We must enact laws that require the debate itself to be open to all who wish to participate. Otherwise, our inherent right (and duty) to be involved in a participatory, constitutional republic has been lost.

There are other steps we can take as well to open up the political process.

End the Manipulation of the Process

We have seen the political decision-making process bought out through excessive contributions to political campaigns. Allowing corporations and other moneyed interests to donate large sums to these campaigns effectively ensures that the government policies these big contributors want will be enacted. I can assure you, for example, that our national dependency on foreign oil and our national preference for environmentally destructive fossil fuels has been secured through massive donations to campaigns.

One of the most amazing reality TV shows I ever witnessed occurred a few years ago, when I happened to be watching CNN at 1:30 in the morning. It was during the Clinton administration, and Congress's failure to reach a budget agreement was threatening to shut down the federal government. Both parties were threatening that unless the other agreed with their respective proposed budgets, the entire funding mechanism for the federal government would be halted.

The deadline for approving the budget in time to keep the government running was just hours away, so the pressure was on. I tuned in to the debate just as members of Congress were revealing that "during the night" "someone" had attached a "rider" to the budget bill. This rider would make it illegal for the Environmental Protection Agency (EPA) to issue any regulations addressing mercury toxicity in the nation's rivers and lakes for three years, allowing for further study.

Now, until then, I was unaware that mercury in rivers and lakes was an issue. I was also unaware of what caused mercury contamination. Apparently, many members of Congress were also unaware of the cause of the problem. That night I witnessed the most impassioned speechmaking I have ever heard by elected officials. Senators were quoting Chief Joseph that "the earth does not belong to us, we belong to the earth." Others were absolutely shocked that someone had the ability to attach this rider. Many knew of the problem of mercury in the waterways and couldn't believe that further study was needed before allowing the EPA to take action.

Can you believe that we have a political system that allows the funding of every federal government activity to be held hostage by an undisclosed power until it gets its way? And to do it in secret, so that we don't even know who is controlling the process?

Interestingly, despite my diligent review of news sources (which supposedly report the daily news), I never heard of this incident again. It took me years to find out why somebody thought it was so important to stop the EPA from regulating levels of mercury in rivers and lakes. Through research, I learned that this contamination results almost exclusively from the burning of coal for electricity.

Exposure to high levels of mercury can be fatal for humans. In Minnesota alone, more than 300 lakes have such a high degree of mercury toxicity that it is not safe to eat the fish. Other state governments all over the country have issued advisories for lakes and rivers warning people not to swim in the water (let alone eat the fish) for fear of exposure to mercury.

Of course, more than 50 percent of the electricity in this country (and 80 percent in Iowa) comes from coal-fired plants. Some contend that this form of power generation is a major cause of the "greenhouse effect," which many scientists believe threatens to significantly change our ecosystem. Other serious environmental degradations—such as acid rain and the depletion of the ozone layer—are also blamed on the burning of coal.

It became clear to me why that rider was attached to the budget bill. The pretense for the rider was that further study was needed before acting "too hastily" in addressing an "unknown problem." What hyperbole when, in truth, many members of Congress were very aware of the issue and knew that mercury toxicity was a problem in the rivers and lakes in their own states. This example is a sad commentary on how the political process in this country is controlled by special interests.

The manipulation is not just at the federal level either. Many people are astonished to discover that special interest groups draft state legislation voted on by elected officials. In 2001, David Miller, a state legislator from Jefferson County, Iowa, wrote in his *Miller Report* that he and other legislators were told by party leaders that they could not change in any way certain legislation, which had been drafted by related lobby organizations, prior to its being voted on. Our own representatives, who are voted into office by the people, were prevented from doing their jobs.

Eliminate the Power of Special Interests

In 1991, Michael Taylor was appointed to the new Food and Drug Administration position of deputy commissioner for policy. Taylor's job was to supervise the formulation of FDA policy on genetically engineered food. A lawyer, Taylor's previous job was representing Monsanto and other members of the biotech industry on food regulatory issues. During Taylor's tenure as deputy commissioner, references to the potentially negative effects of bioengineering were progressively deleted from drafts of the policy statement (over the protests of agency scientists), resulting in a final policy statement that said (a) GE foods are no riskier than others and (b) the agency has no information to the contrary. After he left the FDA, Taylor was re-hired by Monsanto as vice president for public policy.

Unfortunately, this is not the only example of how closely entwined some corporate interests are these days with the government (see Chapter 14 for more). I remember watching another senator on CNN explaining how the Loral Corporation successfully worked its way through the federal government and around campaign finance laws so that it could sell its advanced satellite technology to China. This senator reported that Loral first donated $600,000 to the Clinton election committee, and then requested clearance from the Department of Defense (DOD) to sell its technology to China. The DOD denied the request saying that this was against the law. Loral then appealed to the head of DOD, who reiterated that under DOD guidelines which prohibit the transfer of technology that might aid a potential enemy, the proposed transfer was illegal.

Not to be denied, Loral somehow convinced the federal government to transfer the issue from the DOD to the Department of Commerce (DOC). (How it accomplished this I have not yet discovered.) The company then made the same appeal for permission and was denied once again. The DOC's response was essentially the same as the DOD's—the proposed transfer was illegal under current law. Not yet deterred, Loral appealed to the head of the DOC, who also determined that the transfer could not occur under U.S. law.

But Loral didn't stop there. It eventually was able to convince a senior Clinton administration official to override both the DOD and the DOC, and give it the go-ahead for the transfer of technology. Technology that actually facilitates the possibility of a nuclear attack on the United States was allowed to be sold despite all so-called protections under the law.

When I heard this story, I wondered what kind of a return Loral expected from its $600,000 investment in the presidential campaign. Knowing that there was some risk of failure, I figured it had to be at least a hundredfold. Sure enough, China paid $60 million for Loral's technology. The entire process was purely a business decision by Loral. No big deal, just business as usual.

The campaign finance law passed by Congress this year won't end this kind of abuse. The media, in particular, will have even more power over the process as they will have control over what is printed and aired in the last few weeks of a campaign. It is no surprise that the *New York Times* and other media outlets were so enthusiastic about this so-called reform bill.

In a *Washington Post* article (March 21, 2001), Warren Buffett, the world's most successful investor, explained how he was once approached by a fund-raising senator who, in jest, told him, "Warren, if you'll contribute $10 million to the campaign, you can get the colors of the American flag changed." Later that senator called again, "Let me update you. It will cost you $20 million and you only get to change one color."

Buffett, a humble man who I believe is a genuine American hero, told the *Post* reporter that "If we continue to permit political influence to be dispensed through a market system, we should expect market results. In the private arena, the market works wonders in producing the goods and services that consumer's desire. In the public sector, as well, it will deliver to purchasers what they want."

Fortunately, we still have patriots left in this country who are not afraid to tell the truth about how the political system currently operates.

Enact Genuine Campaign Finance Reform

Many have struggled with addressing campaign finance reform but have been stuck with the concept of constitutionally protected free speech. Isn't limiting these contributions unconstitutional? The Founders would have no problem with this question. They understood that free speech and other unalienable rights were the gift of being born human. They understood that only humans are made in the image of God, and therefore, only humans are blessed with unalienable rights.

In this country, and throughout the world, there has been an inappropriate granting of free speech rights to corporations and other entities that are not human and have no right to vote. Only humans have the inherent conscience and natural concern for the future generations of their brethren and offspring. Corporations exist to make a profit and are willing to spend money to make money. In reality, corporations exist only at the license of the governments that allow their creation. We not only have the right to monitor their activities, we also have the duty.

We must severely limit, or take away entirely, the ability of organizations to influence the political process. If we do so, we can re-establish the possibility of elevating human values to the forefront of political decision making.

Buffett has suggested it is time to enact a bill that (1) entirely bans direct or indirect contributions by corporations and unions; (2) puts increased but strict limits on individual contributions; and (3) requires that all politically oriented donations, including those to independent committees, be immediately disclosed on the Internet. We would suggest taking it even further and banning all campaign contributions by any nonhuman entity.

In regards to individual contributions, Buffett's suggestion for increased but strict limits should be seriously considered. We must look at balancing the right of an individual to vote his conscience by contributing personal funds to a campaign with the right of every eligible voter to have an effective voice in the election process. Also, immediate disclosure of donations made by anyone to influence the process may be more important than a desire for privacy.

It will take courage and commitment to make genuine, restorative changes in the political process. We the people must be willing to take back our responsibilities for the purity of the governmental process and become the masters of the government, rather than the servants of the status quo.

Return Sovereignty to the States and the People

We must elect leaders who have the courage to give the people back their sovereignty. The federal government is involved with societal problems that were never meant to be dealt with at that level. The Founders' vision was to limit the federal government's involvement to only "enumerated powers." That was far more intelligent than what we have allowed to evolve in this country. Shifting power and decision making to the state and local levels would accomplish the majority of the reform that needs to take place in the political process in this country.

Once communities are given back their sovereignty, everyone within that community will have a direct, vested interest in the decisions that are made affecting them and others in the community. What a young voter thinks of an issue will be of vital importance to everyone, as everyone will have to live with those policies every day of their lives. The maximum participation and involvement of the people will be possible as well as necessary. No longer could one claim, "politics isn't relevant to my life."

Encourage Third-party Involvement

To open up the political process, we must encourage third-party involvement. Ballot access must be simple and be encouraged, and third-party candidates for statewide political offices must be able to take part in the debates so that people are exposed to their ideas. Almost every significant reform achieved by the federal government has been initiated by third parties. Given the consolidation of political power in government that naturally results over time, this comes as no surprise.

It is always the existing powers that want to control and limit debate. We must ask if we are more committed to the integrity of the process or to the personalities involved. It has been said that there is nothing so powerful as an idea whose time has come. But if that idea is not allowed to be considered, how powerful can it be?

The watchful eye of the public must be allowed, and encouraged, to oversee the workings of our governments. The Internet is a perfect way to accomplish this. It should absolutely be illegal for anyone or anything to hold the process hostage the way the energy industry did during the budget debate described above. No one should be allowed to create legislation without knowing exactly where that legislation is coming from and who sponsored the legislation.

**We can ensure that our political
process is open to all!**

Electing candidates who have an understanding of the Founders' vision and who are not tied to the status quo offers the greatest opportunity for a return to their vision. I have no doubt that together we can bring about fundamental reforms that will restore the integrity of our political process for everyone. By enacting these reforms, we will once again be able to justly proclaim that we truly have a government *of the people, by the people and for the people.*

Section Three:

The Issues

"At whatever point on the scientific horizon I begin my researches, I invariably reach this one conclusion: The solution to the problems of human relationships is to be found in liberty."

—*Bastiat*, The Law

"The income tax code is a disgrace to the human race."

—*President Jimmy Carter,*
Inaugural address, 1977

Chapter 8. Income Tax: Igniting Iowa's Economy

By Clyde J. Cleveland and Edward F. Noyes, J.D.

Position Summary

We plan to phase out the state income tax over five years. This will create an economic boom in Iowa which will increase economic vitality in the state and thus increase sales tax revenue.

Modest budget cuts will be necessary, but the bulk of them will come from implementing our innovative reforms in the criminal justice system and as a result of allowing communities to regain "local control," i.e., sovereignty. Also, we fully expect a boom in the economy as a result of our property tax reforms, which will result in increased sales tax revenues throughout the state. We will also cut the top salaries in government, starting with a 30 percent cut in the governor's salary. The government workforce will be decreased through attrition, with positions refilled only when absolutely necessary. We will also save money by implementing performance standards for every department of government.

The income tax is a totally destructive tax. It is the second plank of the Communist Manifesto and was recommended by

Karl Marx as one of the best ways to destroy a free society. It does a great job of doing just that. It penalizes hard work, saving, and investing—all of the things Iowa needs to improve its economy. Iowa will never be strong economically with the income tax in place.

Being both responsible and practical, our plan will be extraordinarily effective in improving the quality of life for all Iowans.

The Problem

The first income tax act, passed in England in the 1400s, was so hated that when it was eventually eliminated the English citizenry had all records burned so the "hideous monster," as it was then called, would never be allowed to return. It was not until the early 1800s that the income tax returned, and then to finance the Napoleonic wars. The people paid the tax until Napoleon was defeated at Waterloo. Two weeks later, the people put so much pressure on Parliament that it was eliminated again. The celebration in London was the longest and most impressive celebration in the nation's history. In fact, it dwarfed the celebration of Wellington's victory over Napoleon, which had occurred only weeks before.

Today, the hideous monster lives in Iowa and is a major factor in a vicious cycle of expensive bureaucracy:

• We increase income taxes, along with property taxes and car registration fees, because we don't have enough economic vitality in our state to generate necessary income from the sales tax.

- When we raise taxes and fees, we lose even more companies and successful entrepreneurs; this further reduces economic activity and tax revenues.

- So what do we do? We increase our taxes even more. And on and on it goes!

Iowa ranks near the bottom of all the states in economic vitality, as several studies have shown.

- A 2002 PricewaterhouseCoopers study of venture capital investments ranked Iowa 51st in the nation, down from 50th the year before; Puerto Rico passed us by!

- A 1998 Cognetics study of "entrepreneurial hotspots" ranked Iowa 50th.

- A 2000 Milken Institute "New Economy Study" ranked Iowa 47th in "business starts."

- The Progressive Policy Institute's 1999 "New Economy Index" ranked Iowa 50th in "economic dynamism."

This has been the situation under both Democratic and Republican administrations. Despite that, they have kept on increasing our taxes, which just exacerbates our economic problems by making it even harder to attract venture capital and entrepreneurs to our state. In the meantime, our most valuable resource—our best and brightest young people—leave Iowa to seek more prosperous economic conditions elsewhere.

Those increased taxes, including Iowa's income tax, are financing a bloated state government. Iowa has one of the country's highest ratios of government employees to population, with 601 public employees for every 10,000 people. Most state government employees in other states are paid within 10 percent of what private workers are paid for the same work. We have even seen studies by the Public Policy Institute that report that Iowa pays its government employees over 140 percent of what private industry pays for the same work!

To support that bureaucracy and the ever-expanding state programs, state spending has significantly increased over the years. Iowa's population, however, has not. Our expenditures have gone up by more than the rate of inflation every year, while our population has been stagnant for the last 20 years. It is obvious that previous administrations have allowed our bureaucracy, and consequently our spending, to increase far beyond what is necessary.

In addition to being part of a flawed system, the income tax is a problem because it by nature is a penalty against hard-working people who want to earn more money. It is also a penalty against saving and investing. The income tax discourages everything we need to encourage in Iowa. It discourages people from moving here and moving their businesses here. Our successful young entrepreneurs do not want to pay Iowa's income tax when they can move to states like Alaska, Florida, Nevada, Tennessee, Texas, Washington, or Wyoming, and pay no income tax. The income tax must be eliminated to create prosperity in Iowa.

Money is the fuel that ignites the economy and keeps it running. Like adding wood to a fire, the more money you put into the economy, the more it grows. When you take too much money out of the private sector, it has a dampening effect on the economy, just as taking wood off the fire reduces it. The income tax takes money out of private sector activities.

But it does more damage than that. All taxes are like penalties on whatever is taxed. If you tax interest on savings accounts, people will save less. If you tax income, especially with progressive rates, people will work less. If you tax investment income (capital gains), people will invest less.

There is no popular tax, but the income tax is the worst tax ever invented. The income tax is seen as so unfair that otherwise honest people have been known to cheat in their calculations. It hurts everyone except the very rich, who have exempt foundations to protect their wealth and enough resources to hire the best estate planners to create the necessary tax-avoidance strategies.

The Bottom-up Solutions

We plan to phase out the state income tax over a five-year period. It can be accomplished quicker than that, but we are being very conservative with our projections. Our plan will not affect teachers' salaries. It will not reduce essential services. It will, however, bring us back to the level of spending we had in 1995 and fund our entire state government. Remember, our population today is essentially where it was in 1980.

Iowa State Income Tax Phase-out Plan

Income decrease in (base) tax rate		Income Tax revenue	Other Tax Revenues 8% increase	Total Income	Expenses less 6%
2002	100%	2.4	2.6	5.0	5.0
2003	80%	2.1	2.8	4.9	4.7
2004	60%	1.6	3.0	4.6	4.4
2005	40%	1.1	3.3	4.4	4.1
2006	20%	0.5	3.5	4.0	3.8
2007	0%	0	3.8	3.8	3.5

Note: We use an 8% annual increase in other revenue sources as a conservative estimate of income from all other revenue sources from increased economic activity resulting from the implementation of our phase-out plan. We also add back in, after allowing for the 20% reduction in the base year's income tax revenue, an 8% increase in income taxes collected from the previous year's projected income tax revenue.

Phasing Out the Income Tax

- Government, in general, experiences 10 percent to 15 percent employee retirement every year. Replacement of these workers would be significantly reduced under our plan. Our goal would be to reduce the numbers of government employees to 65 percent of current levels, which should take approximately five years. We believe that attrition combined with the implementation of our proven methods for increasing performance could reduce government spending by approximately 5 percent per year.

- Our plan would cut the pay of top-level government employees immediately, starting with a 30 percent cut in the governor's salary. A study of the discrepancy between state and private workers would indicate where to make further appropriate cuts.

- More authority and freedom would be given to workers based on performance, output, or public appraisals. Incentives for efficient operations would be paid to entire departments for doing more with less. Consolidation of departments would occur where appropriate. We will use the services of organizations like the Mercatus Group, which is now helping our federal government develop performance standards. The Mercatus Group helped move almost two-thirds of New Zealand's public sector employees to the private sector. We will also explore more ways of having services provided by the private sector.

- Appropriate severance packages would be offered to employees in certain circumstances.

- Our plan to move nonviolent offenders from the state's prison system to locally controlled mentor/parole supervision (see Chapter 15) could achieve a major portion of the 6 percent reduction in state spending we have set as our goal. We are very encouraged by the potential of this program to save money and improve the rehabilitation record of our criminal justice system.

A conservative estimate of reductions in expenditures after all cost-cutting measures are implemented, including the hiring freeze and the criminal justice reform program, would be 9 percent to 10 percent per year. We are using only a 6 percent annual reduction for our projections.

We asked William Lynn, Ph.D., a professor of economics at St. Ambrose University, Davenport, Iowa, to review our plan for phasing out the income tax. Here is what he had to say: "I believe your income tax plan should work. It assumes a relatively modest growth rate in the economy. A normal growth rate would be around 3 percent if there were no other inducements to faster growth. I believe the reduced tax rates would increase the growth rate. I think the plan is reasonable."

We agree.

Accomplishing this program will provide immense benefits for our state. Investors, CEOs and venture capitalists from all over the world will be impressed. The investment in capital and new business start-ups will be immediate. Young people with academic and technical skills will no longer be leaving Iowa. Our older citizens will be able to retire in a tax haven here at home. New businesses will move here. Businesses already here will be able to expand their operations and hire more employees. The ripple effect on our economy and way of life will be felt everywhere in Iowa. This program is one of the cornerstones to create the Iowa we all want.

"Don't dwell on what went wrong. Instead, focus on what to do next. Spend your energies on moving forward toward finding the answer."

—Denis Waitley

Chapter 9. Property Tax: Creating a Construction Boom

By Clyde J. Cleveland and Edward F. Noyes, J.D.

Position Summary

Iowa's property taxes are out of control and everybody knows it. Our plan will fix the most onerous problems of the system, which are the disincentive to improve property, unlimited increases in tax amounts, invasive inspections, and an arbitrary system. We will cap the amount of tax a person pays at 1 percent of the last sale price of the property. Each county can decide what level to set taxes, up to that percentage.

This change will create a construction boom as people begin to improve their properties. The resulting increased building and economic activity will, in turn, increase sales tax revenues. Over time, the property tax base will increase naturally as homes increase in value due to improvements and sell for higher prices.

No tax system is perfect, but this will be a very significant improvement.

The Problem

Does this sound familiar to what is currently going on in Iowa?

"Prior to Proposition 13, [California's] property taxes were out of control. People were losing their homes because they could not pay their property taxes. Yet, government did nothing to help them." (Howard Jarvis Taxpayer Association, www.hjta.org)

Iowa's high income tax and high property taxes are preventing companies and individuals from moving here, while at the same time, causing others to leave. We know this from our own gut-wrenching personal experiences of watching our children move out-of-state.

We want our children, and the children of all Iowans, to return to prosperous jobs and a dynamic economy. But Iowa will never attract business unless we create an environment in which people can become prosperous. No government-recruiting effort or tax-tweaking policies will ever compare with significant tax reforms and reductions in our income and property taxes.

Of all of our state taxes, the current property tax may be the most despised. It deserves to be. It is all of the things a tax should not be.

- It is a disincentive to improve property. This creates rundown neighborhoods and failing business districts.

- It is complicated. We don't know anyone who can explain how the appraisal formula actually works.

- It is intrusive. Government can use its police power to force us to submit to inspections of our homes by government officials.

- It is excessive. In some cases, people are paying over 4 percent of the value of their home in property taxes.

- It is arbitrary. One person may be paying 4 percent, while the person across the street or in the next town who owns a similar home will be paying 1.5 percent.

- It punishes seniors, many of whom are on fixed incomes. Over time, senior home owners face higher and higher "assessed" values and pay ever-increasing property taxes.

Awareness of the problem is widespread. In his column in the *Des Moines Register*, David Yepsen reported receiving a letter from an Iowa native now living in California. Julie Stranges, who comes back to Des Moines to care for her aging mother, wrote: "The property tax rates in Iowa are obnoxiously high. I could hardly believe the amount that my mother had to pay. I know how hard Iowa is working to keep people there. But when you can go live in a state where the cost of living is so much lower, where there are no personal income taxes and the list goes on and on, it's a wonder anyone ever stays there at all."

The Bottom-up Solutions

Our vision for Iowa is to go from being one of the highest-taxed states in the country to one of the lowest-taxed states in the country, and do it within four years. We want to become the eighth state in the country to have no state income tax (see Chapter 8 for details). We also want to create a property tax system that not only doesn't discourage people from moving to Iowa, but also encourages those who are here to stay.

Reforming the Property Tax

Our property tax plan will eliminate intrusive government property inspections, increases in property taxes for our retired citizens and farmers, and the huge disincentive for property improvements that now exists. Here's how:

- The "assessed value" of the property would be the last market sale price, eliminating any question as to the value of the property.

- Everyone would pay a maximum of 1 percent of that assessed value. Each county would determine, without need of the state's consent, its own percentage rate, up to a maximum of 1 percent.

- Those who now pay less than 1 percent of the property's last purchase price would not be affected by this change; they would continue to pay their current rate. Those who now pay more than 1 percent would continue to pay their same rate for one year from the date of passage of the new tax law. After one year, their property tax rate would be reduced to 1 percent plus half of the difference between 1 percent and the amount they presently pay. After two years, their rate will decrease to 1 percent.

- Those who are living in a dwelling that has never been sold will have to submit a statement giving their opinion of the current market value of their property. Included in that statement would be the sales prices of at least three comparable properties sold within the last two years, as well as their explanation of the submitted valuation based on the comparables. This will be a simple and inexpensive procedure. The use of local licensed real estate professionals will be encouraged.

- Citizens 65 and over who have been paying property taxes in Iowa for at least 25 years may receive a complete property tax exemption. This would be up to each individual county.

- The state will no longer be involved in collecting or assessing property taxes, and therefore, will be able to save money by eliminating all bureaucracy associated with the collection of the property tax.

- Iowa will enjoy a significant increase in sales tax revenues from this plan as it will trigger a construction boom that will in turn fuel the economy. After a year under the new system, the counties will no longer have to pay any property tax revenues to the state.

- The resulting construction boom will lead to two things: (1) More people having money to build and buy new homes, increasing the homes on the market, and therefore increasing the tax base; and (2) an increase in sales of existing homes, at increased sales values, increasing the amount of taxes paid on that property.

Benefits of Our Plan

With our plan, Iowa will follow in the successful footsteps of California. On June 6, 1978, nearly two-thirds of California's voters passed Proposition 13 reducing property taxes by about 57 percent. The reductions went into effect immediately, and the state still managed just fine financially.

Clyde was a real estate broker in San Diego when Proposition 13 passed and president of a successful real estate company. He saw firsthand the tax revolt that swept the country and made headlines around the world. Proposition 13 started a shift in thinking about the tax burden taxpayers had to bear. It also started a revolution in the use of ballot initiatives as a way for people to gain greater control over their states and communities. (Incidentally, the latest attempt to alter Proposition 13 was defeated 2 to 1 by the voters of California.)

Construction boom. The disincentive to improving property would be eliminated. Hallelujah! California saw a boom in building following the passage of Proposition 13. We are confident this will happen throughout Iowa as well, once we stop penalizing people for doing what comes natural to them, improving and beautifying their homes and other properties.

We also have a model right here in Iowa. In 2001, the City of Keokuk instituted a tax-abatement program, under which property owners will not receive an increase in property tax assessments for three years if they make improvements to their property. Lo and behold, Keokuk is having a construction boom. That construction boom is creating jobs and expanding the economy.

After being informed of the residential property owners' quick response to the tax-abatement program, Gary Folluo, mayor of Keokuk, stated: "We are real excited about the fact that people are using this plan. That means there are people who are doing a lot of construction work…that's just a plus for our community. This will encourage people to come to Keokuk and let them know that this is a progressive community and that we are trying to get people to invest in this community." (*The Hawk Eye*, Sept. 9, 2001)

Overall increase in tax revenues. In California, many of the critics of the new program predicted massive reductions in property tax revenues and consequent reductions in services. That did not happen. In fact, overall property tax revenues went up because houses increased in value as a result of all the improvements people were making to their properties. These improvements would not have occurred otherwise. When these properties were sold, they naturally were sold for a higher price. Therefore, an increase in the tax base, desired by all, is accomplished without the government forcing increased appraisals upon the citizens.

Construction and related economic activity also trigger increases in state sales tax revenue, which will provide additional local and state funding.

Less bureaucracy. This program eliminates the complexity of our current system and eliminates the need for full-time assessors at the local level. This reduction in bureaucracy will help us meet our goal to trim the state budget by 6 percent a year from the current spending level.

Fairness. There will be no more outrageous assessments resulting in inequitable rates between neighbors or even next-door neighborhoods; no more of our struggling farmers will be forced to sell land because of escalating property taxes; and home buyers will know exactly how much they will have to pay in property taxes.

In addition, senior citizens, who are frequently punished the most by the current system, will no longer have to suffer merely because property values are increasing around them: they would not have to pay higher and higher property taxes as their assessed value increases. This cycle has been forcing senior citizens on fixed incomes out of their homes. With "assessed value" being the most recent market sale price, seniors can feel secure that they will not be "taxed out" of their own homes.

No more intrusive inspections. Home inspection by a government official is so foreign to our notion of freedom and property rights that it is amazing we ever allowed our current system to be implemented. Those inspections will be eliminated with this new plan.

No Tax, or Tax Plan, is Perfect

We agree that property taxes are one of the worst forms of taxes. How can you have an inalienable right to property, if that property can be taken away if you don't pay the tax? We are open to eliminating property taxes entirely if a more intelligent solution is available. For now, we will restructure the way property taxes are collected to eliminate the most egregious aspects of the tax.

Even under our new system, some people will try to avoid paying their tax, with phony appraisals and other manipulations. Still, our plan is a vast improvement over our current system and should be implemented. People are willing to pay a tax when they consider it to be simple and equitable, and therefore we predict that cheating will be minimal. Property taxes are already a matter of public record and even available online in many counties. Property sales prices are also public record. Your neighbors will know if you are a tax cheat.

It is possible that in year two or year three of our plan, there could be a slight reduction in county revenues. It is also possible that no decrease will occur, or even that an increase will occur. Every county will be different. The elimination of the amount going to the state (approximately 6 percent of collected revenue) will be a significant factor in keeping most counties from noticing a drop in revenues collected.

In designing our plan, we asked several tax policy experts to review it. William Lynn, Ph.D., is a professor of economics at St. Ambrose University, Davenport, Iowa. His response was: "Property taxes are always a problem. To my knowledge there is no perfect way to tax property. The current system can force people out of their homes because when values rise the taxes also rise. Your plan would protect them. It may not be perfect, but it is probably the best alternative other than no property tax at all. It is clearly a reasonable improvement over our current system."

Now is the time for

genuine property tax reform!

We recognize how important genuine property tax reform is for the people of Iowa. We are committed to changing the property tax system itself in the most innovative way possible so that Iowans can enjoy a new status—as one of the least-taxed states in the Union.

"Human beings have the remarkable ability to turn nothing into something. They can turn weeds into gardens and pennies into fortunes."

—*Jim Rohn*

Chapter 10. Renewable Energy: Powering Iowa's Bright Future

By Clyde J. Cleveland and Edward F. Noyes, J.D.

Position Summary

Our nation stands at the threshold of a new era in energy production. As we see the prices of fossil fuels steadily rise, and the oil and gas supply endangered by geo-political instability, we are increasingly aware that we cannot sustain our standard of living and continue economic growth by relying on fossil fuels.

We Iowans have the answer; we just need to let the world know. Renewable sources of energy are available right now. Iowa alone has the resources to be the nation's leader in the production of clean, agriculturally based energy. The state is already the third-largest producer of wind energy, and along with Minnesota and North Dakota, we can become known as "the Saudi Arabia of Wind."

In addition, our rich soil holds the key to numerous other new energy technologies that utilize "biomass," or energy crops, to produce fuel for electrical generation and transportation fuels. Other technologies—like microturbines powered by methane from livestock or landfills—can add even more opportunities. By distributing generation, Iowa can become an energy exporter, increase grid reliability, and help provide energy security.

Our plan, which is totally revolutionary, will create an environment in which each individual Iowan will reap the economic and environmental benefits of renewable-energy technology. We propose:

- A market-based approach to fulfilling Iowa's energy needs that makes Iowa the nation's leader in cutting-edge energy technology, opens new markets for Iowa's farmers and improves environmental quality.

- A restructuring of Iowa's reverse "net" metering laws, and a grassroots, locally based financing mechanism which will create prosperity for our local communities and each individual Iowan.

The Problem

Iowa gets 87 percent of its electricity from coal, 100 percent of which is imported from out-of-state at the cost of $310 million (in 1995). In addition, we rely on nuclear power and natural gas, both of which are extremely vulnerable economically and pose other risks as well. Only about 3 percent of our energy comes from wind, although Iowa has the potential to produce four times our energy needs from wind alone. We are subsidizing money-losing, out-of-state energy interests, while missing valuable opportunities for boosting Iowa's economy.

Current federal policies have contributed to this decline. Once the United States led the world in wind-generated electricity; we now get less than 1 percent, compared to Denmark's 17 percent. Germany, which had virtually no wind power development five years ago, now produces more wind-generated electricity than any country in the world.

The Hidden Costs of Nonrenewable Energy

There are many hidden costs in the production of energy. For example, the price of electricity generated by burning coal is kept artificially low by coal subsidies, but you still pay in taxes.

And aside from the costs of your electric bill and what you pay at the pump, there are the costs of pollution- and health-related problems. It's been proved that exposure to emissions such as carbon monoxide, acid rain or particulate matter increases the severity of asthma, other pulmonary conditions and cardiovascular disease. Water and air quality are important quality-of-life issues.

B.C. Gerstein, professor emeritus in physical chemistry at Iowa State University, compared wind- and coal-generated energy in a *Des Moines Register* guest editorial (Dec. 3, 2000). Gerstein wrote: "The deferred environmental costs of the spread of nitrogen oxides alone from the burning of coal are about $60 million a year. The Iowa air in the neighborhood of old coal-fired plants kills 300 Iowans a year, with plants in the Des Moines area the worst offenders. Coal-gasification plants of the type that supply electricity for the Iowa population burn 25,000 tons of coal and produce 250 tons of ash a day. The arsenic produced by burning this amount of coal is

765 pounds a day. The uranium in the ash amounts to more than 45 pounds a day. The mercury amounts to about five pounds a day. Being highly volatile, the mercury can easily go out the stack and lead to the type of contamination resulting in the fish kill attributed to the Florida power plant.

"Iowans can be optimistic despite the above news. In 1993, the Union of Concerned Scientists produced a report, 'Powering the Midwest,' in which the wind-energy potential for Iowa was reported to be 45.7 times the electric demand at that time. The economic aspects of wind generators are stunning compared to coal-fired plants. Energy from the wind—including the turbine, substation, transmission, service center, land and indirect/permitting—costs roughly a dollar a watt. This compares favorably to the construction of a coal-fired plant when deferred costs such as health hazards are included. At current rates for the sale of electric power, the payback time for a wind generator is seven years. The lifetime of such a generator is 25 years with the new machines. This means that aside from maintenance costs, there are up to 18 years of free power generation from such a unit."

Since Gerstein wrote his editorial, the expected lifetime of new-technology wind turbines has increased to 30 years, which would result in 23 years of free power generation.

Given the clear advantages of renewable forms of energy (such as wind) for the average citizen, we must ask why government policies continue to promote fossil fuel technologies. We must also ask what fundamental changes need to be made to change this dynamic into one that takes into consideration all of the relevant factors.

Government-sanctioned Ecological Risks

It is common knowledge that burning coal to produce energy results in some of the worst environmental problems. First, the coal must be extracted from the earth. Miners risk black lung disease, while the earth itself is cut open, often by the infamous strip-mining processes. Returning the earth to its previous condition is virtually impossible, with millions being spent in an attempt to restore the land.

Next, the coal must be transported to the site of generation, often thousands of miles away. Those who live next to railroad tracks in Iowa are all too aware of the endless railcars that come through town and the resulting noise pollution.

In addition, burning coal releases heavy carbon dioxide emissions, which many contend are the number one cause of the "greenhouse effect" and global warming. If scientists throughout the world are correct, global warming could seriously change the earth's climate for thousands of years, with unknown consequences.

Sulfur dioxide emissions, another result of burning coal, are the primary cause of acid rain. This is such a problem that many eastern states are considering class-action lawsuits against states that burn coal in regions where the effluents are carried by the wind across state lines.

Coal plants also produce nitrogen oxides, which create smog and soot particles that can invade and lodge in human lungs. Mercury, a toxic metal that accumulates in animals, and fish and in humans who eat them, is another toxin emitted from coal-fired plants. It has so contaminated lakes and rivers throughout the United States that health agencies have issued advisories against entering the water, let alone eating the fish.

Despite the overwhelming environmental and related health problems associated with the burning of coal, 34 new coal plants have been proposed as of September 2001. The U.S. Department of Energy estimates that by 2020 (assuming current policies continue), the nation will use about 22 percent more coal than today. Under our current governmental policies, the utility companies that burn coal and fossil fuels are responsible for almost none of the environmental and related health costs that the people must suffer because of their choice of fuels. Amazingly, the exact opposite is true. As a result of the energy corporations' massive lobbying efforts (as well as the millions of dollars that were contributed to presidential campaigns), President Bush's national "energy plan" provides some $30 billion in tax credits, promotions, and other benefits to these same industries.

The Bottom-up Solutions

We propose:

- A market-based approach, to fulfill Iowa's energy needs that makes Iowa the nation's leader in cutting-edge energy technology, while opening new markets for Iowa's farmers and improving environmental quality.

- A restructuring of Iowa's reverse "net" metering laws, and a grassroots, locally-based financing mechanism which will create prosperity for our local communities and each individual Iowan.

Emissions Credits Trading System and Elimination of Subsidies

Many environmental economists have proposed an emissions credits trading system which would issue credits to interests involved in the offsetting or removal of carbon dioxide and other greenhouse gasses. Plants and trees remove, or sequester, carbon from the atmosphere through photosynthesis. Old-growth forests and prairie grasses sequester the most carbon per acre, followed by other crops. Therefore, farmers would be issued credits dependent on the carbon sequestration potential of their land.

Offsetting emissions is done by replacing the use of fossil fuels with cleaner sources of energy. Wind and solar power produce zero emissions, while co-firing of biomass in older coal-fired power plants, methane recovery, and other agriculture-based technologies produce substantially fewer emissions than burning coal. These facilities would be issued credits on the basis of the amount of emissions releases displaced.

In addition, energy-efficiency measures result in less energy waste, therefore offsetting additional pollution. Credits could be issued to builders and homeowners who utilize energy-efficient building technologies, materials, and other products. Additional fees could be added to products that are clearly no longer environmentally friendly or technologically current, such as mercury vapor lights.

Utilities burning coal or natural gas would be required to purchase the appropriate amount of credits to offset the pollution produced by their plants, thereby reflecting the true cost of fossil fuels to Iowans and allowing locally based energy sources to compete fairly in the energy market. According to Jim Thompson, former governor of Illinois and former head of the National Governors Association Global Climate Change Task Force, the Midwest's diverse industrial, financial, and agricultural economic base makes it an ideal location to demonstrate the effectiveness of greenhouse gas emissions trading.

Perhaps even more effective than this trading system would be the elimination of subsidies. Energy companies receive billions of tax dollars each year. It is difficult to ferret out how much, given the complex tax code, but in *Perverse Subsidies*, Norman Myers and Jennifer Kent identified $21 billion received by the fossil fuels and nuclear power industries. Other estimates range from nearly $3 billion to $80 billion a year.

Renewable-energy companies, on the other hand, receive only about a tenth of that. Myers and Kent calculate that the United States spends about $90 million a year on solar research.

We support both the elimination of subsidies and the establishment of an emissions trading system.

Net Metering Programs

Currently, investor-owned utilities are required by law to purchase power from small producers. This is most commonly done by hooking solar panels, a wind turbine, or other renewable-energy source to the grid. The meter runs forward when producers are using more power than they are producing and backward when they are using less than they are producing.

We will encourage individuals to make use of the net meter-ing opportunity, thereby increasing the reliability of electrical generation across Iowa. This will decentralize energy production, making it much more unlikely that Iowa would ever experience the kind of shortages California expe-rienced in 2001. We believe we should encourage the rugged individualism and independence that is a part of our national and state heritage.

Community net metering. The net metering law needs to be expanded to include county and municipal utilities as well as rural electric co-operatives. This will allow all Iowans to par-ticipate in Iowa's growing renewable-energy opportunities. Access to transmission lines and the power grid by locally based producers is essential to this plan. Nothing would cause energy independence faster than acknowledging the right of counties, municipalities, and rural cooperatives to have equal access to the grid. Environmentalists should also note that nothing would cause a shift towards clean, renewable sources of energy faster than providing this type of economic incen-tive to the local communities.

The economic benefits of renewable energy are already being seen in the vicinity of Iowa's wind farms. Farmers are receiv-ing lease payments averaging $2,000 a year for each turbine on their property, while removing only about a quarter of an acre from production. New jobs are being produced, and local economies are benefiting from the new business.

By adding biomass energy crops, methane recovery, solar, and other renewables to diversify Iowa's farm economy, and stim-ulating new business in the fields of energy production and energy efficiency, Iowa can enjoy sustainable growth, a reliable power supply, and a cleaner environment.

Decentralized energy production. Our vision calls for an aggressive net metering program that would give the vast majority of the profits to the producer of the alternative-energy sources. If each community provided funding for a wind farm through a county or city bond offering, they would then receive profits back from the utility company. Effectively, local communities would receive the benefit of the full retail value of the electricity produced, minus a fair percentage (estimated at 10 percent to 15 percent) for maintenance of the common grid.

Profits would first go to pay off the bond issue. After that, the money would go to the community to be disbursed however the people decide to disburse it. We believe the vast majority of it should go directly back to the taxpayers who financed the original bond offering. This way the people of Iowa would have a source of income that could be used to eliminate property taxes if they so chose. They could also finance local businesses, education, civic projects, charities, nonprofit organizations, and all of the other organizations and enterprises that build civil society.

By financially rewarding communities for taking responsibility for their energy production requirements, we create a powerful motivation for people to remain in their local communities. This cash flow, which now belongs to the communities instead of a utility company, would be available to pass down to succeeding generations as long as they continued to live in the community.

Cost Accountability and Competition

The Founders intended to prohibit the federal government from being involved in the administration of most societal issues. Generally speaking, the federal government was only to be involved in those areas that were "specifically enumerated" by the Constitution. Certainly, the federal government was not to be involved in choosing which energy source should receive extra benefits and promotions from the government. The Founders understood that once you allow preferences, whoever has the most influence would automatically gain the favor of the government.

In our modern version of corrupt government, where the richest entities on earth are allowed to give unlimited amounts of money to elect the politicians of their choosing, it comes as no surprise that the coal, gas, and oil companies receive billions and billions of dollars in benefits while renewable-energy suppliers receive tokens.

Proper use of the Founders' concept of restorative justice provides a tool to level the playing field so that nonpolluting sources of energy have a natural economic advantage over polluting sources. The first step should be to eliminate all government subsidies. Nothing we could do would be more effective in improving our environment than the total elimination of subsidies for all energy producers. However, in addition to the elimination of subsidies, the government has every right (and duty) to impose the costs of pollution on those who pollute. Restorative justice principles would dictate that any entity which harms others would be required to pay the price of "restoring" the victim(s) to their original status.

These principles are based on fundamental civil rights of everyone to be free from harm caused by another.

Under the restorative justice principles, if utility companies continue to choose to burn coal to produce energy, they would be required to incur the costs of damages incurred by the victims of their actions. If these companies were required to take financial responsibility for the consequences of their choices, and their competitors were operating free of those extra costs, you can be certain that they would choose renewable, nonpolluting sources and do so almost overnight. If individuals are held criminally responsible for harming other individuals, why should corporations be allowed to cause harm without paying for the consequences?

The fact is, we the people have every right to compensation for harms caused by corporations that adopt practices that harm us. Once we recognize that right, and insist that our elected representatives not legislate away our protections, we will see the quality of life in our state and nation improve dramatically.

We must also take steps to ensure that the utility companies don't simply pass on to their customers the costs which are imposed upon them if they continue to choose polluting forms of energy production. One way to ensure honesty is by eliminating the monopoly status that utility companies currently possess. Companies that choose nonpolluting, renewable forms of energy production will have an economic advantage over companies that pollute. Vigorous competition along with true cost accountability will naturally result in both the lowest costs for energy and the greatest degree of environmental protection. The "community net metering" concept, where the local communities are encouraged to produce their own renewable forms of energy, would provide further competition and protection from abuse.

The Future is Bright

The future of Iowa is very bright indeed as we acknowledge that the God-given blessings of our state, including natural sources of energy, belong to everyone who lives here. We are committed to giving back to the people the original vision of our nation, which recognized the value of decentralizing power whenever possible. By restructuring the benefits of energy production, we will rightfully proclaim once again, that the people own the power.

"Farmers don't like to hear that we're essentially a ward of the government, that we're on a workfare program."

—*Alan Libbra, Illinois farmer,*
St. Louis Post-Dispatch, *Dec. 5, 2001*

Chapter 11. Agriculture: Returning Prosperity to Iowa's Farmers

By Clyde J. Cleveland and Edward F. Noyes, J.D.

Position Summary

We believe that farming is the most noble and honorable profession there is. We believe that farmers understand nature better than anyone, and that their understanding of nature makes them wise in general. Our farmers are figuring out what has been happening to them over the last several decades. As they continue to seek answers, our administration will be there to help and support them in any way that we can.

We support family farming in Iowa, and we want to help restore prosperity to the local farm communities. We will not tell the farmers what to do; we believe that big problems have been created by people who do not know farming telling farmers how to farm.

What we will do is provide information about solid economic alternatives to conventional farming methods—real solutions that will make them more prosperous and less dependent on large companies and the government. It will be up to farmers to decide whether these alternatives make sense for their situation.

The Problem

In August 2001, Clyde spoke at a conference in Ames sponsored by the Catholic Rural Life Association. At one point, a state senator form northern Iowa made a statement regarding his experience on his recent trip to Japan. He said that the Japanese don't want our soybeans because they are genetically engineered. The Japanese made it clear to him that they would be glad to pay significantly more for soybeans that have not been genetically modified. Then the senator looked out at the audience and asked the question of the day: Why are we continuing to grow a product that people don't want?

We believe this is a very important question. Why would we continue to produce products that don't bring us a price high enough to make a profit, and at the same time, employ growing methods that potentially destroy our own land and our natural resources?

We have heard the same story from farmers across Iowa and the country. The majority of our farmers are locked into a system that they can't get out of, even though they know it is destructive and unprofitable. The cycle seems to be more debt, bigger farms, more expensive machinery, higher-priced inputs, more dependence on government and lower profits.

When you step back and look at what has happened to farming in this country over the last 55 years, it is almost as if a long-term plan to force farmers off the land and into the cities was put into place many decades ago.

> "For people who want to buy corn, there really isn't much choice but to come to us."
>
> —*Bob Kohlmeyer, Cargill Corporation*, Des Moines Register, *Nov. 15, 2000*

That is exactly the view of Charles Waters, who founded *Acres USA* magazine in 1970. Waters has spent a lifetime helping farming entrepreneurs find their way to a profitable bottom line. He has written several books on economics and thousands of articles on eco-agriculture. In his book *Raw Materials Economics*, Waters states, "On the heels of WW 2 in 1946, advisers in the wings of politics said, 'Empty the countryside'…And they knew how to do it…These advisers came on as the American Farm Economics Association, the Committee for Economic Development and the Council on Foreign Relations."

Our current federal subsidy program is so oriented to agribusiness that it has created a system in which taxpayers are subsidizing large corporate farming operations, giving them a huge competitive advantage over small, owner-operated farms. As non-major party candidates, we are not beholden to large corporations. Politicians from both major parties, on the other hand, risk being influenced by campaign money provided by these companies.

Corporate agribusiness has:

- Persuaded farmers to produce raw commodities and then organized agriculture to take care of input suppliers rather than the primary producer.

- Locked farmers into contracts that will not allow them to save seed or to use any products other than those provided by that company. Farmers who have had these seeds drift on to their property have been sued for patent infringement!

- Used its incredible influence with government to have genetically engineered products approved as "substantially the same" as foods produced by traditional breeding practices.

- Convinced Iowa farmers to produce genetically altered crops when over 90 percent of the population of Europe and Japan have refused to have anything to do with any food product that has been genetically engineered.

The Bottom-up Solutions

It seems incomprehensible that our own government would create policies that were intended to destroy the small farmers, but when you look at what has happened, it seems even more inconceivable that it could have happened accidentally. Many of us remember that when President Eisenhower's warning of the unchecked power of the military industrial complex. We wonder if he should also have warned us of the agribusiness/government complex attempting to consolidate all of agriculture into the hands of a few powerful entities.

We attended an Acres-sponsored conference in Minneapolis, on Dec. 6, 2001, that drew about 700 farmers from all over the country. The conference was totally dedicated to helping farmers make the transition to "biological" farming. It was very inspiring to hear story after story from farmers who are now prospering financially and enjoying a new-found independence.

As we campaign, we are asking for input from individuals and groups that are successfully dealing with these issues and breaking out of the system. With their help, we are developing an agricultural platform designed to help give Iowa's family farmers opportunities to engage in farming operations that are profitable and more in tune with nature. Our vision includes farmers big and small who want to be independent of the government and the biotech companies. We will do everything we can to stop the current system that has turned our farmers into serfs.

We have the potential in Iowa to go after truly lucrative markets in Japan, Europe and China, where they are willing to pay a premium for non-GMO produce. A supportive state administration can make it easier for Iowa farmers to take advantage of these markets. There are many practical options to conventional farming that do not require waiting three years for organic certification. We will seek out those options and make that knowledge available to Iowa farmers via the Internet as well as through symposiums and seminars.

Immediate Tasks

As we said, we are seeking advice about specific issues from the farmers themselves over the next several months to develop our agriculture platform, but there are four areas that we know we want to pursue immediately upon election:

1. Allowing farmers the right to grow industrial hemp.

2. Establishing a resource database of proven plans for creating economic viability for our farmers outside of the current corporate ag/government industrial complex.

3. Replacing, or seriously modifying, the current subsidy program.

4. Establishing a well-designed program to help farmers who want to transition to nonchemical, sustainable agriculture.

In addition to the obvious benefit of profitability resulting from our proposed agricultural plan, Iowa's farmers will be able to declare their independence from the government subsidy programs. They will no longer have to put up with restrictive contracts required by the large companies. The loss of topsoil and the loss of trace minerals will no longer be a serious problem. Our farmers will be more prosperous, more independent, have healthier soil and have a good chance of keeping their children in Iowa to take over the family farm.

Beyond Subsidies

We believe the days of subsidies are numbered. They cannot go on forever; the taxpayers will eventually demand a stop to them. The story of New Zealand's farmers may offer some insight as to what may happen here in Iowa when that day comes.

"New Zealand is a farming nation. Agricultural exports underpin the entire national economy. New Zealand is tens of thousands of miles from its markets and faces substantial overseas market restrictions and quotas. Since the Second World War, the standard of living, once one of the highest in the world, declined steadily, By the eighties there were 70 million sheep and untold acres of apples and pears all enjoying government price supports. By the mid-eighties, government resources were no longer available to prop up the failing farm sector and all price supports were removed in the space of one season. New Zealand went 'cold turkey free market'. Farmers and agrifood business were forced to address their customers.

"The result is a remarkable success story. New Zealand now has a diversified agricultural sector with only 30 million sheep, one of the world's largest dairy industries, a thriving organic sector exporting kiwi fruit, apples and pears, avocados, frozen vegetables, etc. The economics of farming are vastly improved. Whereas New Zealand used to produce apples at $9 a case and sell them for $8, they now have a significant production of organic apples which sell for up to $60 a case. The lesson for modern agribusiness is that market orientation is essential. For the farmer, this means there is a need to be flexible and break away from the mold. This is not only a challenge, but it is also an opportunity."

("U.S. Farmers: A word in your ear," a study by Guy Hatchard, Ph.D., March 2002)

Statement from Fritz Groszkruger, Libertarian Candidate for Iowa Secretary of Agriculture

I farm with my wife, Dawn. We have 300 acres of corn, soy, hay; Berkshire (premium marbled) pork—farrow to finish; Angus stock cows; and we feed out the calves. We also have pastured broilers, laying hens, and garden produce we sell to neighbors and townsfolk. We ridge-till, which reduces the amount of chemicals we use, while also reducing erosion.

Peaceable free exchange is the most direct route to prosperity for all.

As secretary of agriculture, I would see to it that within the law people would be held accountable as to the ramifications of their agricultural activities. The visibility of my office would be used to promote free-market solutions to ag problems, instead of just piling on more regulations to complicate the problems that are mostly caused by government interference in the first place.

I would do anything I can to end the pork, and any other mandatory check-offs, as these are not "peaceable free exchange" and so do not abide by libertarian principles.

Another area of interest to me is energy. The fact that ethanol markets are subsidized while oil is as well, through huge defense outlays, takes money out of the hands of the common citizen and hands it over to those with influence on a government that has all but nullified the Constitution that was supposed to limit such spending. As secretary of agriculture, I would promote the idea that each individual should bear the cost of his activity himself. Since the notion that the oil business could defend itself has become a utopian dream,

I would suggest that oil imports be taxed to reflect the true cost of that defense. That cost would then be passed on to the consumer and investment in alternative-energy sources would skyrocket. Unless petroleum was still the best buy.

There is a place for anyone on the land who earns his way there. There is room for factory farms if they can produce the best products at the least cost. If you want to preserve the so-called family farm, go ahead, raise a family and farm. But if you think government coercion is the path to family farm preservation, you are short-changing every family farmer and every citizen. A free-market economy regulated by constitutional law is the least any Iowan should accept.

Animal confinement

In all that I've heard about the animal confinement issue, I find that people on both sides can't see the forest for the trees. They seem blind to the fact that people, as individuals, are basically moral. When that morality is delegated to the state, it is transformed from personal interaction to coercion without conscience.

The real issue is a person's right to own property and do with it what he wants. That issue has been ignored because rather than being responsible for oneself, we have left it to the state (or county). The original intent of government was to settle disputes between people. Now government is expected to make and enforce rules in every aspect of our lives to prevent a possible problem from happening—and they still happen. These rules are too distant from diverse, actual situations to be fair in all disputes.

The only role of government should be to protect our rights, including the property rights of individuals. In promoting regulation of the livestock business the anti-corporate people have transferred the responsibility of people to government. This fact has, in every case, worked against the anti-corporate cause. They shoot themselves in the foot and go on like mind-numbed robots demanding more government intervention in our lives. The corporates smile all the way to the lagoon as they see the rights of the people handed to government and independent farmers quit. Their buildings keep going up and there's nothing we can do, because property rights have become a forgotten concept. If their stench pollutes our picnic we can't complain, because they've complied with the regulations we begged for, and the legislature passed to buy votes. In a world without all these regulations, the stench would be called an infringement on property rights, the building wouldn't have been built, and the picnic wouldn't stink.

Farmer Case Studies

The following case studies illustrate how some of the self sufficiency principles we've described in this chapter are being applied by Iowa farmers

The Madsen Family

Vic and Cindy Madsen operate their family farm near Elk Horn, Iowa. Of the 400 acres they farm, they own the 130 where they live, and rent the rest. They raise about 150 acres each of corn and soybeans, and about 30 acres each of oats and hay. The corn and oats they feed to the 2,000 hogs they finish each year, and they sell the hay and beans.

Their cropping system has evolved since they started farming in 1970. The reason was mainly to find a more economical system, though environmental concerns also played a role. The first change was to leave more residue, and then in 1988 they decided to use ridge tillage. With the switch, they began banding herbicides, which cut herbicide costs in half. They also started doing research trials on nitrogen rates using the late spring soil nitrate test. As a result, they now use half the nitrogen fertilizer they had used before they started doing the research trials.

With the switch to ridge tillage, yields actually increased. There is less compaction, they are not working the soil wet, and they are getting good, even stands. As evidence, in 1991 Vic and Cindy won the conservation division of the District 7 Iowa Masters Yield Contest with a corn yield of 204 bushels from a field that received hog manure in late winter, 30 pounds of nitrogen at planting, and another 30 pounds of nitrogen side-dressed.

Other changes are coming. Last year they did a research trial to look at the impacts of eliminating herbicides in their system. As Vic said, "We are trying to simplify things and make the work more enjoyable, and eliminating herbicides will mean fewer containers to handle and less mixing."

The main question they wanted answered, however, was whether the change would cost them money. Corn yields were 170.7 bushels per acre both with and without a herbicide band, so not using a herbicide saved them $5.40 an acre. They will do another with-and-without-herbicide trial again this year, and if successful they will likely expand the acres grown without herbicides. "Doing trials is an excellent way to test the economies and skills of different systems. We have bills to pay, and so we need to know as much as possible about modifying systems before we go ahead with a change. On-farm trials are an excellent way to do this," he said.

Another change they are contemplating is adding cattle to their system. The idea, in Madsen's words, is to "add value to everything produced on the farm." The hay they grow now is mostly for controlling erosion on the steepest hills and for the rotation benefits. But cattle fit in because, as Vic said, "We want to sell everything we produce as meat, both the grass and grains."

Another purpose is to provide some income from the very rough ground and help clean up corn fields in the winter. They will probably start with some stocker cattle, and their plan is to "ease into it." Their long-term goal is to make the farm as self-sufficient as they can. "That is the reason for the livestock and why we minimize purchased inputs," said Vic. "We also want an enjoyable workplace and work style, and so we are adding other things that will diversify the work."

When Vic was elected president of Practical Farmers of Iowa in January 1993, he said that he would like PFI to take on a third goal in addition to promoting profitable practices and practices that are good for the environment. "I'm afraid we could have profitable, environmentally sound farms, and still have unhappy people. We need to add a third objective, which is to begin doing things that are good for people too. There are a lot of sources for technical information, but we tend to ignore whether or not people are happy. Cindy and I hope that PFI can be a forum for people to visit about things that will help us have fun with our chosen occupations," he said.

(Since this profile was written, the Madsen farm has been moving toward organic on most of their acreage This write-up is based on a "Practical Farmers of Iowa" profile by Gary Huber, Practical Farmer, Spring 1993. Used with permission.)

The Frantzen Family

Tom Frantzen began farming in 1974. Today, the Frantzen farm is managed and worked by the entire Frantzen family, including Irene, Tom's wife, and their children, Jess, Jolene, and James. The Frantzens use holistic management for their farming management model. Their approach to farm management might best be characterized by three words: planning, acting, and evaluating.

"We want to have a good quality of life supported by our diversified farm," said Tom. His definition of sustainable agriculture is also stated simply. He said, "I view sustainable agriculture as a journey towards food and fiber production that will last."

Planning has always been integral to determining the Frantzen family farm goals. They have a long-term vision, create five-year plans, and also do a yearly plan. Their planning book is appropriately named the "Sunlight Harvesting Manual." The entire family takes part in planning, which is typically done from late November to early January. Each year, they write down what is important and create a family quality-of-life statement. They list means of production that will help them to meet their goals and values, and then describe the landscape that will sustain those means of production.

Evaluating, like planning, never stops. They have tried a variety of tillage practices, including moldboard plowing, chisel plowing, no-till, and ridge-till methods. They don't use no-till and also don't plant small grains after corn due to poor experiences with these methods. They do use crop rotation, their current plan incorporating a corn-soybean-oats-hay-pasture rotation.

Specific Frantzen farm goals fall into three categories: quality of life, forms of production, and landscape. Quality of life goals include family involvement, financial stability, a pleasant lifestyle, and quality time. Tom and Irene like to make sure there is plenty of time for the Frantzen children to participate in school activities, especially sports. And Tom and Irene make it a point to attend the sporting events. Says Irene, "Our quality-of-life goals also include having less stress and better personal relationships." One year, the family made a train-trip vacation their goal. Having that goal, and knowing the trip was coming up helped them work through much difficult weather that year.

Forms of production goals include realizing a profit from livestock and determining the appropriate mix of annual and perennial crops, woody crops, and wildlife. The Frantzens currently raise a combination of cattle, hogs, soybeans, oats, forages, and alternative crops on their 335 acres. They pasture their sows and on occasion graze cows and sows together. Trees play an important part on the farm. They use multipurpose shelterbelt trees in their pasture-farrowing system and are working to establish hazelnuts to add to this already diversified enterprise. For their landscape, they strive for an attractive farmstead, effective water and mineral cycles, capturing the sun's energy effectively, plant succession, covered soil, no erosion, and diverse crops. To further these goals, they have put in a pond and planted wildlife and shelterbelt areas.

The Frantzens do on-farm research to gain information that can help them move their farm in a sustainable direction. Each trial is chosen for a specific reason. They have conducted research to examine profitability, learn how to reduce pesticide use, examine rotations that will work best for their farm, and investigate nonchemical means of suppressing quackgrass.

The Frantzens have enjoyed improved profitability and have improved the look of the farm. Along the way, these practices have helped develop their ecological conscience and a greater appreciation for the land, which they steward in a way that involves the entire family. Strong advocates of sustainable agriculture, the Frantzens put their beliefs into practice and share what they learn along the way.

(Since this profile was written, the Frantzen farm has moved to organic on most of their acreage. This write-up is based on a "Practical Farmers of Iowa" profile by Jenny Kendall, Practical Farmer, Spring 1998. Used with permission.)

Doug Alert

Doug Alert's start in farming was not typical. His parents quit farming in 1966 when he was four, so he did not have access to the machinery, buildings, and grain handling facilities that are available to most people who begin farming.

Doug got a chance to farm when he was in junior high and his parents moved to a place near Mason City that had 30 acres of cropland. Doug was 14 when he purchased his first piece of equipment, a John Deere B he bought for $400. He then equipped this tractor with a two-bottom plow, a single-wing disk, a 10-foot field cultivator, and a two-row planter and corn cultivator. The only item he bought new was a sprayer, and he traded his labor for the use of a combine.

After farming the 30 acres for several years, Doug and a high school classmate rented a nearby 80 acres, which brought the total to 110 acres. He used the income to buy a John Deere 720 diesel, a four-row planter and cultivator, a three-bottom plow, and a tandem disk.

Doug continued to farm this land while attending Iowa State University in the early 1980s. In 1986, he began farming 200 acres of rented land near Sheffield. The land was well-fenced and included a set of buildings, so Doug began diversifying into livestock by buying six beef cows and some bred gilts. He eventually built his sow numbers to 45 and his beef cow herd to 25 head. Most of the 200 acres was planted to corn and soybeans, but he included as much oats as needed to establish hay for his beef cows. According to Doug, adding the livestock was one of the reasons he survived the drought years of 1988 and 1989. Thus, one of his strategies for success is diversification.

Doug went from renting 200 acres to 320 in 1987, and then added another 80 in 1988, bringing the total to 400. When the original 200 and the 80 he added in 1988 were sold in 1991, Doug relocated to a 320-acre farm southwest of Hampton. He now operates this farm and a 120-acre farm just down the road from where his Dad was raised, bringing the total to 440 acres. With the relocation, Doug sold his livestock because the new place had no fences for the cattle or facilities for raising hogs. However, in keeping with the strategy of diversification, he started a farm equipment business, called Conservation Tillage Systems. His plan is to get back into cattle over time as he builds fences, eventually expanding to about 40 cows.

In the mid-1980s, Doug deviated from his second strategy for success, which was containing costs. Until then, nearly all of Doug's equipment "was older than I was," but the farm economy in the mid-1980s brought down new-equipment prices to the point that he decided to purchase a new 160-horsepower tractor. He has since sold this tractor because it was no longer needed as the result of another move Doug made to contain costs—a change in his tillage system. He had decided in the early 1980s that ridge tillage provided the best opportunity to reduce costs. However, he could not change completely to ridge tillage until recently because his landlords wanted him to use a moldboard plow or a chisel plow. As he changed farms or convinced landlords that ridge tillage was a good system, he was able to make the switch. This enabled Doug to downsize his equipment; a 100-horse-power tractor is now his biggest. He also eliminated some equipment altogether, and now his machinery investment is about 40 percent of what it was several years ago.

Doug has also contained costs by reducing his use of nitrogen and herbicides. He typically puts on 50 pounds of nitrogen with the planter and then side-dresses more, if needed, based on results from late spring soil nitrate tests. Also, though he sometimes uses a burndown on soybeans, he applies his herbicides in a band with the planter. And in 1993, about 10 percent of his row crop acres had no herbicides applied.

Doug has done on-farm research as a PFI cooperator. Being a cooperator is a good opportunity because "it gives me a framework to attempt to document whether my practices are working or not," he said.

(*Since this profile was written, Doug Alert has moved to organic on most of his acreage. The write-up is based on a "Practical Farmers of Iowa" profile by Gary Huber, Practical Farmer, Fall 1993. Used with permission.*)

The Welsch Family

A bale of hay, a sack of dyfonate and death in the field prompted the Welsch family of Lansing, Iowa, to bring down the curtain on 20 years of toxic chemical farming. The trigger mechanism was an empty bag of the above-named pesticide that remained undetected for several months. When the contaminated hay was fed to the cows, 40 became sick and 14 died.

That did it. The Welsch family had become disenchanted with low profits and environmental damage in any case. Now the older generation—Bill and Esther Welsch—and the family started looking for production models that did not rely on toxic technology.

They found answers enough to make their 200-plus acres turn a profit. All the crops, it turned out, could be grown without chemicals of organic synthesis, the crops being oats, corn, barley, legumes (alfalfa and clover), most for on-farm use.

Gary and Kim now do most of the work, with Dad and Mom Welsch in retirement. Greg Welsch, the only extension agent in Iowa trained in organiculture, spends the weekends on the Des Moines-area farm, almost always deeply involved in the clean production that has become a Welsch family hallmark.

The crop nowadays is 50,000 chickens that range out from their pole barn quarters, some 25 slaughter steers and 600 finished hogs, all raised according to eco-friendly methodology.

(*Reprinted from* A Farmer's Guide to the Bottom Line, A Handbook to Secure Success and Profits on the Family-Scale Farm, *by Charles Walters. Copyright © 2002 Acres U.S.A. Used with permission.*)

The Manges Family

Marvin and Carol Manges of Yale, Illinois, farm 700 acres in the east-central part of the state. The farm was originally Carol's home place and they began farming it in 1977. Carol says she became interested in ecology while still in college and enjoyed discussions about Rachel Carson's *Silent Spring*. Even so, when they began farming they went conventional, but became very unhappy with chemical farming in the mid-1980s. They now have 400 acres certified organic by OCIA. The remainder of the acres, some newly purchased, are also headed for organic certification.

By every measure of results, they are highly pleased with their program. The previous high costs for fertilizer and chemicals are gone, soil health is greatly improved and they enjoy growing markets. They have organic markets for white food-grade corn, for red, yellow and specialty popcorn, wheat, yellow corn, and Clear Hilum soybeans. The white corn goes to tortilla chips and the soybeans go to Eden Foods for soymilk.

They have good yields with their organic methods of crop rotation, ridge-tilling and rotary hoeing. Under their system, something green must be growing at all times. Still, there is no hard-and-fast rotation. Corn yields range from 100 to 125 bushels per acre. Soybeans generally yield 44 to 55 bushels per acre. "We take a lower yield than conventional farmers, but our markets more than compensate for that. In any case, our soybean yields are high average for the area, and our market advantage more than compensates us," says Marvin.

Marvin and Carol agree that the soil is God's greatest gift and "we are the caretakers, not the owners of this gift. If we take care of the soil, it will take care of us. Our stewardship involves a total system approach. With crop diversity and rotations, and cover crops which recycle plant nutrients, we are seeing soil life return to our once compacted and lifeless soil."

Conversion is never an accident. It answers a plan made, as a plan anticipates a bottom line.

(Reprinted from A Farmer's Guide to the Bottom Line, A Handbook to Secure Success and Profits on the Family-Scale Farm, *by Charles Walters. Copyright © 2002 Acres U.S.A. Used with permission.)*

Fred Kirschenmann

Frederick (Fred) Kirschenmann left his Windsor, North Dakota, organic farm last summer to become the director of the Leopold Center for Sustainable Agriculture at Iowa State University in Ames.

When Kirschenmann is asked what the key to successful organic farming is, he'll answer, "Management. Essentially, I substitute management for capital." Kirschenmann diligently applies a five-year rotation plan of wheat, rye, buckwheat or millet, sunflowers and clover to his 3,000-acre organic spread. During a 12-month stretch ending in July of 1988, his crops received only 1.3 inches of rain. Another 1.5 inches of rainfall on August 1 enabled him to harvest a crop 80 percent of normal. Some of his neighbors never even got a chance to plant.

Fred's wheat yields are also the envy of the state, running more than 40 percent higher than the county average. "We have to be open to the idea that there are energies in nature we can't quantify, but are nevertheless there," Kirschenmann says. He added that when he stirs together his biodynamic soil preparations in the presence of neighbors they joke that, "I'm making my witches brew." But Kirschenmann doesn't mind their humor. He's too busy running to the bank with his $7-per-bushel wheat while his neighbors are struggling to make ends meet with lower yields and $4-per-bushel wheat.

Bookkeeping includes production crop records from season to season as well as financial transactions. Together, good records mean good management.

(Reprinted from A Farmer's Guide to the Bottom Line, A Handbook to Secure Success and Profits on the Family-Scale Farm, *by Charles Walters. Copyright © 2002 Acres U.S.A. Used with permission.)*

Duane Hager

Duane Hager likes to think of himself as an average Minnesota dairy farmer. In many ways he is, but he is far ahead of the crowd by farming ecologically. Both he and his father before him have farmed without toxic pesticides and herbicides—adding up to about 50 years of clean land stewardship.

Duane farms 220 acres near the southeastern Minnesota town of Kellogg, close to the scenic bluffs along the

Mississippi River. His land has soil types ranging from sandy to heavy clay. He raises corn, soybeans, oats and hay (alfalfa plus orchard grass and timothy).

As he has taken rented land that had been farmed conventionally and converted it to biologically active land, Duane has been fascinated by the visible changes and improvements. Without toxic chemicals and strong salt fertilizers, earthworms soon increase dramatically, along with a noticeable improvement in soil health. In 1993, the day after a four-inch rain, he was able to drive on a field that had many worm castings without mud sticking to his tractor tires.

Duane relies on judiciously applied manure for much of his crop nutrition, along with corn and alfalfa starter fertilizers. He collects dairy manure in a liquid storage pit and spreads it in the fall. His manure collection method is a less common gravity-flow system. He has another pit for solid manure from feed lots, and he can spread it at various times, giving him more flexibility.

The 40 Holstein and Guernsey cows are milked in a tie-stall barn. During the warm months, the dairy cattle eat green-chopped hay and are pastured on rotational grazing. In the winter, the cows stay in the barn and get corn silage and baled hay. Milk production runs around a 15,500 rolling herd average, with 3.5 to 4.1 percent butterfat and 3.2 percent protein. Duane has won milk quality awards for his dairy in past years. Keeping the ration adjusted to changing feeds is always a challenge, he noted.

Duane also raises about 30 beef cattle, either Angus, Hereford or Angus-Hereford cross. This farm is correctly positioned for the innovative structure now abounding in eco-agriculture.

(*Reprinted from* A Farmer's Guide to the Bottom Line, A Handbook to Secure Success and Profits on the Family-Scale Farm, *by Charles Walters. Copyright © 2002 Acres U.S.A. Used with permission.*)

The Thompson Family

Richard and Sharon Thompson, Boone, Iowa, are outstanding in their field. In fact, Sharon often introduces her husband that way, with a slide of—you guessed it—Richard out standing in his field.

It all started in 1967, because the university/UDA-touted system wasn't working any longer. Crops were faltering and livestock exhibited the effects. That's when this Iowa couple decided to go back to basics, and then marched forward with innovations that comply with nature's rhyme and seasons. This meant rotations—corn, soybean, corn—and growing rather than buying feeder cattle. The fences that had been removed under the Svengali-like spell of the get-bigger chant were replaced. Pigs were farrowed on-farm, and the Thompsons looked to using valued manures rather than buying commercial fertilizers. As a matter of fact, no factory-acidulated fertilizer entered the system for decades.

The goal, of course, was to farm without contaminating land, water or food. Compost suggested itself, and—in time—a potassium shortage made soil testing necessary.

There was a time when the Thompsons figured the crops and weeds would have to report the condition of the soil. This worked to such a degree, with soybeans, corn, oats and hay, that the Thompsons were pulled into the national limelight.

But then just selling clean beef and red meat was not enough. The world demanded scientific proof. The Thompsons held to their opinion that castrated beef didn't entirely measure up, thus no castration for young animals, and only a rubber band treatment later on.

Those 300 Thompson acres do not measure for much with those who think they have to farm several sections and end up losing the farm. But those 300 acres have provided for a family of four children, two of them farming. The economic numbers reveal that conventional-wisdom corn loses $30 an acre. Thompson's corn, in a five-year rotation, grosses $50 an acre and saves at least $45 on toxic supplements—a $90 differential.

The Henry A. Wallace Institute for Alternative Agriculture wants these facts to become common knowledge, for which reason the Institute has sponsored record keeping and testing that make the Thompson experience more enduring than ever.

(Reprinted from A Farmer's Guide to the Bottom Line, A Handbook to Secure Success and Profits on the Family-Scale Farm, *by Charles Walters. Copyright © 2002 Acres U.S.A. Used with permission.)*

"We are at that very point in time when a 400-year-old age is dying and another is struggling to be born—a shifting of culture, science, society, and institutions enormously greater than the world has ever experienced. Ahead, the possibility of regeneration and individuality, liberty, community and ethics such as the world has never known, and a harmony with nature, with one another and with the divine intelligence such as the world has always dreamed."

—*Dee Hock, Founder and CEO Emeritus,*
VISA International

Chapter 12. The Environment: Restoring our Natural Resources

By Clyde J. Cleveland and Edward F. Noyes, J.D.

Position Summary

Just improving our environment is not enough. We need to think much bigger than that. The total restoration of our natural resources in Iowa is our goal. We believe in the compatibility of political freedom and environmental restoration. In Iowa, the key problems are agricultural-related pollution and the burning of fossil fuels to provide our energy needs. Our energy and agriculture policies (Chapters 10 and 11) deal directly with these problems without the use of coercion.

The fundamental principles of Libertarian philosophy are based on an understanding of natural law. That understanding provides a model for restructuring our institutions for maximum personal evolution as well as resolving our environmental problems.

It is already happening. Buildings are now being built according to natural principles that do not create pollution. Farming methods that mimic nature allow us to grow crops profitably without damaging the environment. Manufacturing processes that are based on observing natural processes are already gaining acceptance. As William McDonough writes in *The Next Industrial Revolution*, "It is time for designs that are creative, abundant, prosperous, and intelligent from the start. The model for the Next Industrial Revolution may well have been in front of us the whole time: a tree."

We propose to accelerate the changes already taking place by promoting them and making some critical changes in corporate law and campaign finance law. In addition, changing government from a top-down to a bottom-up system will play a critical part by eliminating institutional resistance to environmentally friendly technologies.

The Problem

The environmental problems in Iowa are severe. The state Department of Natural Resources cannot possibly deal with the severity of the damage that is being done to our natural resources. The problem is primarily coming from two areas: burning fossil fuels for our energy needs and agricultural pollution.

Agricultural Pollution

Our current program of government subsidies encourages farmers to cultivate their lands to the hilt. This has resulted in larger farms and more intense applications of fertilizers, pesticides and herbicides. Unfortunately, this has also led to less land devoted to trees, wetlands, and other conservation buffers that would help control run-offs of chemicals.

With the increased pesticide and herbicide use, the cities and towns downstream have to devote more resources to purifying their water before it can be drunk. It also is contributing to the creation of dead zones in the oceans, sometimes thousands of miles from shore.

Water quality in Des Moines and other cities has become a serious problem. The countryside throughout the state has been awash in fertilizers, pesticides, herbicides, and animal wastes. This has led to over 150 fish kills over the past six years leaving 5.7 million fish floating dead in rivers and lakes and temporarily closing half the state's beaches in 2001.

Energy-related Pollution

Eighty percent of the electricity in Iowa comes from coal-fired plants. We now know that the burning of coal is the cause of high levels of mercury in our water. Exposure to high levels of mercury can be fatal for humans. State governments all over the country have issued advisories for lakes and rivers warning people not to swim in the water (let alone eat the fish) for fear of exposure to mercury. Other serious environmental degradations such as acid rain and the depletion of the ozone layer have been blamed on the burning of coal.

As explained in Chapter 10, the deferred environmental costs of the spread of nitrogen oxides alone from the burning of coal are about $60 million a year. The Iowa air in the neighborhoods of old coal-fired plants kill 300 Iowans a year, with plants in the Des Moines area the worst offender. Coal-gasification plants of the type that supply electricity for the Iowa population burn 25,000 tons of coal and produce 250 tons of ash a day.

The Bottom-up Solutions

Our platform for addressing environmental problems takes place on two levels simultaneously—that of the individual and that of the organization. Both levels are crucial to restoring our environment. We believe noncoercive solutions in both areas will be the most effective approach.

The Individual Level

> "I live badly because life is bad. Life is bad because people, we live badly. If we the people, lived well, life would be good and I should not live badly. I am included in the people. And if I cannot make all people live well, I can at least do so myself, and thus can improve, however little, the life of other people and my own. What confronts this reasoning is that if everyone adopted it—and this reasoning is irrefutably just—then life would be good for everyone."
>
> —*Tolstoy*, Last Diaries

Every individual makes daily decisions that affect the environment. What car they purchase, how much they drive, what kind of light bulbs they put in their home, how they farm, how they insulate their home, how they build their home, what kind of food they eat—the list goes on and on.

We believe that every human being is naturally an environ-mentalist. No one would choose to breathe dirty air when they could breathe clean air, or drink polluted water when they could drink pure water. It is not our nature to do this. However, it is true that some people are more aware of and concerned about what is healthy than others.

It is up to us to do whatever we can as individuals to make environmentally sound decisions. This is where it all starts, with us. And everything we do makes a difference. Once we become skilled and knowledgeable about how to reduce pol-lution in every area of our lives, we can spread that knowledge to our friends and neighbors.

The amazing fact is that, in almost every instance, there is an economic incentive already built in to being environmen-tally aware. Insulation retrofits on homes usually pay for themselves within 18 months. After that it is pure profit. In addition, there are now several companies in this country that offer automobile retrofits that will increase mileage two to four times! These retrofits usually pay for themselves within 14 months. Again, after 14 months, it is all profit.

The fundamental principle that lies at the basis of our free society is that we are free to do what we want as long as we do not harm others. When an individual's actions harm the air that their neighbors' breathe or spoils the water that someone downstream drinks, then it is that individual's responsibility to compensate those who have been harmed. Upon reflection, it is obvious that if the harm comes from a corporation or other business enterprise, the same principles must apply. Our Constitution is based on the premise that all power comes from the people, not from the government.

Therefore, we the people have every right to assert our will on both the government and any government-sanctioned commercial entities, in whatever form created. Clearly, we would never provide greater rights to nonhumans than we would to humans. Neither should we ever allow nonhumans to be free from the same restraints that individuals naturally must obey. Otherwise, we allow a veritable "monster" to have dominance over the people.

We therefore recognize that corporations and all business enterprises must be held to the same standards as individuals who cause harm to another. The Founders' concept of restorative justice defined a "crime" as an infringement upon the liberty or interests of another. When enterprises choose business practices that harm the environment, they must be held accountable for those business decisions. By holding them accountable, they will naturally choose those business practices that cause the least (or no) harm. One of the most important actions our administration will take to protect the environment is to restore and make use of civil law and civil courts. The laws of the state must not protect those who damage property or infringe on the rights of others from facing full responsibility for their actions.

Paul Hawken (of Smith and Hawken) details in his groundbreaking book *The Ecology of Commerce* how restorative justice principles can be applied to all forms of commerce. He writes, "A cyclical, restorative economy thinks cradle-to-cradle, so that every product or by-product is imagined in its subsequent forms even before it is made. Designers must factor in the future utility of a product, and the avoidance of waste, from its inception. If this proposal sounds radical, it is, because it gets down to the root causes of pollution and toxicity. Responsibility belongs to the maker, not merely the user, and certainly not with the victim…By placing both the responsibility and the cost of mitigation with the originator of the problem, vast and compelling incentives are created for companies to redesign, even re-imagine, their business and processes."

Hawken envisions a market system that "creates, increases, nourishes and enhances life on earth," and competition that "improves living and cultural systems." This occurs, he explains, as a result of "a public-private partnership in the economy that reverses the incentives so that economic success is tantamount to biological success."

> "Of liberty I would say that, in the whole plenitude of its extent, it is unobstructed action according to our will. But rightful liberty is unobstructed action according to our will within limits drawn around us by the equal rights of others. I do not add 'within the limits of the law,' because law is often but the tyrant's will, and always so when it violates the right of an individual."
>
> —*Thomas Jefferson,*
> *to Isaac H. Tiffany, 1819*

It is not surprising that visionary, successful business owners who are committed to reversing environmental damage, such as Hawken, are turning to the concept of restorative justice.

This fundamental principle, based on liberty and equal justice for all, is at the heart of our Constitution and Libertarian philosophy. There is no question that the Founders would have required the originators of environmental damage to pay for the costs of correcting that damage. After all, how long can we continue giving corporations greater rights than individuals?

Community-based financial incentives that encourage individuals to be more environmentally conscious have also been shown to be effective. If done properly, these programs can have wide community support and foster good relations among people who are working together to improve the quality of their community.

The current programs that are top-down, command-and-control dictates from Washington, D.C., such as low-capacity toilets for the whole country, are not constructive. The long-term effect of this type of solution is resistance, resentment, and a feeling that all environmentalists are oppressive government bureaucrats.

The difference in environmental quality between West Germany and East Germany before they were united, and between North Korea and South Korea, provides striking evidence of how environmental problems are handled in a free society versus a command-and-control society. In a free society, the people have at least some control over the situation and will demand some level of action regarding damage to the environment. Whereas in South Korea and East Germany, the people had absolutely no ability to demand anything. The environmental damage in those two countries was extreme compared to their free counterparts.

A government that has no accountability to the people is never a good steward of the environment.

When people have an opportunity to use their free will, they grow in awareness the fastest. Therefore, it is essential to have maximum individual freedom. People resent force, and usually rebel against it even if it is "good for them." As governor and attorney general, we will do whatever we can to bring working models of community-based non-coercive environmental solutions to the awareness of Iowans.

The Re-emergence of Individual Rights

Fortunately, courts are beginning to recognize that inalienable rights of individuals are paramount to laws passed at the insistence of big industries. In October 2001, for example, the Center for Rural Affairs reported the following in its monthly newsletter:

"In Orange City, Iowa, a judge has ruled that a statute that gives large livestock farms immunity to nuisance lawsuits is unconstitutional. Sioux County District Judge John Ackerman said that such farms could interfere with the use of a neighbor's property and right to seek compensation. The ruling was in response to a brief filed by the Iowa Civil Liberties Union.

"The judge's decision will allow Joseph and Linda Gacke of Rock Valley to continue with their lawsuit against Pork Xtra LLC, a Sioux County company. The couple sued Pork Xtra last year, claiming the company's 4,000-head hog farm near their home was a nuisance that attracted bugs and harmed their emotional and physical health. They are seeking punitive and compensatory damages, as well as an injunction that could halt the operation of the farm."

A top-down society frequently results in those who have the most money controlling the political process to the detriment of the people themselves. The creation of legislation that provides exemptions for industries that are a nuisance to existing property owners is just one example. Naturally, the people will want "local control," as that control frequently offers the greatest protection against undesirable industries that might come into their counties, cities, or neighborhoods. By enlivening civil law and recognizing the legal rights of individuals and communities as paramount, we have the best chance to protect against continuing encroachment of civil rights. We must recognize the importance of decentralizing decision making whenever possible by giving individuals and communities the primary responsibility to make decisions (such as if and where to allow the placement of a confinement operation). Not only must individuals have their civil rights protected, but communities as well must be able to make important decisions for themselves rather than leaving the decision making to the politicians in Des Moines or Washington, D.C.

It should provide some comfort that the Founders understood these rights as well as the danger of allowing the consolidation of political power. We are committed to their vision and to the primacy of individuals and communities over top-down, government-imposed restrictions and exemptions favoring the powerful.

Organizational Level

A revolutionary and evolutionary way of approaching environmental problems is beginning to take hold in our country. This new approach is more in tune with the bottom-up approach described in Chapter 3 and is a more natural approach to the problems we face. As we move in this direction, we will see much more effective solutions to our environmental problems. We are seeing people coming together in a noncoercive manner to create alternative institutions, rather than relying on regulatory agencies to solve environmental problems.

Here are three examples of this new principle in action.

Lobster coalition. In one of the country's most interesting experiments in cooperative self-government, a coalition of lobster fishermen, restaurant owners, environmentalists, and other interested parties are working together to protect and preserve Maine's lobster market. Reporter Alan Ehrenhalt described the group's efforts in "Lessons From the Lobster Legislature," *Perc Reports*, June 2001.

More than 7,000 individuals are engaged in lobster fishing in Maine. In a good year, they bring in 50 million pounds of crustaceans, worth half a billion dollars—roughly 2 percent of the gross state product. So the health of the industry is central to Maine's economy.

Of course, when things are good in the industry, anyone can enter the business, and that is exactly what has happened in Maine in the past. Before long the number of lobsters begins to dwindle, and there are not enough to support the families who are dependent on that way of life.

Overfishing and gradual depletion of sea life are more the rule than the exception. In recent years, it has happened with Alaskan king crab, scallops, shrimp, and sea urchins, and it has begun to happen with cod, halibut, and sea bass. Last year, the U.S. Commerce Department reported that 98 different species were overfished; in other words, there are fewer or smaller fish each year due to too much fishing. Since 1994, the federal government has spent $160 million on subsidies to those hurt by overfishing.

This is a classic "problem of the commons," a situation in which the relentless pursuit of self-interest by members of a community eventually destroys the livelihood of everyone within it.

But it is now a different story in Maine. The lobster coalition created local legislative bodies that made regulatory decisions without bureaucratic input from Washington, D.C. The group divided the state into seven lobster-fishing zones. Each zone contains between eight and 14 districts, and every district has 100 licensed fishermen. The job of each of these units is to cooperate in crafting rules that will prevent overfishing and stave off the dreaded intrusion of the federal bureaucrats. The first thing the local legislative bodies did was to agree that they wouldn't put a limit on fish; instead, they would put a limit on the number of traps each fisherman could put in the water.

A form of grassroots government created in response to a difficult situation has been able to make hard political choices that have eluded mainstream government.

Buffalo ranchers. In the Great Plains states, there is another example of stakeholders getting together and realizing that they are better off working together to solve their problems than continuing to do battle with each other.

The Great Plains Institute for Sustainable Development (GPISD) is a group of state and federal agencies, local residents, and conservationists who came together to discuss their issues instead of waiting until problems occurred. The people who made this program work are the farmers, storekeepers, ranchers, and students who are currently living on the land. These are the people who face the challenges each day of making a living and who see environmental stability as the driving force behind a functioning economic system.

The group is counting on significant income from hiking, biking, expeditions, camping, and hunting. For these new noncoercive alliances to work, the rewards from conservation must outweigh the immediate benefits to be gained from its sacrifice. The involvement and serious commitment of the people at the local level are essential to achieving sustainable, long-term, environmental protection.

William Funk reported on the group's efforts in his article, "Buffalo Commons: An Ecological and Economic Restoration of America's Great Plains," which appeared on the GreenWave.com web site earlier this year. Funk wrote: "Eco-tourism, wherein visitors have an opportunity to safely enjoy the wilds in a manner not damaging to the resources, succeeds when residents of the area are employed to share their knowledge, history and expertise in exchange for payment, an interaction that both strengthens and preserves indigenous cultures and ecosystems."

Livestock and wildlife grazing. The Quivira Coalition, a group of southwestern ranchers based in Santa Fe, New Mexico, is tackling the problem of grazing. They have successfully bridged the gap between those who believe that grazing creates no environmental problems at all and those who believe all rangeland should be cleared of cattle to protect nature.

The coalition is a group of ranchers, environmentalists, pub-lic-land managers, and other members of the public interested in sustainable ranching. They believe that wildlife, wetlands, and livestock can coexist on the same parcel of land, and even help each other if properly managed. The mission of the coalition is to define the core issues of the graz-ing conflict and develop a position based on common interests and common sense.

They have already proved that ecological and economic health can exist simultaneously. In an article in *Acres USA,* Courtney White, one of the founders of the Quivira Coalition, explained, "Our aim is to build bridges between all reasonable people involved in the grazing debate… It is not a theory, it already exists; it is simply a matter of spreading the news." ("The Quivira Coalition: Creating 'The New Ranch' in the Southwest," by Robert Gerard, January 2002)

Chaordic Models for Change

These are three examples of environmental problems being solved without coercion. They represent an incredibly important and positive development for our environment and our freedom. The irrefutable conclusion when compar-ing top-down coercive environmental programs with these noncoercive bottom-up approaches is that the bottom-up approach is actually more effective at dealing with the envi-ronment. This will always be the case, because it more effectively incorporates human nature in the solution.

The three models share the principles that Dee Hock used to build VISA International, outlined in his book *Birth of the Chaordic Age*. We cannot overstate the importance of Hock's achievement in creating an organization from principles he defined by observing nature at work. We have much to learn from his story. Those who draw on his principles will help form the alternative structures in our society, and our state, and be instrumental in restoring our environment.

 Hock defines a "chaordic organization" as a self-governing system that:

- Harmoniously blends characteristics of order and chaos.

- Is patterned in a way dominated by neither chaos nor order.

- Is characteristic of the fundamental organizing principles of evolution and nature.

By following the bottom-up model described in Chapter 3, VISA became the largest commercial enterprise on the planet. It also became the most profitable consumer service in the financial services industry and reduced the cost of unsecured credit for individuals as well as the cost of handling payment instruments. The organization created thousands of new industries and new ventures.

Environmental problems can be solved much more effectively in a noncoercive way and with the bottom-up approach to governing. We are convinced that the constant struggle between environmentalists on the one side and property owners and freedom lovers on the other side will disappear once we experience a paradigm shift to a bottom-up approach to governing.

The role of the federal government in environmental matters, if any, would be to provide the guidance to create chaordic models for solving problems involving the commons.

> "But with nature's help we can draw distinctions between right and wrong, and between honorable and shameful actions. Our own common sense gives us the first principles of understanding, and impresses them on our minds, so that we connect honorable qualities with virtue and all that is disgraceful with vice. It is folly to suppose that such judgments are matters of our own opinion and not natural instincts. Not by opinion, but by nature do we judge the excellence of a tree or horse. This being so, whatever is either honorable or shameful we must judge with the help of nature."
>
> —Cicero

"To summarize then, the model for a highly evolved society: Beings live in clusters, or what you would call small intentional communities. These clusters are not further organized into cities, states, or nations, but each interacts with the others on a co-equal basis. *There are no governments as you would understand them, and no laws.* There are councils, or conclaves, usually of elders. And there are what could best be translated in your language as 'mutual agreements.' These have been reduced to a triangular code: Awareness, Honesty, Responsibility."

—*God, to Neale Donald Walsch,*
Conversations with God 3 *[Emphasis added]*

Chapter 13. Response to the Green Party: Green and Free!

By Clyde J. Cleveland

There is vast common ground between our Libertarian-oriented environmental solutions and the efforts of long-time environmentalists who have become frustrated at the slow progress of environmental improvement. The Green Party in particular supports many of the same ideas that we do. In fact, our bottom-up approach to creating more effective organizations and institutions embraces the goals of Green principles addressing human dignity, fairness, equality and justice, as well as environmentally sound policies.

In this chapter, I give my position in response to each of the core values of the Green Party.

Respect for Diversity

We must honor cultural, ethnic, racial, sexual, religious and spiritual diversity within the context of individual responsibility to all beings. We must reclaim our country's finest shared ideals: the dignity of the individual, democratic participation, and liberty and justice for all.

I absolutely agree. The sovereignty of the individual and the individual right to act in accord with our own free will is only limited by the rights of others to do the same. In other words, do what you want as long as you act responsibly and respect the rights of others. What we find as we develop and evolve is that freedom is limited when those around us are not also free. When you are truly a free individual you cannot help but do whatever you can to create freedom for others. It becomes impossible to allow others to be treated with less dignity than you would have others treat you; it would be seen as a restriction on your own freedom.

Social Justice

We must respond to human suffering in ways that promote dignity. We must encourage people to commit themselves to lifestyles that promote their own health. We must have a community-controlled education system that effectively teaches our children academic skills, ecological wisdom, social responsibility and personal growth. We must resolve personal and group conflicts without just turning them over to lawyers and judges. We must take responsibility for reducing the crime rate in our neighborhoods. We must encourage such values as simplicity and moderation.

This is music to my ears. Encouraging people to follow a lifestyle that enhances their health and to resolve issues without attorneys is teaching self-reliance. We have to stop depending on government, particularly a government that is thousands of miles away, to solve our own individual and community problems. We have to teach self-sufficiency and responsibility. I would add that education has to include the teaching of fundamental core values: at our school these values are taught in relationship to natural laws that are common to all religious and cultural traditions.

Grassroots Democracy

We must develop systems that allow and encourage us to control the decisions that affect our lives. We must ensure that representatives will be fully accountable to the people who elected them. We must encourage and assist the "mediating institutions"—family, neighborhood organizations, church groups, voluntary associations, ethnic clubs—to recover some of the functions now performed by the government. We must learn the best insights from American traditions of civic vitality, voluntary action and community responsibility.

In 1835, French statesman and author Alexis de Tocqueville came to America and was astounded to find that government was "invisible." It was nowhere to be found. Everything was done on the local level by an amazing array of civic organizations. Service organizations, associations, church groups, charities, school groups and the like were pervasive and well attended by enthusiastic members. This is an example of a civil society based on the principle of no force prevailing over a political society which has force as its essential element. Civil society is the essence of a society based on bottom-up versus top-down management.

Feminism

We must replace the cultural ethics of dominance and control with more cooperative ways of interacting. We must encourage people to care about persons outside their own group. We must promote the building of respectful, positive and responsible relationships across the lines of gender and other divisions. We must proceed with as much respect for the means as the end (the process as much as the product of our efforts). We must learn to respect the contemplative inner part of life as much as the outer activities.

Domination and freedom are inherently opposed to each other. Thomas Paine was a passionate spokesperson for both the abolition of slavery and women's rights. He believed that America's manifest destiny was to be the shining example of freedom for the world, and that both slavery and the degrading treatment of women were foreign to the core principles of our new country.

The qualities of respect, caring and ethical behavior toward all—regardless of race, skin color, ethnic background or gender—are directly tied to a person's level of consciousness. Unfortunately, a higher level of personal evolution cannot be legislated. Our Founders did what they could to create an environment for personal growth. That is what freedom does: it creates an opportunity for people to evolve as quickly as possible. I personally believe that they did a remarkable job, considering their circumstances.

It is now our responsibility to take what they started to a new level. We need to take the foundation that they built and revitalize the core underlying principles. We also need to use the recently discovered technologies that are available now in the field of human development and make those technologies widely available. I believe this is best done through civil society, not political society.

As far as the "contemplative inner part of life," I am right with you. I have spent a great deal of time in both prayer and meditation during my life, and I continue to pray and meditate as a regular part of my daily routine.

Community-based Economics

We must design our work structures to encourage employee ownership and workplace democracy. We must develop new economic activities and institutions that will allow us to use our new technologies in ways that are humane, freeing, ecological and accountable and responsive to communities. We must establish some form of basic economic security, open to all. We must restructure our patterns of income distribution to reflect the wealth created by those outside the formal monetary economy: those who take responsibility for parenting, housekeeping, home gardens, community volunteer work, etc. We must restrict the size and concentrated power of corporations without discouraging superior efficiency or technological innovation.

Over the years, I have founded or co-founded 29 commercial enterprises—seven corporations and 22 limited partnerships. Those entities had hundreds of employees, and it is obvious to me, as an entrepreneur and businessman, that people work harder and perform better when they are treated with dignity and respect, and are given a high degree of freedom to accomplish their tasks. Sharing equity or profits is another tremendous way to generate happy, productive associates.

Only foolish business people fail to realize the power of these concepts. I believe deeply in these principles and that the marketplace will eventually demand that businesses adopt these ideas. Those that don't will not be able to compete with companies that utilize these principles. I do not, however, believe that the relationship between a businessperson and employee should be legislated.

Corporations need to be removed from the political process. Corporations, unions, PACs, and other nonpersons are not sovereign individuals created by the Creator. They are not protected under the Constitution and should not necessarily be granted the same rights to participate in the political system. I would work to eliminate all donations, of any kind, to individual candidates and political parties from any organization. This will go a long way in the fight to reduce the role of corporations, or any other institution, in the political system. Many companies will breathe a sigh of relief that they no longer have to bribe politicians with political contributions.

Corporate acts of irresponsibility—such as the recent tobacco scandal, environmental damage, and intentional actions that damage health or take lives—are not acceptable. Simply fining the corporations after the fact for these acts is a complete waste of time and energy, except for the attorneys who collect hundreds of millions in fees. The tobacco companies just raised prices to pay for their fines; the customers paid the price for the decision-maker's gross negligence. We have to re-think what requirements we place on all business enterprises. By requiring corporations to take responsibility for all of the effects of their business decisions, and imposing those external costs on the originator of the problems, we take a huge step toward providing the kind of market incentives necessary to change the way they do business. Corporations will think twice about the choices they make in developing their goods or services if they know that 100 percent of the detrimental effects of their choices will be imposed on them.

We also need to look at the issue of determining what degree of personal liability should exist when corporate directors and office holders make a conscious decision to conduct business in a way that they know will cause significant harm to others. An individual cannot hire someone to commit a crime for them and then claim they're not accountable; just so, we need to consider whether we should allow an individual to hide behind a corporate veil when they know their choices will cause direct harm to others.

All corporate welfare should be abolished. It is obvious that when government power is allowed to exist beyond the limited form of government envisioned by the Founders, those who are most powerful will subvert the political process to their advantage. The billions of dollars of corporate welfare benefits doled out by politicians will end once we return to a libertarian form of government.

We should also consider eliminating all forms of income taxes, including corporate income taxes, as they are simply passed on to the consumers as higher prices. This is, in effect, a hidden sales tax and results in what is actually a regressive tax, hurting those in the lower income brackets the most. The extremely high cost of complying with a corporate income tax is simply passed on to the consumer and is a complete waste of resources to all concerned.

Decentralization

We must redirect power and responsibility to individuals, institutions, communities and regions. We must encourage the flourishing of regionally based cultures, rather than a dominant mono-culture. We must have a decentralized democratic society, with our political, economic and social institutions locating power on the smallest scale (closest to home) that is efficient and practical. We must redesign our institutions so that fewer decisions and less regulation over money are granted as one moves from the community to the national level. We must reconcile the need for community and regional self-determination with the need for appropriate centralized regulation in certain matters.

This is totally in line with Libertarian principles. We believe that energy, drug abuse, food production, currency, welfare, education, health care, and retirement are all dealt with most efficiently and practically at the local level. We recommend the Ithaca hour currency system (see http://www.lightlink.com/hours/ithacahours) as a way to create local prosperity and even to finance a local health care system. The American Liberty Currency, a voluntary gold- and silver-backed currency, could be a supplemental currency that could be used in local communities and statewide.

Our entire campaign platform is based on bringing local control back to Iowa communities in every sphere possible. For instance, our energy platform (Chapter 10) explains how Iowa communities can become self-sufficient using wind energy.

Ecological Wisdom

We must operate human societies with the understanding that we are part of nature, not on top of it. We must live within the ecological and resource limits of the planet, applying our technological knowledge to the challenge of an energy-efficient economy. We must build a better relationship between cities and countryside. We must promote sustainable agriculture and respect for self-regulating natural systems. And we must further biocentric wisdom in all spheres of life.

The fundamental principles of the Libertarian philosophy are based on an understanding of natural law. It gives us a model for restructuring our institutions for maximum personal evolution, as well as for resolving our environmental problems. Buildings are being built now according to natural principles that do not create pollution. Farming methods that mimic nature allow us to grow crops profitably without damaging the environment. Manufacturing processes that are based on observing natural processes are already gaining acceptance. All of these changes are already taking place; we just need to promote them and make the changes in corporate law and campaign finance law I've described here. It is the huge corporate interests and their control of government that holds back these innovative developments.

Imagine having the governor of Iowa be someone who lives in a house designed according to ancient principles for being in tune with nature and built with natural materials, and a first lady who is a commercial organic grower.

Nonviolence

We must develop effective alternatives to our current patterns of violence at all levels, from the family and the street to nations and the world. We must eliminate nuclear weapons from the face of the Earth without being naive about the intentions of other governments. We must constructively use nonviolent methods to oppose practices and policies with which we disagree, and in the process reduce the atmosphere of polarization and selfishness that is itself a source of violence.

Nonviolence is the fundamental Libertarian principle. Nuclear weapons should be eliminated. But the priority must be the elimination of genetically engineered organisms, which are an even more urgent environmental danger. Force cannot be used to create nonviolence; the two are incompatible. This means that we have to set an example of nonviolence in our personal lives, our families, our communities and our nation. Our international relations should be based on respect and good will. We should not be involved militarily in any foreign nation. We should not interfere with other nations, we should not arm other nations, we should have a very strong defense, and we should only target aggressors, never civilians.

Personal and Global Responsibility

We must be of genuine assistance to grassroots groups in the Third World. We must help other countries make the transition to self-sufficiency in food and other basic necessities. We must cut our defense budget while maintaining an adequate defense. We must promote these ten Green values in the reshaping of our global order. We must reshape the world order, without creating just another enormous nation-state.

The current United Nations is just that, another enormous nation-state with a growing military and subject to the same special interest influences that currently control our national government. It is corrupt at the top levels. We would favor the elimination of the UN, the World Bank, the International Monetary Fund and the World Court. We would replace it with a Sovereign United Nations (SUN), based on the principles of individual sovereignty, national sovereignty and noncoercion. It could never have an army, police force, currency, bank or court. Its bureaucracy would be a fraction of the size of the current UN, and it would function as an enabling organization to foster communications between nations. The people involved with the SUN would be trained in what is called "chaordic leadership," which is a system of organizing institutions that is in harmony with natural law. (For more on chaordic leadership, go to www.chaordic.org.)

The World Interactive Treaty Signing (WITS) event—a world cooperative civil, commercial, and military space program designed to replace the war industry—is a perfect example of a chaordic international organization. The key legislation, the Space Preservation Act of 2002 (H.R.3616) introduced by Congressman Dennis Kucinich, Democrat from Ohio, would end the arms race in 2002 *before* space-based weapons are deployed, while stimulating a new space economy. This new economy would have enormous benefits for the entire world.

If we follow the principles outlined here, we will set an example that the entire world will want to follow. True free trade and mutual respect between nations will increase prosperity and quality of life for all.

Future Focus

We must induce people and institutions to think in terms of the long-range future, and not just in terms of their short-range selfish interest. We must encourage people to develop their own visions of the future and move more effectively toward them. We must judge whether new technologies are socially useful and use those judgments to shape our society. We must induce our government and other institutions to practice fiscal responsibility. We must make the quality of life, rather than unending economic growth, the focus of our future thinking.

We encourage, inspire and motivate people to think long term, and we certainly agree to induce government to be more fiscally responsible.

A high quality of life will attract prosperous people who will help us create more prosperity. We have a bold vision for Iowa. The rest of the country will be looking to the people of Iowa to learn how to generate widespread prosperity while halting the degradation of our environment. We will do this by holding firm to our core principles. We will recreate a state that is organized from the bottom up rather than the top down. A revitalized civil society will be able to solve the problems that have seemed intractable for so many years, because instead of depending on others, we will solve them at the level of the community.

We are the heart of America's heartland, and it is fitting that this new vision of politics for the nation and the world should start here and flow outward. This is a revolution based on the qualities of love. Love is the most powerful force on the planet. Love is unifying, and we should work together to unify all people in the state who share our vision.

"Regardless of what the biotechnology industry wants us to believe, agricultural genetic engineering is an imprecise science. It relies on methods that include the haphazard insertion of genetic elements into a plant's genome. This in turn may result in the disruption of complex gene interactions and may lead to potentially catastrophic results."

—*Dr. Michael Hansen, and Ellen Hickey,*
Global Pesticide Campaigner, *April 2000*

Chapter 14. Genetic Engineering: Bio-Tech or Bio-Deception?

By Clyde J. Cleveland

Position Summary

Genetic engineering has enormous implications for Iowa. Unfortunately, neither of the major political parties in Iowa appears to have questioned the biotech industry's assumptions regarding the economic, health, and environmental impacts of this technology.

We have, and what we found are some very disturbing facts unknown to most Iowans.

What is worse, the more we look into it, the more alarmed we become should Iowa continue to blindly follow these companies down the biotech path. There are huge financial incentives for those who play ball with these large corporations, but we need to analyze whether this is the best long-term strategy for our state.

Our concerns have to do with economic and freedom issues as much as with health and environmental issues. Most Iowa farmers have been affected by the economics of genetically engineered foods in the last few years. The industry's claims of increased yields have not materialized, and market resistance has been far greater than expected. In fact, the massive resistance shown by consumers all over the world toward food products made from genetically modified organisms (GMOs) is unprecedented in terms of resistance to a specific type of agricultural product. We believe this consumer resistance will only grow as people become aware of the concerns shared by world scientists regarding the health and environmental risks associated with GMOs.

We also believe that the decision by the U.S. Food and Drug Administration to treat GMO products the same as it does traditional products could be overturned. There has already been one lawsuit against the FDA regarding its approval process, and we expect that there will be others. An FDA reversal would dramatically affect the industry.

Faced with these serious issues about GMOs, the question for Iowa farmers is whether to continue being involved with an experiment. We think that's a bad idea, especially since there are viable alternatives.

The Problem

We are not against biotechnology or biotechnology companies. In fact, my company, UIG, raised research funds for biotech projects. But these projects did not involve recombinant DNA technology, that is, the forcible and unnatural transfer of DNA from one species to that of another species.

The long-term consequences of this transfer are unknown and unpredictable. This technology could create potentially life-damaging substances.

In 1992, the FDA ruled that these GMO products were to be classified the same as conventional products. Since then, GMO products have flooded the marketplace, without adequate testing to ensure their safety.

There are four major problems with GMO technology:

- The unknown long-term health and environmental consequences, an issue of grave concern to scientists worldwide.

- A poor return on investment for farmers.

- Increasing evidence of uncontrollable contamination of non-genetically engineered crops by genetically engineered crops.

- An illegal approval process by the FDA, which could dramatically affect the industry once the facts become widely known.

The Big Unknown

The biotech industry has had a tendency to accuse its critics of being Luddites or eco-terrorists. The truth is that, all over the world, people from literally every walk of life are highly concerned about this technology. The potential health and environmental consequences are too significant to allow self-regulation by those who benefit financially. Many of the world's leading scientists have expressed their deep concerns.

Steve Jones is one of the world's most prominent geneticists and someone who consistently reveals a serious disdain for the ecology movement. Jones, a professor of genetics at University College in London, once compared the Green movement to Nazism. Despite his loathing of environmentalists, he had this to say about genetically modified foods: "The genes you put in may actually leak out and get to places where we can't control them...Genes can leap in the most extraordinary and alarming way. There's no reason to say the same thing cannot happen in genetically modified plants. It only has to happen once. The dangers are really quite real."

He went on to say, "I definitely think we need more knowledge before we make the same mistakes with GM foods that we made with penicillin—and I most clearly think we should stop doing this until we know more about it." ("Where does the truth lie," *The Guardian*, Feb. 26, 1999)

Erwin Chargaff, professor emeritus of biochemistry, Columbia University, and discoverer of Chargaff's Rules, which laid the scientific foundation for the discovery of the DNA double helix, is another scientist skeptical of GMOs: "I have a feeling that science has transgressed a barrier that should have remained inviolate...you cannot recall a new form of life...it will survive you and your children and your children's children. An irreversible attack on the biosphere is something so unheard of, so unthinkable to previous generations, that I can only wish that mine had not been guilty of it." (*Genetic Engineering, Food, and Our Environment*, by Luke Anderson)

Chargaff and Jones are renowned scientists and clearly not alarmists, Luddites, or eco-terrorists. This issue affects us all and the truth has been ignored. The industry's public statements are a distortion of the facts, while the opinions of Chargaff and Jones speak to the heart of the issue of genetically engineered foods. We simply do not know how these organisms will affect our environment or our health. This is a critically important issue to everyone—we potentially face irreversible damage.

Poor Economics for Farmers

The predicted economic benefits of GMO products for farmers just haven't happened, as the following documentation shows.

- A 2001 study done by Guy Hatchard, a research scientist and director of market research, Genetic ID, found that "U.S. corn farmers alone lost more than $12 billion in 2000. This was partly offset by $4.3 billion in government support programs, giving a net loss of $7.7 billion. This compares with a net profit of $1.4 billion in 1996, the year GMOs were first commercialized."

- With major European food giants such as ASDA (owned by Wal-Mart), Tesco, Sainsburys, and Aldi all demanding non-GMO products, it does not look good for GMO-producing countries to ever recapture these markets. According to Hatchard, "The key assumption underlying simple global supply and demand models of commodity price trends is one of homogeneity. Homogeneity implies that all lots of commodities can be traded between nations on an equal footing. The GMO issue has disrupted this homogeneity condition by introducing significant discontinuities in commodity markets."

- After analyzing the 2000 USDA report "Cost and Return," the University of Iowa concluded that there has been no economic on-farm benefit of GMO soy and corn crops to counter falls in prices. The USDA report surveyed 350 Iowa farms, gathering data on yields compared to costs of fertilizer, herbicide, and seed.

- A 2001 study done by Michael Duffy, Iowa State University, concluded that there "does not appear to be any difference" in the per-acre profitability between the Bt [brand of GM] corn and non-Bt corn." He found similar results with soybeans. An earlier study, done in 1999, showed essentially the same results.

Why have so many farmers purchased the products if there is no increase in profitability? The reasons appear to be related more to convenience and flexibility, rather than profitability. Advertising is also a factor.

Farmers may also need to be concerned about issues other than yield. In an article in the Iowa Farm Bureau *Spokesman*, Jerry Rosman, a farmer in Shelby County, Iowa, describes how birth rates in his pig herd dropped by almost 80 percent between October 2000 and August 2001. After considerable testing to determine the source of the problem, all to no avail, Rosman learned that four other producers in his area were seeing the same pseudopregnancies in their herds. The only common denominator among the producers was that they were all feeding their pigs the same Bt corn hybrids.

"Laboratory tests revealed their corn contained high levels of fusarium mold...One of the producers subsequently switched back to known tested pure corn, and pseudopregnancy is no longer a problem within that herd," wrote reporter Tom Block.

"...An agronomist has told [Rosman] that a regular rotation of corn and soybeans might not get rid of whatever gene has contaminated his corn ground." ("Pseudopregnancies puzzle swine producer," April 29, 2002; www.ifbf.org/publication/archive/)

No government agency has required testing to find out how Bt corn affects the reproduction rates of animals. Nor have there been any studies of the effects on humans who consume Bt-fed animals.

Contamination of Other Crops

The European Environment Agency (EEA), the European Union's environmental regulating agency, published a study this year concluding that gene flow can occur over long distances and that some varieties of genetically modified crops interbreed with others more often and at greater distances than previously thought. The study also states that genes will inevitably escape from genetically modified crops, contaminating organic farms, creating superweeds, and driving wild plants to extinction.

The new information confirms environmentalists' worst fears and will make it very difficult for any government to approve the commercial planting of GM crops. Pollen from the GM crops traveled much farther than the official "isolation distances" laid down to prevent interbreeding by separating them from ordinary crops, making a mockery of the safety precautions. Cross-pollination by GM oilseed rape was recorded about 2.5 miles away from the crop, compared to an isolation distance of just under a half mile (600 meters). As reported by the London *Independent* (March 24, 2002), the EEA report warns that "over time even small amounts of gene flow can have important effects on evolutionary change." It predicts superweeds, those that are resistant to herbicides, to become "common" if GM crops are grown and warns that organic farmers will find it hard to sell their produce once it has been infiltrated by GM genes. Finally, the EEA report states that the interbreeding could lead to natural wild relatives of the crops becoming extinct.

> "We cannot afford to jeopardize our commodity grain."
>
> —*Larry Johnson, head of Iowa State's Center for Crops Utilization Research*

The Europeans are not the only people concerned about this, of course. Closer to home, the Iowa Farm Bureau Federation has called for a formal review of regulations governing both field testing and commercial production of GM crops; several Midwestern states are collaborating on a study of pollen drift; and the National Academy of Sciences has recommended closer regulatory scrutiny of GMOs. In addition, a coalition of environmental and consumer groups, called Genetically Engineered Food Alert, plans to call for a halt to open-field testing of the new class of transgenic crops to prevent contamination. The coalition contends too much is at stake to permit the production as long as field-to-field gene flow is a possibility.

An article by Anne Fitzgerald in the *Des Moines Register* on March 17, 2002, described similar concern among Iowa farmers, who worry that the pollen from high-tech corn varieties that are genetically engineered to yield pharmaceutical and industrial products could drift to nearby fields and contaminate other crops. Corn is a cross-pollinating crop that relies largely on the wind and gravity to carry pollen from tassels atop one plant on to the silks of another plant. As John Nason, an assistant professor of botany, Iowa State University, told Fitzgerald, corn plants are "basically just broadcasting piles of pollen out into the air and hoping it lands where it's needed."

As Fitzgerald's article describes, pollen drift has already contributed to massive recalls of corn-based food products and a drop in export sales. Two years ago, StarLink, an Aventis brand of corn approved for animal but *not* human consumption, was found in taco shells and other food products. Although StarLink was planted on less than 1 percent of U.S. acreage in 2000, it was found in 10 percent of the corn harvested that year. Potential causes of the contamination were found to be pollen drift; inadvertent mixture of the specialty seed with conventional corn, either in packaging or during handling; and "volunteer" field growth of kernels left in the field after harvest.

Contamination of food grains by genetically engineered grains designed for industrial or pharmaceutical use is a frightening concept. Farmers, organic growers, environmentalists, and even some proponents of the new class of engineered crops have all voiced concern about this. They also worry that pollen drift will contaminate so-called commodity grains destined for export, resulting in the closing of major foreign markets to U.S. producers. The long-term effects of contamination could be catastrophic, particularly for Iowa, which produces about one-fifth of all U.S. corn.

"...There are scientifically justified concerns about the safety of genetically engineered foods and some of them could be quite dangerous...It is because I view the FDA's policy and practices regarding genetically engineered food to be irresponsible—and because I regard the consequent risk posed for public health to be substantial—that I have taken the step of joining the lawsuit as a plaintiff."

—*Philip J. Regal, Ph.D., Professor of Ecology, Behavior and Evolution, University of Minnesota, and one of nine scientists joining as plaintiffs in the Alliance for Bio-Integrity lawsuit against the FDA*

The FDA's Deception

In 1999, in an attempt to overturn FDA policy, the Alliance for Bio-Integrity filed a lawsuit challenging the FDA's claim that genetically engineered (GE) foods do not pose greater risks than conventional foods. The suit alleged that in allowing GE foods to be marketed without safety testing, the agency was violating federal statutory law and its own regulations. In an unprecedented move, nine eminent scientists and numerous religious leaders joined as plaintiffs.

During the litigation, the FDA was required to turn over more than 44,000 pages of internal documents to the plaintiffs. After reviewing these documents, we believe that any objective person would conclude that the FDA approved GE foods only by disregarding the warnings from its own scientists about the unique health risks of these foods, covering up these warnings, and then going so far as to deny their existence.

The court ultimately upheld the FDA on technical aspects of administrative procedural law. Among other things, it ruled that the FDA's politically appointed bureaucrats had the discretion to disregard their scientific experts. But the court neglected to discuss the fact that the bureaucrats not only ignored what their experts said, they then lied about it. This irresponsible behavior of the FDA bureaucracy has contributed to the sad state of affairs Iowa farmers now face.

Most of the FDA scientists who commented on bio-engineered foods identified reasonable grounds for doubting the safety of these foods, while several issued strong warnings. The predominant view was that genetic engineering entails distinct risks and that GE products cannot be regarded as safe unless proven to be through appropriate studies.

The Alliance for Bio-Integrity lists many of the FDA scientists' comments on its web site (www.biointegrity.com). Here is a sampling.

- "There is a profound difference between the types of unexpected effects from traditional breeding and genetic engineering," according to FDA microbiologist Louis Pribyl, Ph.D.

- The director of the FDA's Center for Veterinary Medicine stated, "…CVM believes that animal feeds derived from genetically modified plants present unique animal and food safety concerns." He explained that residues of unexpected substances could make meat and milk products "harmful to humans," and called for bio-engineered products to be demonstrated safe prior to marketing.

- The head of the FDA's biological and organic chemistry section chided agency bureaucrats for turning prior policy "on its head" in attempting to equate bio-engineered foods with their conventional counterparts. He also pointed out that the lack of definitive evidence that a GE food is dangerous does not assure safety, noting that "in this instance, ignorance is not bliss."

- Linda Kahl, Ph.D, a compliance officer, protested the agency was "trying to fit a square peg into a round hole…[by] trying to force an ultimate conclusion that there is no difference between foods modified by G.E. and foods modified by traditional breeding practices." She declared, "The processes of G.E. and traditional breeding are different, and according to the technical experts in the agency, lead to different risks."

- FDA Biotechnology Coordinator James Maryanski, Ph.D., acknowledged in a letter to a Canadian official on Oct. 23, 1991, that there was not a scientific consensus about safety. He also admitted, "I think the question of the potential for some substances to cause allergenic reactions is particularly difficult to predict."

Despite the dissent among its scientists, on May 29, 1992, the FDA issued a statement asserting that there is overwhelming consensus among scientists that genetically engineered foods do not entail different risks. This policy presumes every GE food is as safe as its conventional counterpart unless demonstrated otherwise. The FDA does not require any testing or labeling, and testing is purely voluntary and left to the manufacturer's discretion.

There is a very serious disconnect between the truth about genetic engineering and what most people have been told.

It is clear that FDA leadership was more concerned about promoting the biotech industry's agenda than following the law. There was no consensus that these organisms were safe, and if FDA had followed the law, these products would not be on the market. The truth about this issue, however, is not getting out to the people. The national media has ignored the evidence of the FDA's cover-up, as well as the warnings about the health risks of GE food that have been voiced by FDA scientists and other experts. What has been reported has been incomplete and distorted. In the meantime, self-serving statements by GE proponents claiming that these foods are safe receive widespread coverage.

Two years ago Monsanto sponsored a huge worldwide media campaign designed to make everyone believe that the only way to feed the world was genetic engineering. Not everyone was convinced. For example, the following statement was signed by all 24 of the UN delegates from African countries:

"We strongly object that the image of the poor and hungry from our countries is being used by giant multinational corporations to push a new technology that is neither safe, environmentally friendly, nor economically beneficial to us. We do not believe that such companies or gene technologies will help our farmers to produce the food that is needed in the 21st century. On the contrary, we think it will destroy the diversity, the local knowledge, and the sustainable agricultural systems that our farmers have developed for millennia and that it will thus undermine our capacity to feed ourselves." (*Genetic Engineering, Food, and Our Environment*, by Luke Anderson)

There is a vast difference between the truth about genetic engineering and what most people know about it. Media consolidation, biotech industry consolidation, the revolving door between government regulators and corporate interests, and good propaganda techniques are all part of the reason for the gap. To understand the issues of genetic engineering, you need to understand how all of these factors relate. Then it becomes obvious that genetic engineering is not just an environmental issue, it is a freedom issue as well.

Media Consolidation

The consolidation of the media in recent years has been incredible. There are now just five companies that essentially own the entire media industry, and thus control what the American people see and hear. These chilling statements from top-level media insiders tell the story.

- "We are going to impose our agenda on the coverage by dealing with issues and subjects that we choose to deal with." Richard M. Cohen, former senior producer, of CBS Political News (*Losing Your Illusions*, Gordon Phillips)

- "We paid $3 billion for these television stations. We will decide what the news is. The news is what we tell you it is." David Boylan, Fox News (*Genetic Engineering, Food, and Our Environment*, by Luke Anderson)

- "Our job is to give people not what they want, but what we decide they ought to have." Richard Salant, former president, CBS News (*Losing Your Illusions*, Gordon Phillips)

In an excellent article about Edward Bernays, considered the "father" of modern-day public relations, well-known libertarian author Claire Wolfe explains the mindset of those who desire to control everyone else and how they manipulate the media to do their bidding:

"Bernays believed that he and other members of the elite were exactly the leaders we needed to save us from our primitive, animal-like selves. 'If we understand the mechanism and motives of the group mind,' he wrote, the elite could 'control and regiment the masses according to our will without them knowing it...just as the motorist can regulate the speed of his car by manipulating the flow of gasoline.'

"He further said, 'The duty of the higher strata of society—the cultivated, the learned, the expert, the intellectual—is therefore clear. They must inject moral and spiritual motives into public opinion.'

"Bernays and the intellectual, governmental elite for whom he practiced his new 'science' literally believed that they must 'create manmade gods...who assert subtle social control' to 'bring order out of chaos.'

"Of course, another word for 'chaos' is freedom—the millions of free choices made by individuals.

"That pattern has continued to this day—with thousands of (tax-exempt!) research foundations aggressively promoting everything from genetically engineered foods (with funding from Monsanto, DuPont, and Coca Cola) to citizen disarmament, and with charitable foundations provoking anxiety over an endless stream of new, 'scientifically proven' problems." ("How to Recognize a Skunk or Why Most Americans Can't Think—But You Can," by Aaron Zelman and Claire Wolfe, Feb. 2002)

Food Industry Consolidation

GMOs must be seen in the context of the drive to control the world's food supply. The profits and power that would accrue to the companies that have this control are immense. All of the scientific and political issues must be considered from the perspective of what is at stake for the companies involved.

GMOs are only a part of the picture. The same companies that control GMOs, also own the vast majority of the seed companies in the world. They also own or control most of the global pesticide market. If you add Bayer and Dow to the list, they dominate over 90 percent of the agrichemicals sold in the world.

Because Iowa farmers are part of a much bigger plan for these companies, they must ask themselves how likely it is that these global food giants are thinking about their best interests while going about their business of globalizing the food industry. In his book, *Genetic Engineering, Food, and Our Environment*, Luke Anderson articulates the range of the consolidation occurring in the food industry around the world:

- In three years, from 1999 to 2001, Monsanto spent $8 billion on acquisitions, incorporating seed companies, genetic engineering companies, and other related interests.

- In December 1998, Germany's Hoechst and France's Rhone-Poulenc merged to form Aventis, "the world's biggest life science company," with combined sales of $20 billion.

- UK Zeneca and Astra AB of Sweden have announced their intent to merge in what will be the largest-ever European merger. At more than $70 billion, the combined assets will be larger than the 1997 gross national product of 93 countries.

- In March 1999, DuPont announced it would pay $7.7 billion to buy the remaining 80 percent stake in Pioneer Hybrid International, the world's largest seed company.

- In November 1998, Cargill, the world's largest grain exporter, announced a merger that would allow it to control 45 percent of the global grain trade.

- 40 percent of U.S. vegetable seeds come from a single source. The top five producers control 75 percent of the global vegetable seed market.

- On July 9, 1999, Cargill Inc., the nation's largest privately held company, won approval from the Clinton administration to acquire the grain-trading operations of its primary rival, Continental Grain Inc. The approval came over the objections of the attorneys general in the farm states, the Farmers

Union, consumer organizations and green groups, which charged that the union will create a near monopoly in the grain business. Combined, the two companies will control 94 percent of the soybean and 53 percent of the corn market.

Luke Anderson goes on to quote Dwayne Andreas, CEO of ADM, who boasted to Reuters that he wanted ADM to dominate [saying that] "there's simply nothing more powerful than controlling the world's food supply...The food business is far and away the most important business in the world...Everything else is a luxury. Food is what you need to sustain life every day. Food is fuel. You can't run a tractor without fuel and you can't run a human being without it either. Food is the absolute beginning."

> "This is not just a consolidation of seed companies, it's really a consolidation of the entire food chain."
>
> —*Robert T. Fraley, Co-president of the agricultural sector, Monsanto*

The Revolving Door between Industry and Government

The FDA admits it has been operating under a policy "to foster" the U.S. biotechnology industry, a policy initiated by Reagan/Bush and carried on by Clinton/Gore and Bush/Cheney.

In 1991, the FDA appointed Michael Taylor to the new FDA position of deputy commissioner for policy. Taylor's job was to supervise the formulation of FDA policy on GE food. A lawyer, Taylor previously represented Monsanto and other members of the biotech industry on food regulatory issues. During Taylor's tenure as deputy commissioner, references to the potentially negative effects of bioengineering were progressively deleted from drafts of the policy statement (over the protests of agency scientists), and the finalized policy states (a) that GE foods are no riskier than others and (b) that the agency has no information to the contrary.

After he left the FDA, Taylor was hired by Monsanto as vice president for public policy.

Taylor isn't the only crossover. The list goes on and on. Here is just a sample.

Biotech executives who are now high-level advisers to President Bush

- Linda Fisher, deputy director, Environmental Pollution Agency (EPA); for vice president and chief lobbyist, Monsanto

- Donald Rumsfeld, secretary of defense; former president of Searle Pharmaceuticals, owned by Monsanto

- John L. Henshaw, assistant secretary of labor, Occupational Safety and Health Administration; a 20-year veteran of Monsanto

- Ann Veneman, secretary of agriculture; formerly on the board of directors of Calgene Pharmaceuticals, owned by Monsanto

- Mitch Daniels, director of the Office of Management and Budget; former vice president, Eli Lilly Pharmaceuticals

Biotech executives in the Clinton/Gore administration

- Marcia Hale, assistant to President Clinton in the area of intergovernmental affairs; went on to a senior position with Monsanto, coordinating public affairs and corporate strategy in the United Kingdom and Ireland

  L. Val Giddings, a biotechnology regulator for the Department of Agriculture (USDA/APHIS); went on to serve as vice president of the Biotechnology Industry Organization (Giddings was at the first meeting of the Open-Ended Ad Hoc Working Group on Biosafety Protocol as a member of the United States delegation; he attended the second meeting as the representative of the Biotechnology Industry Organization.)

- David W. Beier, chief domestic policy adviser to Vice President Al Gore; former head of government affairs for Genentech

- Josh King, former director of production for White House events; went on to become director of global communications in the Washington, D.C., office of Monsanto

- Margaret Miller, deputy director of human food safety and consultant services, Center for Veterinary Medicine, FDA; former chemical laboratory supervisor for Monsanto

- William D. Ruckelshaus, chief administrator of the EPA; served on Monsanto's board of directors for the last 12 years

The Bottom-up Solutions

As I've said, there is nothing inherently wrong with biotechnology as long as the processes used do not create potentially life-damaging substances, but the effects of crossing DNA between species are totally unpredictable at this time. We don't have to risk these unknown consequences. Real alternatives exist and they are all based on the bottom-up model.

Capitalize on the Opportunity

Seed companies and farmers who can supply a non-GMO product can attract a premium price. Corn processors can recapture European Union export markets. Every level of the agrifood industry now has the opportunity to join in a non-GMO food network which facilitates the sourcing of ingredients and dismantles obstacles to trade.

Traditionally, American grains have helped feed the world, while U.S. commodity markets have set global prices. The introduction of GMOs has put this market system at risk. Iowans can benefit from this situation by using our creativity and acting on the opportunity, or we can be left holding the bag, as Hatcher explained in his study:

"Already an Internet-based electronic market for international trade in organic goods is planned to open in Europe, funded by the giant telecommunication player BT. Under present market conditions, similar start-up companies trading in conventional GMO-free commodities will soon become key-holders for international trade. North America will be left out of this process, unless the separate identities of GMO and conventional grains are preserved throughout the processing chain. Without rigorous segregation, a two-tier grain commodity market will develop, with U.S. grains selling in the lower tier and U.S. farmers footing the bill until they can no longer carry on."

Spread the Truth

If the truth about GE was widespread, we would have the natural, free-market, libertarian solution—no market for the product, hence no regulation necessary. A truly free press would have informed people about the dangers, and this whole controversy would not be an issue; the biotech industry would already be on to something else. That is why we will be speaking out about this issue. That is why we will be sponsoring seminars about this topic in Iowa. We are talking about the survival of our species. This is not the time to be political or cautious. This is a time for truth.

Enforce the Law or Eliminate the FDA

Many people who are aware of the dangers of recombinant DNA are taking action to force the FDA to follow the law and reclassify genetically engineered foods properly. This would mean that these organisms would be removed from the market until proven safe. We believe that this effort will be a complete waste of time and energy.

There could not be a more dramatic example of the corruption of a federal government agency than the fraudulent approval of genetically engineered foods by the Food and Drug Administration. Anyone who has studied the track record of this agency knows that it has been corrupt since its inception. We believe it is time to abolish the FDA and replace it with a noncoercive organization based on the principles we have outlined in earlier chapters.

A strong reliance on local solutions should predominate in the regulation of products that are potentially hazardous to the environment. We believe that the people of Iowa, if properly informed, can best make the decision about this issue. Therefore, we will endeavor to get the appropriate information to all the people of Iowa. We will ask *all* interested and affected parties in our state to participate in a debate about this subject. When this process is allowed to progress to its natural conclusion, without power politics and money controlling the process, the people of Iowa will make the right decision.

Grow Your Own Food or Buy Locally from People You Know

The more people who grow their own food, the better. It is possible to do more than feed your family with a greenhouse. One family in our town built a 2,000-square-foot greenhouse, which is financially supporting a family of five. They sell their non-GMO produce to a local restaurant as well as the health food store. Others here heat and cool their greenhouses for free with the amazing earth tube technology (described in Appendix 4 page 323). It is possible to grow food all year long in any climate, saving money and ensuring that your family eats good-healthy produce with no genetic contamination whatsoever. The more people who do this, the less power the agribusiness/government complex have over us.

This is an outstanding business opportunity for small farmers in Iowa. It is a way to make a good living on a very small amount of land. For those who want to transition to non-chemical farming, a large greenhouse and a few acres of crops planted for human consumption could prove to be very profitable.

We have presented many case studies of farmers who are not using GMOs, in Chapter 11. The financial benefits are positive for those who choose the non-GMO path.

Demand Labeling

We believe that people have a right to know what is in the food they eat. Companies should not have a problem with disclosing the ingredients in their products. If they do, that indicates they have something to hide. Food should be labeled so that people can exercise their free will and make informed decisions about buying it. In all the polls we have seen, a large majority of the American people want genetically modified foods to be labeled. How can people have freedom of choice if they do not have the required information to make that choice?

Become a Community Activist

In Oregon a political action committee was formed specifically to use the ballot initiative process to address the issue of labeling genetically engineered foods. In Denver, an initiative is under way to require only non-GMO food to be served to the public schoolchildren until proper long-term testing is completed (the same testing required by the law but ignored by the FDA).

These initiatives are very good models of bottom-up government in action. Unfortunately, our state politicians have
squelched all efforts to bring the initiative process to Iowa.
Our administration would support this valuable process,
which allows people to take direct action to circumvent powerful institutions that have gained control of government.

A Better Way

Iowa Governor Tom Vilsack has turned out to be the nation's
chief proponent for the biotechnology industry. In fact, the
Biotechnology Industry Organization named Vilsack
"Governor of the Year," citing his support for both the industry's growth and continued agricultural biotech research. Our
governor was praised for creating the Governors'
Biotechnology Partnership, a bipartisan coalition of governors aimed at spreading biotechnology information. The
group started with 13 members, but more than half of the
nation's governors now participate.

Obviously Governor Vilsack believes strongly in biotech's
potential for Iowa. We think that the Republicans and
Democrats are both so completely lacking in creative solutions for bringing prosperity to Iowa that they have climbed
on the biotech bandwagon as their great hope to save the
state economically. That is a recipe for disaster. The policies
we are advocating throughout this book will bring economic
and environmental health to our state.

Genetic engineering is an issue that affects us all. In our opinion, it is a serious economic and freedom issue. It is also very
likely the most important environmental or health issue this
planet is facing or has ever confronted. Remember: you can

make a difference. Don't take our word for it, do your own research. Several excellent sources are listed in the Appendix and on our web site (www.clevelandforgovernor.org).

> "Either you're going to go along with your mind and the truth, or you're going to yield to fear and custom and conditioned reflexes. With our minds alone, we can discover those principles we need to employ to convert all humanity to success in a new, harmonious relationship with the universe. *We have the option to make it.*"
>
> —*R. Buckminster Fuller*

"According to drug court advocates, keeping a defendant in the drug court program costs $4,000 per year. The cost of jailing the state's 30,000 prisoners comes to more than $22,000 per prisoner per year. According to a recent study of the state's drug courts by researchers at Virginia Tech, the number of participants who have successfully completed the program is running at 68 percent, up from 60 percent in 1999. Only 7 percent of the graduates have received new convictions, the study found."

—The Week Online with DRCNet
(Issue 233, April 19, 2002)

Chapter 15: Criminal Justice: Creating a Humane AND Effective System

By Edward F. Noyes, J.D.

Position Summary

Iowa, like states throughout the nation, has accepted the inevitability of building more and more prisons and incarcerating more and more of our citizens in a never-ending war against crime. Our nation now has the distinction of imprisoning a higher percentage of its citizens than any nation on earth. As fast as we build new prisons, they are filled and then we plan for more. Is this trend truly our only destiny, or can we redefine what constitutes success in criminal justice for our families, neighbors, and communities?

The need to reform the criminal justice system is very clear. All we have to do is take a look back at how the Founders viewed (1) the relationship between government and the people, (2) the role of government when one citizen harmed another, and (3) the ideal relationship between citizens when one fell below the level of dignity expected by the community.

If Iowa would redefine success at the level of the community, and apply the resources of each community to address criminal behavior, we would have a unique opportunity to lead the nation in a new paradigm of criminal justice. This new paradigm would simultaneously offer the greatest chance for the rehabilitation of the offender, provide for the restoration of the victim, and incur the least cost for its citizens. Not coincidentally, it also honors the best of our religious and political traditions.

What is Liberty?

When I speak to groups about the criminal justice system, I first ask the audience for their definition of liberty. We are all familiar with the concept of liberty and understand that it is an important principle in our nation. Most believe that the wars fought by Americans—including the Revolutionary War, World War I and World War II—were fought so that we, and others throughout the world, could obtain or retain our liberty. France gave the Statute of Liberty to our country to symbolize what the United States represents to the world and what it offers to all of those who come to its shores. In the state of Iowa, our flag declares "Our Liberties We Prize and Our Rights We Will Maintain."

If liberty is such an important concept that we would erect monuments, put it on our flags, and fight world wars to defend it, then it must be worth taking some time to consider its meaning. When Thomas Jefferson spoke of the pursuit of happiness, he clearly was referring to the natural right of every man and woman to exercise their liberty, to make choices, and to exercise their God-given free will. It is clear that liberty does not dictate absolute freedom but provides for the right of the individual to pursue happiness in whatever way he or she chooses, as long as they do not interfere with the rights of others.

> **Liberty: The freedom to make choices for yourself in the exercise of your free will, in the pursuit of personal happiness, as long as you do not interfere with the rights of others.**

The Problem

The United States has come a long way from the Founders' vision of an ideal criminal justice system. The so-called war on drugs is a reflection of our modern-day approach to criminal justice. Almost all would agree that this effort has done nothing to stop the use of illegal drugs in this country. Despite billions of dollars spent, the building of hundreds of new prisons, and the imposition of a virtual police state throughout the nation—combined with the highest citizen incarceration rate of any nation in the world—the use of recreational drugs has actually increased. As a further consequence, by focusing our attention on punishment rather than on rehabilitation, we have not only imprisoned others, we have imprisoned ourselves as well, with ever-expanding crime and taxation levels.

Learning from Prohibition

A brief study of Prohibition shows the futility of the majority trying to dictate the personal choices of the minority. Making the sale and transportation of alcohol illegal:

- did not change the desire of millions to consume alcohol; instead, these millions became "criminals."

- forced people who were otherwise law-abiding to be in the company of true criminals.

- attached the stigma of "criminal" to the family members of those breaking this new law.

- put families on welfare when the breadwinner was arrested.

- made the now illegal business of selling and transporting alcohol very profitable.

- encouraged gangsters to arm themselves to defend their turf.

- led to corruption of officials.

- took away many people's right to privacy.

- bred disdain for the law and law enforcement personnel.

- resulted in overcrowding the judicial system, jails and prisons.

Alcohol usage among the public actually increased each year during Prohibition, proving that criminalizing pervasive victimless conduct did very little if anything to address the issue.

The citizens of this country were intelligent enough to put an end to Prohibition. They eventually realized that attempting to manage the private lives of citizens was counterproductive, as the Founders knew.

The present-day war on drugs is an even a bigger failure than Prohibition. Neighborhoods have turned into battlegrounds because gangs are now involved in drug dealing. This should come as no surprise given the vast financial incentive that exists, just as it did during Prohibition.

Who benefits from the war on drugs? This is an excellent question to ask regarding any government program, but it is particularly important in issues concerning our criminal justice systems and policies. Anyone who has watched the expansion of police power and corresponding government spending over the past several decades should be able to answer this question. The beneficiaries have been the "tough on crime" politicians who have gained the votes of the people. Once again, they have played on the fear of the people and promised to solve a problem that never was the politicians' problem to solve in the first place.

The Difference between 'Demagoguery' and Genuine Leadership

I believe it is vital for the American people to gain an understanding of the difference between demagoguery and genuine leadership. Webster's defines a demagogue as "a leader who makes use of popular prejudices and false claims and promises in order to gain power."

Certainly, Adolph Hitler was a very successful demagogue. As we know, the majority of German citizens endorsed his policies and were highly moved by his rhetoric. That rhetoric appealed to their fears and to their base desire to blame someone else for their problems. It also appealed to their desire to feel superior to others. Of course, we know it worked all too well.

What forms of demagoguery should we watch out for today? Whenever a politician promises to solve a problem, whether it is an individual's problem or the community's, we should stop and ask ourselves if we are about to improperly delegate away our own duties and responsibilities. In the context of alcohol and substance abuse, I believe history has shown us that it is our personal responsibility to refrain from overindulgence and that we should work within our families and communities to solve these problems. In this way, we incur the least expense and have the greatest possible opportunity for success.

Of course, just because a politician promises to solve a problem if elected doesn't mean he or she can or will. In October 1989, Senator Charles Grassley stated that the government "would take back the streets today and provide for a drug-free America tomorrow." In reality, the statistics will show that despite the billions of tax dollars spent by government, the imposition of a virtual police state, and resultant erosion of civil liberties, drug usage has actually increased since the war on drugs started.

We cannot single out Grassley as the only politician who has made these types of claims. Virtually all candidates for public office have made promises to solve our drug and crime problems for us. In fact, any politician depicted as soft on crime by other candidates or the media has been virtually guaranteed defeat. The public's nearly epidemic level of distrust of politicians today stems from the endless promises they have made to solve our problems—problems that almost always cannot be solved by the government, even with all the power and money in the world at their disposal. The solution to most societal problems simply does not exist within the politicians' or the government's domain.

Giving Away Our Power

One way to look at these issues is to ask ourselves whether we have improperly delegated (to the government) our responsibility to deal with fundamental human problems. An honest assessment of the past shows that this delegation has never worked, and it never will. Such "unnatural" delegation has cost us dearly in ever-expanding taxation and the inability to allow for a genuine opportunity for personal, family, and community growth. By returning the "jurisdiction of the issue" to the people and the local communities, we naturally avoid the expense of attempting to solve a problem, such as crime, at a level where the solution cannot be found.

Who Benefits from the War on Drugs?

Who has benefited from the war on drugs? In addition to the politicians, it has been the career prosecutors and those within the prison industry who gain status and power as the incarceration rates go up. To my disgust, I once heard an aspiring prosecutor make the statement, "I own Billy Jones," as a way of impressing the attorneys within earshot. It amazes me to see how certain career prosecutors view adding another notch on their belt (by sending another human being to prison) as the prime motivating force for their career. Unfortunately, the truth is that we, the people, have given prosecutors this power, hoping they would solve our problems for us.

The Founders were aware of man's base desire for power and control over others. They were also very aware that power corrupts. Former career bureaucrats in the Iowa criminal justice system have admitted that they were quick to learn that the way to advance their careers and expand their power (and earn more money) was to add more staff and increase the budget for their department. Of course, this process is nothing new and is prevalent within all branches of government, from the local to the federal level. We therefore must be vigilant to prevent their assumption of power whenever possible and to return to the community any and all functions that can be handled more efficiently and effectively at that level.

The Bottom-up Solutions

Iowa has a unique opportunity to lead the nation in a new paradigm of criminal justice that simultaneously protects the public, offers the greatest chance for the rehabilitation of the offender, provides for the restoration of the victim, and incurs the least costs for its citizens. Not coincidentally, this paradigm honors the best of our religious and political heritage, while respecting and encouraging the humanity and dignity of us all.

The new paradigm includes the following elements.

Decriminalize the War on Drugs

The Founding Fathers and Libertarians would say that it should be up to the individual first, then his or her family, and then the community to address personal issues. We agree.

By decriminalizing drugs, we would automatically take away the profit incentive that now provides the lifeblood of violent gangs. It would also free up the court system. According to Cedar Rapids attorney David M. Elderkin, "More than 50 percent of the 1.3 million Americans in jail today are there for drug crimes, many for mere usage. We have consumed an estimated 60 percent of the trial time of our judiciary and have occupied the time of a half million police officers." (*Des Moines Register*, July 31, 2001)

Many people wonder if by decriminalizing certain drugs, will we be encouraging their use? In fact, the exact opposite is true. Once we end the government's involvement in this issue and reassume our sovereignty and personal responsibility for ourselves, our families, and our communities, we will have the greatest chance of success in reducing harmful drug use. All of the human and financial resources misused at the governmental level can be directed to the local level, where we actually can make a difference.

Let me ask you a question. If individuals were free to be open about their inappropriate drug usage without fear of criminal prosecution, wouldn't that create the greatest chance of dealing honestly with the problem? If all of our resources were available for rehabilitation, wouldn't we have the greatest chance of success? Do we not have a duty to be honest about these issues, rather than putting our heads in the sand and assuming the government in all its forms will solve it for us?

End Mandatory Sentencing Practices

Recently, a young man was sentenced to 15 years in federal prison because the authorities found a single .22 caliber bullet in his house. Although he had never used a weapon in his criminal activity, he was classified according to federal law as an armed, violent criminal. Mandatory sentencing guidelines imposed by the federal government forced the judge to sentence the young man to 15 years in prison, where he will be housed and fed by taxpayers.

By taking away the judge's authority to make a sentencing decision, these laws prevent the use of common sense. An editorial in the *Des Moines Register* sums it up well: "Mandatory minimum sentences strip judges of the power to use their experience and common sense to weigh the circumstances of each case. The sentencing guidelines tie federal judges' hands in precisely the same way as mandatory minimums by prescribing criminal sentences through a rigid formula." ("Stop Handcuffing Judges," Jan. 28, 2002)

In that same article, Senator Tom Harkin admitted that mandatory minimum sentences are a mistake, even though he voted for them. He said, "I was wrong. I think it's turned into a sentencing nightmare."

Believe me, you won't hear many politicians admit that they were wrong. How many other policies not in the people's best interest have been enacted by "get tough" politicians? As citizens, we need to ask ourselves how we have contributed to these policies by allowing the advocates of centralization to take away our power to deal with problems at the local level. Because we believe in local control and maximum intelligence in decision making, we support ending maximum and minimum sentencing requirements and returning as much of the decision making to the people as possible.

End Zero-tolerance Policies

Zero-tolerance policies in schools are another perfect example of top-down decision making that precludes common sense. While many incidents are not defined as "crimes," they frequently exact punishment as if a crime had been committed.

Too many honor students have been prevented from graduating from high school because of a nonsensical interpretation of a zero-tolerance policy. In one instance, an Eagle Scout and honor student innocently left a hatchet in his car and then parked in the school parking lot. Despite being no threat whatsoever, the student was suspended. The school administration said it had no choice but to punish him severely.

In another incident, an honor student was prevented from graduating after he wore a traditional Scottish kilt to his senior prom. The kilt has a small pocket containing a small knife, a traditional part of the uniform. No choice, said the school administrators.

In yet another example, two eighth-grade girls were suspended from school because they were seen hugging each other, thereby violating the zero-tolerance policy of no touching. Of course, their hugs were perfectly natural among girls their age (and healthy, I might add), but this did not matter to the "no choice" administrators.

What is the impetus for zero-tolerance policies? It is clear that administrators want to be seen as fulfilling their responsibility to protect students and to be tough on crime. In fact, by invoking this policy, they abdicate any real decision-making ability and declare that common sense plays no role in

their jobs. Once again, top-down imposed policies and decision-making that deprive local communities of reality-based
decisions take away liberties.

Understand Our Relationship to Each Other

To address any reformation of the criminal justice system, we
must honestly ask ourselves whether our primary objective is
punishment or rehabilitation. The following news release
from Texas Tech University says much about how the two
approaches work.

"Four years ago, Adrian Corral sat in a dank prison, wracked
by convulsions from cocaine withdrawal and filled with
thoughts of hanging himself with a bed-sheet. He survived
his four-year sentence for drug dealing only because he lacked
the nerve to kill himself. Now Corral, 34, is going to college
under a program at Texas Tech University that gives recov-
ering addicts scholarships for staying clean, getting good
grades and attending recovery meetings.

"The addicts-to-scholars program, started four years ago at
the Texas Tech Center for Addiction Studies, may be the first
program of its kind in the nation. Corral, who had only a
high school education, is getting a bachelor's degree and
hopes to attend medical school and become a pathologist. 'I
wanted to be a part of law enforcement, and I realize that I
can't do that because of my history,' he said. 'But at least this
way I can be a part of the process.'

"Carl Anderson, director of the center and himself a recov-
ering alcoholic, founded the program. 'This isn't a situation
where you've got someone in charge who doesn't know what
he is dealing with,' said Anderson.

"The money for this program comes from private sources, including rehabilitation groups and former students. The amount a student gets depends on grades: a 4.0 average earns $2,000 per semester, a 3.5 is worth $1,500, a 3.0 gets $1,000 and a 2.5 earns $500. Participants pay the rest of their expenses." (Published as a guest editorial in the *Des Moines Register*, Aug. 27, 1999.)

Anderson said only 5 percent of participants have reverted to drug or alcohol abuse. Why does this new program work while the get-tough policies haven't? I believe it works because it acknowledges the inherent desire of most people to improve themselves. It also acknowledges that humans often react positively when they are treated with dignity by others.

Remember this incredibly wise advice? "He who is without sin cast the first stone." We must decide whether we are going to follow this admonition or continue down the path of choosing judgment and punishment over rehabilitation. If we choose the path of love and mutual recognition of our universal capacity to sin (as well as recognizing our inherent divinity), we will then have the context necessary to adopt a system of criminal justice that is truly just. Such a system provides the greatest opportunity for rehabilitating those who have crossed the line into criminality, and therefore will ultimately be the most effective and inexpensive system.

Not coincidentally, the Libertarian vision encompasses the maximum involvement of the community in the criminal justice system, providing the greatest opportunity for each one of us to truly be our brother's keeper.

Honor the Human Desire to be of Service

Remember what happened in Iowa during the flood of 1993? It was the worst flood in memory, and it presented unique challenges for our state. I'll never forget the "call to arms" for volunteers to help sandbag various towns against the encroaching floodwaters. In the town of Dubuque, the need for volunteers was so great that area prison officials were asked whether the prison inmates could help. Despite the concern expressed by many that these inmates could not be trusted, their help was requested. After a hard day of work sandbagging, one of the inmates told the local paper that he was "very grateful for the opportunity to be of service to others."

I also recall the female inmates who volunteered to make quilts for the survivors of the September 11 terrorist attacks. These women expressed the same gratitude for the chance to help others. If we actively acknowledge the higher nature of those who are in prison, would this affect their chances of success outside of prison?

Parents of high-achieving young men and women can attest to the success of instilling in their children a faith in themselves and downplaying any so-called mistakes. Father Flanagan, the founder of Boys Town, once said that there is no such thing as a bad boy. I am certain that the young men he taught and mentored committed many bad acts, but because of the way Flanagan related to them, they came to recognize their own intrinsic value and not see themselves as failures.

On a personal level, when you make a mistake, how do you wish to be related to? Do you feel that you are forever condemned to failure?

By embracing the Libertarian (or Founders') approach to criminal justice and a civilized society, we can redirect our efforts into programs that will have the greatest opportunity for success. While government may not be able to provide the kind of hands-on support and mentoring that humans require, an extended family, neighborhood, or community has both the incentive and motivation to provide that support.

Adopt a True Community Parole and Probation System

Iowans who have watched the debate over the years involving the parole and probation system in Iowa have heard much talk of implementing a "community correction system." Those within the system have begun to recognize that it is impossible to effectively manage significant numbers of people in a centralized parole or probation system. Once again, government officials are admitting that there are not enough resources, including man- (or woman-) power, to deal with the day-to-day realities of helping individuals effectively transition from incarceration to a productive life.

We have all heard the stories of individuals who are released from prison and then almost immediately commit a heinous crime. It is obvious that a centralized system of monitoring inmates is inadequate when it comes to making a real-world assessment of the likelihood of an inmate's success or failure when released. We need to acknowledge that many factors are involved, including the individual's ability to become successfully employed, level of family and community support, state of mind, self-perception, and level of commitment.

Frankly, we cannot blame those who work within the current criminal justice system for the failure of the system to rehabilitate inmates. Once again, it is the fault of the system itself, and not of those who work within the system that we need to address.

It is a joke among local county attorneys and criminal defense attorneys how the same individuals continually re-emerge within the system with new charges, including probation and parole violations, and essentially provide guaranteed full-employment for these attorneys. Some would argue that this is a good reason for throwing away the key when it comes to these re-offenders. However, it also forcefully argues that the system itself does not work. Clearly, people are not being rehabilitated while in jail or prison. In reality, exposure to career criminals only increases the likelihood that individuals will re-commit and return to prison.

The criminal justice system, as it presently exists, is based on the assumption that punishment and humiliation will somehow lead to rehabilitation. Genuine rehabilitation however usually requires the uplifting of the individual. While the concept of community corrections has the potential to lead to rehabilitation, such a system does not appear to have been implemented to date.

A Libertarian approach to parole or probation might be to base any decision on whether to grant parole or probation on whether that individual has a solid, genuine support structure within their community. Such a support community could perform the following:

- Help ensure that the parolee has a safe, functioning place to live.

- Meet with the parolee on a regular, if not daily, basis to monitor his efforts and to provide inspiration and coaching.

- Provide the moral support that can only be given in a trusting relationship.

- Help the parolee to find suitable employment.

- Monitor the parolee's efforts to remain alcohol and/or drug free.

- Act as an informed liaison to the local probation or parole officers.

Some may question whether people would care enough to volunteer for this type of support or mentorship team. I contend that the exact opposite is true. If communities were given the opportunity to offer this support, the individual's friends and family members, churches, fraternal organizations, and other groups would step up. I also believe that if communities were rewarded with a reduction in taxes and with less crime, there is no question that they would take advantage of such an opportunity. We could have such a system if only we had what I call "truth in government."

Establish Truth in Government

Truth in government is the acknowledgement that the level of taxation within a state or a nation is directly proportionate to the level of government services required by the citizens. Therefore, the greater the level of self-sufficiency within a community—that is, the degree to which a community takes responsibility for the needs of the community and is success-ful—the less the people must be taxed.

The Founders clearly understood this correlation. They envi-sioned a country where the functions of the government were limited to the maximum degree, with people taking responsi-bility for themselves, their families, and their communities. They also understood that it was only in this way that the majority of human needs could be met.

Today, we are a far cry from the Founders' vision. In every election, we are bombarded with political rhetoric that the government will solve all our problems (as long as we keep paying over 50 percent of our incomes in taxes). We are told that the government will solve the "war on crime," the "war on drugs," and now the "war on terrorism." (The "war on poverty" rhetoric seems to have subsided since federal poli-cies have clearly increased poverty. Remember the government housing erected in the 1960s and 1970s, only to be demolished 15 years later after being literally destroyed by the recipients of those "favors"?)

Have we learned anything about human nature and the value placed on government handouts? A familiar adage forcefully illustrates the distinction between government handouts and efforts that lead one to true independence: "Give a man a fish and he eats for a day; teach him to fish and he eats for the rest of his life." Truth in government would acknowledge that citizens respect self-sufficiency and abhor dependency.

Reward Communities

By acknowledging the direct relationship between the cost of incarceration and the level of taxation required to pay for that imprisonment, we have taken the first step toward truth in government. The people themselves should then be rewarded with a reduction in taxes to the degree that they take responsibility for their communities.

We propose that this cost-savings be passed on to the communities through a reduction in the state sales tax within that community. Sales tax rates already differ around the state, such as when local option sales taxes are added. Communities already have the option of not renewing these local option sales taxes after their original purpose is fulfilled. Therefore, sales tax rates need not be uniform throughout the state if communities differ in their dependency on government services.

Our philosophy is that by returning sovereignty on fundamental issues, such as criminal rehabilitation, to the communities, the communities should receive a corresponding reduction in their taxes when they demonstrate responsibility and success. In this way, we have the potential to become not only the state with the least number of citizens in jail and prison, but the least taxed as well.

Acknowledge Human Nature

It is human nature to occasionally "cut loose." People have always seemed to "imbibe spirits" and experiment with substances that alter their consciousness, and every generation of young people wants "to party." Imagine what a community could do if it acknowledged this pattern rather than making these natural desires illegal. As a community, do we prefer to catch criminals or to prevent a crime from ever happening? For example, would it be preferable to prevent the crime of "operating a vehicle while intoxicated" or to bust drivers when they commit the crime?

Some of the most sensible crime-prevention efforts I have seen have involved high school graduation activities in many cities in Iowa. Acknowledging the inevitable, common-sense parents and community leaders have hosted private parties and provided adequate transportation and safe drivers. As a result, their children have had a safe environment to do what they would have done anyway, without the potential for an arrest. In contrast, a tough-on-crime approach would be to drastically increase police patrols and arrest every kid who even slightly swerves his car.

What would happen if communities were to encourage police officers to make themselves and their autos available to transport partygoers (whether in public or private establishments) to their homes, rather than to hide themselves in parking lots across the street in hopes of catching someone who might cross a centerline? Which of these approaches is more adult-like and which would have the greatest chance of lowering drunken-driving rates? Which approach is most respectful and tends to improve community and police relations? Which approach helps to preserve the status of drivers' licenses and lessens the need for court involvement? Finally, which approach would you want for your own family members?

Return to Restorative Justice

In the Founders' vision of criminal justice, the power of government should be used to restore the victim, not fund the government. The criminal justice system today is primarily focused on exacting hefty fines from people, filling the coffers of government. We also effectively "imprison" state taxpayers with the costs of incarceration when we send someone to prison. If a criminal justice system could be devised that would make incarceration unnecessary, as well as restore the victim, we could avoid punishing ourselves with the burden of housing and feeding an inmate. Perhaps this is what Jesus meant when he said, "Judge not, lest ye be judged."

We believe the criminal justice system should focus on making sure that when someone is genuinely harmed by another, the victim is "restored" to their original status by the wrongdoer and receives something more for the trouble they endured. The emphasis would be on protecting personal rights and property rights, and not on legislating morality.

Learn from Experience

In a letter to the editor of the *Des Moines Register*, David Helman, a retired federal warden with 27 years of experience in the federal judicial system, wrote:

"In the course of my career, I have come to know thousands of prison inmates. While many are true predators requiring lengthy imprisonment, many are not. They, too, must be punished for criminal acts, but I sense they are decent people who can change for the better. Overcrowding, longer prison terms, mandatory minimums, three strikes, so-called truth in sentencing, and abolition of parole in some jurisdictions have limited corrections professionals in their ability to deal with prisoners as individuals.

"Good corrections officers have always seen themselves as role models and agents for change. Increasingly, these workers are overwhelmed by sheer numbers and the lack of incentive for prisoner betterment. As the situation continues, the prison environment becomes even harsher, and the prospect for change is less.

"Political expediency has largely driven a national belief that imprisonment is the be-all-and-end-all solution to crime. Yet, as we see often in the political arena, that which makes good politics does not necessarily translate to good justice. A free nation must continually reflect on how it treats its citizens. Is it not troubling that a nation holding personal freedom and liberty as its greatest virtue imprisons more of its citizens than any other? Are we pleased that prison construction is stripping resources from school construction and that we are hiring prison guards at a faster rate than teachers? Imprisonment is, indeed, vital to public safety, but it should not be taken lightly. Times change. People, economics and societies change. Alternatives evolve. Reform should be ongoing." (Printed March 10, 2002)

Conclusion

We have an opportunity to incorporate into our criminal justice system the wisdom of those who have been involved with the system for decades as well as higher understanding of human nature. We also have the opportunity to take advantage of the natural desire of people to be of service by supporting others to become productive, fulfilled members of their communities. By encouraging communities to "take responsibility for their own," we can become the safest, most humane and least taxed, state in America.

"The aim of public education is not to spread enlightenment at all; it is simply to reduce as many individuals as possible to the same safe level, to breed a standard citizenry, to put down dissent and originality."

—*H.L. Mencken*

Chapter 16. Education: Developing Iowa's most Valuable Resource

By Clyde J. Cleveland and Edward F. Noyes, J.D.

Position Summary

We individuals are as different as leaves on a tree. Each of us can do one special thing better and with less effort and more joy than anyone else on the planet. The goal of education should be to help students find out what their unique potential is and then help them to develop it.

Our schools do not do enough to develop individual potential. This lack leads to deep dissatisfaction among young people, which in turn leads to drug abuse, crime, depression, and societal breakdown.

It is vital that we restructure education in this country and that we do it on the local level. The federal government will never create the kind of education we need. Parents must be involved, and local communities must have the freedom to develop education in the way that works best for them. When it comes to education, one size does not fit all.

We support giving back to the local communities the right to choose how to deliver quality education. We also believe that the tax dollars now funding the U.S. Department of Education bureaucracy should be returned to the states and the local communities. Doing so will provide more than enough resources to educate our children. These two changes will enable us to move to an educational system that is without equal anywhere in the world.

The Problem

A recent study ranked the United States of America 21st out of 21 industrial countries in the effectiveness of its educational system. Within the United States, Iowa still has comparatively good schools, and education remains one of the strongest selling points for people moving into our state. But we can and must improve the system before the trends causing the decline in education around the country infect Iowa.

For many years, the United States has operated under the fallacy that the more we spend on education, the better it will get. This just isn't true. The amount spent per student has continued to increase, and yet, the quality of educational has declined. In fact, there is increasing evidence that home-schooled students are outperforming all others on tests and in college classrooms.

As with so many government efforts, throwing more money or more regulations at this problem does not fix it. The best way to end the crisis in education is to deal with the main cause, government involvement itself.

The politicians who run the public schools keep creating new regulations and mandating new programs. As these are imposed on local schools, we have more bureaucracy and less innovation, more red tape and less creativity, and more resources spent on regulatory requirements. So the cost of education goes up and the quality of education goes down.

The federal government keeps 75 percent of the money you send to Washington, D.C., for education! Only 25 percent of what goes to the federal government for education comes back to the states, and then it comes back with strings attached—strings that cost the schools money!

Does anyone think that the 75 percent that stays in Washington helps educate our children?

The Bottom-up Solutions

Allowing local communities to choose the education model that best fits their situation will dramatically improve the quality of education. Many superb models exist throughout the United States and the world.

It is our commitment to open up the public school system in Iowa to allow every community to choose among the very best programs available, without the federal government or even the state imposing a system that by its very nature requires uniformity. We would also encourage educators to attend statewide conferences that focus on the most success-ful education technologies. By doing so, the state would have a low-cost, minimalist role in facilitating the most intelligent choices for each community.

Our solution achieves the Founders' vision of ultimate choice, based on the inherent desire of the people to choose what they believe is best for them and their children. The marketplace of ideas will rule, instead of a centralized government, dramatically reducing taxes and allowing the people's funds to directly support their local schools.

Charter Schools

Charter schools are publicly funded schools run by parents, educators, and sometimes companies. Iowa is one of only 14 states without a charter school law. But the proof is in the pudding—a 2001 study by the Rand Corporation found that, with charter schools, parents are more satisfied, children are well integrated, and academic achievement tends to grow after the child's first year. The report also suggests that, to help foster equity for children and ensure that an adequate supply of charter schools are available, policymakers should ensure that multiple chartering authorities exist.

The most successful charter schools are generally in states with laws that provide local communities and parents the most freedom. We will work for a charter school bill in Iowa that will allow the maximum amount of freedom and choice for our local communities.

We support charter schools as one option for communities to improve their children's education. There are many other models for improving education at the community level as well. Once we establish the fundamental principle of bottom-up government in the state of Iowa, we will have the flexibility to consider the full range of models that have been successfully implemented in communities throughout the world.

The Montessori method is one example. It focuses on developing the child's natural interests rather than using formal teaching methods, and is used in schools throughout the world. Although Montessori schools are private and currently receive no support from state or federal governments, the principles on which these schools are based have much to offer should our school system in Iowa be opened to the full range of educational opportunities and technologies available.

Maria Montessori, Ph.D., founded the Montessori method based on her belief that learning is a natural, self-directed process that follows certain fundamental laws of nature. As explained on the International Montessori Society web site (www.montessori.com), in 1907, she discovered that young children come into complete harmony with their environment—or "normalize," as she called it—when in an environment committed to such principles as observation, individual liberty, and preparation of the environment. The normalization she saw in children came from the adults' commitment to these Montessori principles, which nurture the child's true nature with its spontaneous desire for goal-directed activity, serious intellectual development, and a genuine thirst for knowledge and academic achievement.

Observing definite stages of normal mental growth in children from three to 18 years of age, Montessori evolved a series of materials and lessons to support normalized development. These which comprise the Montessori method of learning.

Please note that while we are impressed with the success that the Montessori method has achieved throughout the world, we believe that local communities have the right to choose whatever educational model they feel is most advantageous for their children. We trust that local educators, school boards, and especially the parents will create the best educational environment for their students when given the freedom to develop what they feel is the best system.

> "A new education from birth onward must
> be built up. Education must be reconstructed
> and based on the laws of nature…"

> —Maria Montessori,
> Founder of the Montessori Method

Merit Pay for Teachers

We believe in merit pay for teachers. It is interesting that the reason many teachers give for opposing merit-based pay is that the administrators will play favorites with the teachers. The teachers will then be in the same situation as their students, dependent on the whims of their teachers and unable to leave for a better classroom.

Many teachers will not allow for any accounting of quality besides the highly dubious seniority system currently in place. With our current system, there is no reason to pay our best teachers more than what we pay our worst.

The easiest way out of this mess is to have total school choice and charter schools. This way, if teachers or students aren't happy with the school they are in, they can switch. If administrators play favorites with the teachers at their school, it will become readily apparent in the quality of education. The administrators' pay should also be based on results.

Quality teachers are bound to rise to the top of the profession. Those who have been complacent will have reason to improve their performance. Competition does work. Only by allowing choice and competition into our current closed system will we ever see an increase in the quality of education and teachers being paid what they deserve.

Details of Our Plan

As your elected representatives we would:

- Work with the other governors in the country to eliminate the U.S. Department of Education and all other federal agencies and programs that deal with education. Return to the people of each state all of their tax dollars that currently go to the U.S. Department of Education.

- Encourage legislation that would make it possible for every school in Iowa to be a charter school.

- Decentralize education as much as possible, taking the decision making out of Washington, D.C., and Des Moines, and putting it where it belongs: at the local level.

- Promote merit pay for teachers. Why shouldn't teachers be graded on performance as other professions are?

- Help create an Internet-based, interactive networking system between state educators, so that ideas and solutions can be instantly and effectively shared between schools.

- Facilitate the sharing of ideas and innovations between Iowa educators and parents and those around the country.

- Constantly motivate and inspire parents to get involved in their children's education. No amount of money or government policies will substitute for parental involvement.

- Create a prosperous economic environment that will facilitate parents who want to spend more time at home with their children during their formative years.

We support the unimpeded right of parents to provide for the education of their children however they deem best, whether in public, charter, home, private, or religious schools. The authority and responsibility for educating children rests with the parents.

Children are of utmost importance to us all. We must not allow the forces of top-down, centralized government to destroy the future many generations have dedicated their lives to achieve. Our legacy is our children and their children to come. By understanding, and implementing, the Founders' vision of a free society, unencumbered by governmental power and excess, we can implement an educational system in Iowa that will be envied and unrivalled throughout the world.

> "Everything that is really great and enter-prising is created by the individual who can labor in freedom."
>
> —*Albert Einstein*

"Number of physicians in the U.S.: 700,000

"Accidental deaths caused by physicians per year: 120,000

"Accidental deaths per physician (U.S. Dept. of Health and Human Services figures): 0.171

"Number of gun owners in the U.S.: 80 million

"Number of accidental gun deaths per year (all age groups): 1,500

"Accidental deaths per gun owner: 0.0000188

"Statistically, doctors are approximately 9,000 times more dangerous than gun owners. Not everyone has a gun, but everyone has at least one doctor. Please alert your friends to this alarming threat. We must ban doctors before this gets out of hand."

—Benton County News Tribune *(reprinted in* Alternative Medicine, *May 2002)*

Chapter 17. Guns and Peace: Restoring a Natural Right

By Clyde J. Cleveland and Edward F. Noyes, J.D.

Position Summary

History records that freedom and the individual's natural right of self-defense are intimately connected. Societies that encourage their peace-loving citizens to be self-sufficient in the defense of their homes and persons have maintained the most individual liberty.

We are firm believers in the Second Amendment. No government should ever stand in the way of an individual's natural right of self-defense. We are also firm believers in gun safety and proper training for those who own guns. At a time when our nation wishes to become more secure, it is vital to "decentralize" our national defense through the fulfillment of the intent and purpose of the Second Amendment.

Our administration will see that law-abiding Iowans who wish to carry a firearm for self-protection are not denied their constitutional rights. Rather than licensing those who wish to carry, we propose a plan that rewards those who participate in regular training programs by waiving the sales tax on purchases of ammunition and firearms.

The Problem

Too many Americans do not understand that a firearm is an inanimate object that can be used for both good and bad purposes. Guns can be used to protect and preserve life and liberty, or they can be used to take them away. The media, along with many in government, have heavily promoted the image that all guns are evil. But a society in which law-abiding citizens are unarmed is a society dependent on government.

All free societies have had an armed citizenry. There is nothing to fear from an armed citizenry. It is not the citizens who try to amass power over their fellow citizens. In the United States today, we need to worry instead about the government having too many guns. People don't start wars. Governments, and those special interests who control governments, start wars.

Law enforcement cannot prevent crimes from happening. In almost all cases, law enforcement does not get involved until a crime has occurred. When people are armed, crime is reduced, because criminals won't perpetrate a crime against a potential victim who they think may be armed. States that have "carry laws" have experienced a reduction in crime. Countries like England, Canada, and Australia, which have eliminated the right of law-abiding citizens to own guns, have experienced an increase in crime.

We believe that the fundamental problem is a lack of awareness of:

1. the true causes of violence in our society,

2. the natural laws upon which our Founders based the founding documents, and

3. the advantages that accrue to societies that use guns intelligently to reduce crime as well as reduce the need for a large, standing army.

The Bottom-up Solution

The bottom-up solution for drastically reducing crime, creating world peace, and reducing the need for a large defense budget is an armed citizenry. Americans need to wake up to the fact that one of the best solutions for keeping America out of war is to let the world know that Americans have the will and the means to fight for freedom to the last man or woman.

We will start a "Truth about Guns" campaign in Iowa to counter the constant negative propaganda regarding individual ownership of firearms. We will also promote changes in state laws to bring Iowa in line with the U.S. Constitution. Clearance for a gun purchase should be "while you wait" or within a maximum of 24 hours. After all, it only takes law enforcement computers a few seconds to do a criminal background check. A person who needs a gun for personal safety should not be made to wait three days to be able to defend his family.

Our administration will make it a priority to ensure that Iowa honors the natural right of the individual to protect his or her life and the lives of their family members. If a law-abiding citizen feels the need to carry a weapon for protection, there should be no government barrier.

On the other hand, we do not promote the idea of people carrying guns without the benefit of proper training. We strongly recommend that anyone who owns a gun receive training from a qualified instructor. In addition, we will sponsor matches and other events to promote the safe and responsible use of firearms. We also strongly recommend that when you purchase a gun for the first time, you also buy at least one of the books listed in the Appendix.

Iowa will be a safer place if those individuals who are buying guns are trained in the safe use of those weapons. To that end, we will promote laws that make it easier for individuals or groups to set up outdoor rifle or pistol ranges, and influence the Iowa Department of Natural Resources to maintain or expand its ranges now open to the public. Having a safe place to practice is important to good marksmanship, which is part of being a responsible gun owner. We will also create incentives for ongoing training by allowing all purchases of firearms and ammunition to be free of sales tax for those who show proof of training.

Switzerland does not have a large national defense. The percentage of its GNP devoted to national defense is small relative to most nations. Therefore, Switzerland requires all male citizens from the age of 18 to 55 to carry, train, and bear arms. It does not have a top-down defense, only bottom up. Despite the abundance of guns, Switzerland has a very low crime rate. More interesting, it has not been at war in over 600 years! Who would be foolish enough to attack a country where every man is a well-armed and highly trained adversary? It is true that Switzerland has natural barriers to invading armies, but the impact of its citizen militia cannot be overlooked as one of the significant reasons for hundreds of years of peace.

An increase in properly trained, armed citizens will decrease crime in our state. We will do everything in our power to remove all unconstitutional guns laws at the federal, state, and local level.

> "A well regulated Militia, being necessary to the security of a free State, the right of the people to keep and bear Arms, shall not be infringed."
>
> —*U.S. Constitution, Second Amendment*

Even a cursory analysis of our Founders' discussions regarding the Bill of Rights and the Second Amendment will lead any reasonable, objective person to the conclusion that the amendment is a combination of two principles:

- That a citizen militia is comprised of the "whole people," which means that the Founders wanted literally every citizen to be armed and well trained in the use of weapons. They knew that there would be little need of a large standing army if the citizens were well armed.

- That the right to bear arms is based on an eternal and universal principle—the natural law of self-defense that all people are born with and that cannot be taken away by anyone or any institution.

To believe that the Second Amendment refers to a "government right" (National Guard ownership only) and not an "individual right," you would have to believe that the following phrases from the Bill Rights all refer to individuals:

- "...right of the people peaceably to assemble"

- "...right of the people to be secure in their homes"

- "...enumeration's herein of certain rights shall not be construed to disparage others retained by the people," and

- "The powers not delegated herein are reserved to the states respectively, and to the people."

However, you would then have to believe that "the right of the people to keep and bear arms" *refers to the government!*

You would also have to believe that the Second Amendment, which was ratified in 1787, refers to the National Guard, when the National Guard was created by an act of Congress in 1917!

And you would also have to believe that the National Guard—funded by the federal government, occupying property leased to the federal government, using weapons owned by the federal government, punishing trespassers under federal law—is a state militia!

In a discussion between Cokie Roberts and George Will on one of the Sunday morning television news shows, Will gave an accurate account of the Second Amendment. Describing it as one of the fundamental principles in the Bill of Rights that protected individual rights from government encroachment, he explained that the argument purporting that the

Founders were limiting the right of individuals and giving that right only to a state militia was absurd.

Amazingly, Roberts, who is an ardent gun control activist, actually agreed with him regarding the meaning of the amendment. Then she went on to explain that her animosity toward guns had to do with the fact that so many people were killed or injured in accidents, and that guns contributed to violence.

As the opening quote of this chapter points out, relative to other causes of injury and death in this country, there are very few deaths or accidents related to guns. The last time we checked government statistics, there were more deaths attributed to bathtub accidents than to firearm accidents.

Any death or accident is a tragedy to the victim's family, whether it is caused by a car, baseball bat, knife, bathtub, or gun. We believe that effective training in the proper use of guns can further reduce the number of accidents. It is clear, however, that the frequency of gun use to prevent or stop a crime far exceeds the number of accidents by individuals or the misuse of firearms by criminals.

Despite Roberts' statement, we believe that most Americans are intelligent enough to realize that an inanimate object does not cause violence. What does cause violence? Stress in the home, prescribed and nonprescribed drug use, exposure to violence via movies or real-life situations, and more. Watching a movie like *Natural Born Killers* over and over certainly could influence a mindset that might lead to violence. The student shooters at Columbine watched that movie many times, literally preparing themselves for a reign of terror.

We would like to bring harmony to the discussion of gun control in this country by suggesting that people on both sides of the issue begin working together. If we all focus on doing whatever we can to reduce the root causes of violence in our communities, substantial progress would be made. A better understanding of the Second Amendment, and of the thinking behind it, should help us begin the process of working together to end needless violence in our country.

Our philosophy regarding the Second Amendment is best summed up by these quotes from three of the Founders:

- Joseph Story: "The right of the citizens to keep and bear arms has justly been considered, as the palladium [safeguard] of the liberties of a republic; since it offers a strong moral check against the usurpation and arbitrary power of rulers; and will generally... enable the people to resist and triumph over them..."

- George Mason: "To disarm the people is the best and most effectual way to enslave them."

- Patrick Henry: "The great object is, that every man be armed...Everyone who is able may have a gun...Where and when did freedom exist when the sword and the purse were given up from the people? Unless a miracle in human affairs interposed, no nation ever retained its Liberty after the loss of the sword and the purse."

The Ultimate Top-down, Command-and-control Solution: International Gun Control

Earlier this year, the United Nations hosted a meeting in New York on "small arms" to discuss international gun control efforts. Some of the delegates attending this meeting made it clear that they favor a binding UN resolution that would ban private ownership of all firearms, with the exception of some specialized hunting weapons. The resolution states that "Such weapons distort societies, they make it harder for the State to regain the legitimate monopoly of force…compromising the effectiveness of police forces and encouraging law-abiding civilians to arm themselves for protection…."

Notice the diametrically opposed philosophical concepts characterized by the UN language and the language of America's Founders. The advocates of internationalism favor a government monopoly of force.

Our country was founded on the concept of individual sovereignty, not government sovereignty. This is ultimately the difference between freedom and slavery. The Second Amendment illustrates so dramatically the American philosophy that government power comes from the bottom up, whereas in most of the world it is from the top down. It is vital that we elect people, at both the state and federal levels, who understand what is happening to our country and are absolutely committed to individual sovereignty in all areas.

We can create peace in our homes, communities, nation and world by increasing human freedom and restoring bottom-up government. Infringing on the natural right of all humans to defend their lives, liberty, and property is counterproductive to world peace.

> "In 1996, Britain banned handguns; since then, gun crimes have risen by 40 percent...Australia also passed severe gun restrictions in 1996 and made it a crime to use a gun defensively. In the subsequent four years, armed robberies rose 51 percent, unarmed robberies by 37 percent, assaults by 24 percent, and kidnappings by 43 percent...The problem with these harsh gun laws, experts say, is that they take guns away from law-abiding citizens, while would-be criminals ignore them, leaving potential victims defenseless.

> "The U.S. has shown that making guns more available is actually a better formula for law and order...In the U.S., 33 states have right-to-carry laws. In those states, deaths and injuries from multiple-victim public shootings fell on average by 78 percent."

> —"Gun Control Misfires in Europe," by John Lott, Jr., Wall Street Journal, April 30, 2002

"The cure for these problems? Remove the state backing from the AMA and FDA, and unleash the power and creativity of the free market. Many people have been brainwashed into thinking the state protects them. The truth is the exact opposite."

—*Morris Fishbein*

Chapter 18. Health Care: Promoting Preventative Care

By Clyde J. Cleveland and Edward F. Noyes, J.D.

Position Summary

Naturally, we would like to make all Iowans healthy. Government, however, is not responsible for the health of its citizens. Each adult is responsible for her or his own health, while parents are responsible for their children's health, as well as for teaching them to take responsible care of their health as they mature.

That said, every Iowan should understand that we do not have a health care system in this country. We have a disease care system. In other words, our system comes into play only after a person gets sick or injured. This is foolish. Health care resources are all geared to taking care of problems after they have manifested as a disease or injury.

A much more effective way to think about health care is to think about what can be done to prevent sickness or injury in the first place. Our administration would facilitate a system that would help Iowans help themselves in creating a disease-free life. This would involve education in preventative medicine, including proper diet, exercise, rest, stress release techniques, environmental concerns, and so on.

We would encourage communities to offer these courses through adult education programs and the schools. This is a community function *and should not involve state funding*. The role of the state would be to offer knowledge and support, and to create the communications infrastructure for sharing information about successful preventative health programs in communities around the state, country, and world.

The Problem

Health care for every Iowan is intertwined with the national policies of the health care industry and the federal government. The following is a summary of the Libertarian Party diagnosis of our health care system.

"Twenty years ago, health care was a $42 billion per year industry. Today, health care costs Americans more than $2 billion per day, more than 14 percent of our Gross Domestic Product. These soaring costs are putting enormous financial pressures on American businesses, forcing thousands of small businesses to reduce or drop benefits for their employees. Moreover, health care costs are an increasing burden to already strained family budgets. At the same time, nearly 35 million Americans lack health insurance.

"Proposals for socialized medicine are worse than the disease. These plans would increase costs, destroy jobs, impose broad new taxes on the American people, and lead to the rationing of care.

"The only health care reforms that are likely to have a significant impact on America's health care problems are those that draw on the strength of the free market. The Libertarian Party has developed a comprehensive proposal for health care reform that will reduce health care costs, while extending access to care."

As with virtually everything in our country, the health care industry has suffered from centralization.

The Bottom-up Solutions

We believe that individuals are ultimately responsible for their own health, families are responsible for family members unable or unwilling to take care of their own health, and the community is next in line for taking care of the health concerns of its citizens. State government should be involved only to the extent that the citizens want it to be involved. The federal government should not be involved in health care at all.

Deregulate the Health Care Industry

There should be a thorough examination of the extent to which government policies are responsible for rising health costs and the unavailability of health care services. America can help lower health care costs and expand health care access by taking immediate steps to deregulate the health care industry, including elimination of mandated benefits, repeal of the Certificate-of-Need program, and expansion of the scope of practice for non-physician health professionals.

In the workplace, employee-controlled "family coverage" health insurance plans based on cash value life insurance principles are a constructive development.

Privatize Medicare and Medicaid

The current Medicare and Medicaid systems have clearly failed. Costs are skyrocketing. Patients are receiving second-rate care and providers are being shortchanged. The time is ripe for drastic reform. The federal government should begin to restructure the system to give Medicaid and Medicare recipients more flexibility to purchase private health insurance.

In Iowa, the state Medicaid program provides state aid for those who cannot afford health care. We would not repeal this safety net until a community-based program and the other changes we are recommending are in place.

Replace the FDA

The regulatory agencies of other countries are able to safeguard their citizens for far less and still allow innovative products to enter the marketplace. The U.S. Food and Drug Administration (FDA) has probably protected fewer people than it has let die waiting for new therapies to come to market. In addition, it is a significant factor in the cost of bringing drugs to market, a process that can cost a manufacturer more than $200 million.

The FDA is clearly an unnecessary burden on the American health care system. There is no evidence that the agency offers Americans any real protection, but there is massive evidence that it is causing great harm by driving up health care costs and depriving millions of Americans of the medical care they need. The agency should be abolished and replaced with voluntary certification by a private-sector organization, similar to the way Underwriters Laboratories certifies electrical appliances.

Promote Choice

The first principle that libertarianism is based on is that you own yourself. Only you know how best to live your life. You have the right to make your own mistakes, and the responsibility to do what is best for you.

When the supply of medical care is controlled by the federal government, then officers of that government will determine which demand is satisfied. The result will be the rationing of services, higher costs, poorer results, and the power of life and death transferred from caring physicians to unaccountable political overseers.

There are many ways to reduce the costs of health care and simultaneously increase quality and choice. A critical measure is to expand the scope of services offered by health care professionals other than physicians. One excellent example is having midwives provide prenatal care and attend deliveries. In Europe, more than 90 percent of the women who are pregnant never consult a physician during their pregnancies and childbirth. Midwives see these women from the beginning of their pregnancies onward, helping them to remain healthy and deliver healthy babies. The rate of problematic births is significantly lower in Europe than it is in America. The cost of the European system is significantly less as well.

Patients, if they want to and feel able, should also be allowed to choose which drugs they want for their care. We all want the best for ourselves, but if second-best costs half as much, shouldn't we be able to make the decision for ourselves? Our current system offers no real choice for the patient.

We affirm the freedom of choice of practitioner and treatment for all citizens. Individuals should have the absolute say over the care of their bodies. If they feel a particular treatment is the best one for them, it should be their choice, right or wrong.

"We in the Congress have a moral and constitutional obligation to protect the value of the dollar and to understand why it is so important to the economy that a central bank not be given the unbelievable power of inflating a currency at will and pretending that it knows how to fine-tune an economy through this counterfeit system of money."

—*Ron Paul, M.D.,*
U.S. Congressman (R-Texas)

Chapter 19. Monetary System: Reverting to Real Value

By Clyde J. Cleveland and Edward F. Noyes, J.D.

Position Summary

It could be argued that the single most important act of our Founders was to give us a sound monetary policy. Money must reflect real value. When a nation's money has no value, and it becomes fiat money, the people lose power and those who control the money control the government and eventually all of the country's institutions, including the media. Peter Kershaw, author of the 1994 booklet, "Economic Solutions," summarized the problem as follows:

"The Founding Fathers of this great land had no difficulty whatsoever understanding the agenda of bankers, and they frequently referred to them and their kind as 'friends of paper money.' They hated the Bank of England, in particular, and felt that even were we successful in winning our independence from England and King George, we could never truly be a nation of freemen, unless we had an honest money system. Through ignorance, but moreover, because of apathy, a small, but wealthy, clique of power brokers have robbed us of our Rights and Liberties, and we are being raped of our wealth. We are paying the price for the near comatose levels of complacency by our parents, and only God knows what might become of our children, should we not work diligently to shake this country from its slumber! Many a nation has lost its freedom at the end of a gun barrel, but here in America, we just decided to hand it over voluntarily. Worse yet, we paid for the tyranny and usurpation out of our own pockets with 'voluntary' tax contributions and the use of a debt-laden fiat currency!"

The Founders established a system of coin money that was designed to prohibit the "improper and wicked" manipulation of the nation's medium of exchange while guaranteeing the power of the citizens' earnings. It is time to educate Iowans, and the rest of America, regarding this extremely important issue. We plan to do that. Our educational process will be the first step to returning this state and our country to true prosperity.

The Problem

There is no more fundamental problem to every Iowan than our current corrupt money system. It is virtually impossible for the people to ever be truly prosperous with our current debt-based system. It is also virtually impossible to have true freedom when we have given the politicians the ability to borrow unlimited amounts of money.

The federal government has departed from the principle of coin money, as defined by the U.S. Constitution and the Mint Act of 1792, and granted unconstitutional control of the nation's monetary and banking system to the private Federal Reserve System. These violations now threaten the economic stability and survival of our country's republican form of government.

> "If all bank loans were paid, there would not be a dollar of coin or currency in circulation. Someone has to borrow every dollar we have in circulation. We are absolutely without a permanent money system."
>
> —*Robert Hemphill, Federal Reserve Bank, Atlanta, as quoted in the foreword of* 100% Money, *by Irving Fisher*

> "By a continuing process of inflation, governments can confiscate, secretly and unobserved, an important part of the wealth of their citizens. There is no subtler, no surer means of overturning the existing basis of society than to debauch the currency. The process engages all the hidden forces of economic law on the side of destruction, and does it in a manner which not one man in a million is able to diagnose."
>
> —*John Maynard Keynes*

Our Founders clearly understood the danger of allowing bankers to control the monetary system in this country. As James Madison noted, "History records that the money changers have used every form of abuse, intrigue, deceit, and violent means possible to maintain their control over governments by controlling money and its issuance."

The Bottom-up Solutions

It is essential to every Iowan, and every American, that we reform the monetary and banking system of our country. We should do all that we can to make this come about. In the meantime, there are things that can be done to protect us and bring more prosperity to our state.

Local Currencies

We propose that Iowa counties establish alternative currencies, redeemable in something of value. Not only would this bring an increase in prosperity, our example would hasten the reform process of our federal monetary system.

The concept of local currencies is spreading across the country (more than 70 cities now have them). Local currencies have helped restore prosperity in communities like Ithaca, New York, where the "Ithaca Hour" is a unit of currency based on one hour of labor. The increase in prosperity in Ithaca after adopting this currency was so dramatic that Ithaca serves as a model for other cities and even foreign nations.

Each county in Iowa could establish its own currency patterned on the Ithaca Hour model. Local currencies encourage people to shop locally and thus support local businesses and local farmers who sell their products within the county.

Monetary Education

Our administration will begin a very intense and massive effort to educate every Iowan about the nature of money. John Adams once said that if we ever lost our freedom in this country, it would be due to the people's ignorance of the nature of money. He was right, and we want to start right here and now in our communities in Iowa to fix that situation. Our government-managed educational system will never reveal the truth about our fatally flawed monetary system.

There are three possible solutions to our current debt-based monetary system which you can begin to study right now:

- The system presented in "Billions for Bankers—Debts for the People," by Sheldon Emry, reprinted in Appendix 4

- The plan presented by Cleon Skousen in "The Urgent Need for Comprehensive Monetary Reform" (see Appendix 3, Money, Banking, and Currencies)

- The plan presented by Theodore Thoren in *The Truth in Money Book* (see Appendix 1, Money, Banking, and Currencies)

All three of these plans eliminate the Federal Reserve and fractional reserve banking. They are all correct on those two points. Beyond that there are differences that require analysis and careful review.

We have turned our monthly constitutional study program into a working group dedicated to analyzing these and any other plans we find, to determine the best course of action for our country. People in communities throughout the country should be doing the same thing. When the time comes to eliminate the current monetary system—and it will, soon—we need to have a substantial, well-educated group of citizens ready to implement an alternative. It is absolutely essential that we the people understand this subject well enough to make sure that what has happened to us in this country never happens again.

> "All the perplexities, confusion and distress in America rise, not from defects in the Constitution or Confederation, not from want of honor or virtue, so much as from downright ignorance of the nature of coin, credit, and circulation."
>
> —John Adams, in a letter to
> Thomas Jefferson, 1787

Federal Reforms

On the federal level, the reforms that must be taken are as follows:

1. Restore the nation's official medium of exchange to be compliant with the U.S. Constitution and the Mint Act of 1792.

2. Establish a new American dollar that is a coinable commodity money.

3. Prohibit all fractional reserve banking.

4. Repeal the Federal Reserve Act and transform the current Federal Reserve banks into clearing houses only.

Our administration will work with other state governors to create a groundswell of popular support for these essential reforms. Without them, we cannot be a sovereign nation or a sovereign state. The power we have given to a small group of individuals is so immense that calling our nation a free country under the current circumstances is a joke. If you don't believe us, please ponder these words of the former President of the United States who signed the Federal Reserve Act in 1913. Spoken in 1916, these remarks by President Wilson obviously show that he realized he had made an enormous mistake.

"A great industrial nation is controlled by its system of credit. Our system of credit is concentrated [in the Federal Reserve System]. The growth of the nation, therefore, and all our activities are in the hands of a few men…We have come to be one of the worst ruled, one of the most completely controlled and dominated governments in the civilized world—no longer a government by free opinion, no longer a government by conviction and the vote of the majority, but a government by the opinion and duress of small groups of dominant men."

The incredibly good news is that by returning to the monetary system envisioned by the Founders, we can virtually eliminate inflation, the national debt, and almost all federal taxes including the income tax. By not requiring the federal government to "borrow" from the private Federal Reserve (instead, having the federal government re-assume its constitutional prerogative to create its own money), we will no longer have to pay interest on money we create ourselves. We also gain the right to charge commercial banks throughout the country a modest interest (say, 3 percent) on funds which they then loan to their customers. This interest, paid to the federal government, would be sufficient to pay for the essential, and constitutional, services provided by the federal government. There would be no need for an income tax, national retail sales tax, or any other kind of federal tax.

> "If the American people ever allow private banks to control the issue of their currency, first by inflation and then by deflation, the banks and corporations that will grow up around them will deprive the people of all property until their children will wake up homeless on the continent their fathers conquered."
>
> —*Thomas Jefferson, in a letter to Albert Gallatin, Secretary of the Treasury, 1802*

"You cannot bring about prosperity by discouraging thrift. You cannot strengthen the weak by weakening the strong. You cannot help the wage earner by pulling down the wage payer. You cannot further the brotherhood of man by encouraging class hatred. You cannot help the poor by destroying the rich. You cannot keep out of trouble by spending more than you earn. You cannot build character and courage by taking away man's initiative and independence. You cannot help men permanently by doing for them what they could and should do for themselves."

—*Abraham Lincoln*

Chapter 20. Welfare: Community Solutions

By Clyde J. Cleveland and Edward F. Noyes, J.D.

Position Summary

America's welfare crisis is a government-induced crisis. Taxpayers should never be forced to assume the cost of providing welfare services for others. We encourage all Iowans to rebuild the infrastructure of our civil society by taking care of all welfare at the local level. We encourage individuals and families to fulfill their personal responsibility to help those in need through tithes, offerings, and other acts of charity.

Our plan calls for model structures similar to local parole/mentor boards, staffed by local volunteers, that will create the local programs necessary for eventually replacing Iowa's current welfare system. These community systems will treat people with dignity and be more effective in getting them off welfare, as opposed to the current system of institutionalizing welfare. We will reward communities that are successful in eliminating poverty within their counties with a reduction in overall taxation rates, such as the sales tax.

The Problem

We are endowed with life, liberty, property, and the right to pursue happiness. It is up to us to care for the needy, the sick, the homeless, the aged, and those who are otherwise unable to care for themselves. It is an American tradition and the natural inclination of humans to help those in need.

As we recreate Iowa on a bottom-up model, we will develop the institutions necessary to take care of everyone in need. However, these institutions should never be based on the principle of force. Forced charity is an oxymoron. It is impossible to feel charitable when the government is confiscating the money from one family to give it to another—especially when we know that the federal government keeps over two-thirds of what is budgeted for welfare for its own bureaucracy.

Governmental social and cultural policies have undermined the work ethic, even as the government's economic and regulatory policies have undermined the ability of our citizens to obtain work. Exorbitant taxes have tragically limited the ability of families to take care of themselves, let alone have the abundance to give generously to others.

When this country revolted against England, most Americans were paying about 5 percent of their incomes in taxes. Today the average American pays well over 50 percent of their income to cover the cost of government. This percentage includes federal, and state, income taxes; property taxes; sales taxes; excise taxes; travel taxes; duties; hidden corporate taxes passed on to consumers, etc.

With all these taxes, have we gotten rid of poverty? The great "war on poverty" institutionalized poverty among the poorest

Americans and moved the entire middle class into a near state of poverty by forcing it to support a gargantuan government bureaucracy.

Charity, and provision of welfare to those in need, is not a constitutional responsibility of the federal government. Under no circumstances should taxpayers be obligated, under penalty of law through forced taxation, to assume the cost of providing welfare for other citizens. Neither should taxpayers be indentured to subsidize welfare for persons who enter the United States illegally.

> "The war against illegal plunder has been fought since the beginning of the world. But how is …legal plunder to be identified? Quite simply. See if the law takes from some persons what belongs to them, and gives it to other persons to whom it does not belong. See if the law benefits one citizen at the expense of another by doing what the citizen himself cannot do without committing a crime. Then abolish this law without delay…If such a law is not abolished immediately, it will spread: multiply and develop into a system."
>
> —*Bastiat*

In many cases, federal welfare provisions are not only misdirected, but morally destructive. It is the intended purpose

of civil government to safeguard life, liberty, and property—
not to redistribute wealth. Such redistribution is contrary to
the command against theft inherent in all the world's religious traditions.

We find it amazing that food stamps have a depiction of the
Founding Fathers signing the Declaration of Independence.
What could be more ironic than linking dependency on the
federal government for food with the "independence" of the
people? Here in Iowa, we have the richest soils in the world.
By redirecting our efforts we have the opportunity to provide
for the basic needs of the people, without the federal government's involvement.

The Bottom-up Solution

Poverty has increased as freedom has decreased. If we want to
reduce poverty, we must increase freedom. This is a natural
law proven over and over again throughout 5,000 years of
history. Everything done through the government that could
be done privately increases government power, raises taxes,
and reduces freedom and opportunity.

All social problems, including poverty, are best taken care of
on the local level. A local-level, bottom-up solution will be
much more likely to solve the problem, rather than perpetuate the bureaucracy set up to do the job for us.

Our solutions for the current welfare system are very similar
to those for reforming the criminal justice system. Every
county has volunteers who would willingly be part of men-
tor/sponsor teams for people in need. The priority would be

to help individuals who cannot support themselves find work in the community, so that they do not have to go on welfare in the first place. Those who are already in the system would work with their mentor/sponsor team in developing a plan to get off welfare as soon as possible.

Our solutions are based on natural human compassion to help others. The meaning of compassion is to "suffer with." In other words, compassion is a personal response to another human being's situation. It is a voluntary action and cannot be forced. This is the essence of why government-driven welfare or charity or compassion will *never* work. When we rediscover the beauty of bottom-up government, however, people will naturally come forward to help others, and new noncoercive systems will be developed in response to the particular conditions in the communities.

We know that there are many people in every community who would be willing to take on these challenges. And they would do it for free out of the goodness of their hearts. The role of the mentor/sponsor team would be to draw on community support to keep the person or family out of the welfare system. As an incentive, the resulting reduction in welfare payments to the county would be matched with a reduction in that county's sales tax rate for the following year.

The creation of this community-based infrastructure is the first step to eliminating the incredibly wasteful and destructive role of the federal welfare bureaucracy. Once we have proven models, we can quickly phase out the federal programs, saving enormous amounts of money for every American family and community.

The next step would be to phase out the unnecessary state bureaucracies as the community-based programs become more reliable and effective. This would provide additional savings for the taxpayers and further reduce the number of people who have to experience the vicious cycle of welfare dependency.

Section Four:

This is YOUR Campaign!

"If you don't run your own life, somebody else will."

—*John Atkinson*

"The greatest pleasure in life is doing what people say you cannot do."

—*Walter Bagehot*

Chapter 21. What Can YOU Do?

By Clyde J. Cleveland and Edward F. Noyes, J.D.

We believe we can win our elections, otherwise we would not be running. We heard from many skeptics when we first launched our campaigns, but no more.

In this chapter we lay out for you why we can win and what you can do to help us to win. In addition, we provide some very valuable information regarding actions you can take immediately in your communities to start the process of building self-sufficiency and taking back your sovereignty.

Why We Will Win

It is the sad reality of our system today that it takes money to win campaigns. It hasn't always been that way. In fact, the Founders would have found the concept of campaigning unthinkable. Unfortunately, things have changed.

We started asking for donations soon after we announced our campaigns. The first people we approached did not think we could win, and therefore did not want to "waste" their money. So we put our heads together and listed all of the reasons why we sincerely believe we will win. Although we compiled our points early in the campaign, within weeks we knew our 10 points were valid.

"Only those who dare truly live."

—*Ruth Freedman*

1. Jesse Ventura proved that if you have a well-articulated third-party message, you can tap into the vast well of discontent among the citezenry. When running for governor of Minnesota, Ventura's message in his debates and speeches was basically libertarian. Ventura proved that having the right message at the right time can overcome two extremely well-known major party candidates. It should be easier the second time because more people will believe it can be done.

2. Iowa has a high percentage of nonaligned registered voters. There are about 550,000 Democrats, 580,000 Republicans, and 700,000 "no party declared." Then there are another 200,000 or so eligible, nonregistered voters. Again, Ventura showed that "no-party" and nonregistered folks can be brought to the polls.

Out of the 1.8 million registered voters in Iowa, only slightly more than half voted in the last gubernatorial election (956,415 out of 1,818,289 registered). More than 850,000 people didn't even bother to vote! Our campaign will identify these people; reach out to them with targeted, issue-specific messages; and inspire them to go to the polls. Imagine how much different the 2002 election would look compared to 1998 if even 200,000 more votes are cast, let alone more than 500,000! Enough to tip the scales!

3. It comes down to credibility. And credibility starts with money. Sun-Tzu observed that most battles are won or lost before they start. We realize that we have to raise enough money and put together a big enough organization early on to be considered viable in the eyes of the media and those countless people who would vote Libertarian if they didn't feel their vote was being wasted. No Iowa Libertarian candidate has been able to get past these early hurdles. We will. Our early start gives us a solid foundation to build on.

4. We have a professional staff and great candidates. Deborah Williamson is a real organizational pro. As our campaign manager, she has already put together a statewide organization that is unprecedented in this state for third-party campaigns. We will be hiring others to complement her work as the campaign builds steam.

Clyde is an excellent promoter and speaker. He speaks passionately about what he believes in, and freedom is his passion, making him an outstanding campaigner and candidate. We believe having a venture capitalist running in a state that ranks 51st in the nation in venture capital (behind Puerto Rico) will appeal to Iowans. The rest of our ticket is as strong, with Ed as attorney general and Richard Campagna as lieutenant governor. Other very credible Libertarian candidates complete the ticket (see Appendix 1 for a list of these candidates).

5. Libertarians all over the country have a stake in ensuring a successful campaign in Iowa. Remember, we are the first presidential caucus state. We will be soliciting money and support for our campaign from all over the country. Imagine what it would mean for a future Libertarian candidate for president to come here and be greeted by a Libertarian governor.

6. Dissatisfaction with the current administration is intense. Our current governor has a plan called Vision Iowa 2010, which involves bringing immigrants into the state to fill positions our children could fill if they didn't leave after getting their education here. One reason many of our children flee the state is the ridiculously high taxes and resultant lack of economic opportunities. One poll suggested that over 80 percent of Iowans oppose the governor's plan. Our plan will be based on keeping our kids in Iowa by eliminating all the reasons why people don't stay or move here. Iowa has one of the very highest income taxes in the country, a very high property tax, and a fairly high sales tax. Why on earth would someone voluntarily move into a state with such high taxes? We are killing ourselves with taxes.

7. No candidate for governor has made a greater commitment. Clyde began campaigning full time early on and will continue to do so. He is committed to raising the necessary finances. But more than anything, he has a clear vision for a freer Iowa, with specific government-trimming, people-empowering steps to get us there.

8. This campaign is about truth. We are honest with voters (novel idea for a political campaign, don't you think?), for nothing else will set them free. Our great advantage over our Democratic and Republican opponents is that, unlike them, we are not going to be influenced by huge institutional campaign contributors. That means we will actually be able to tell you what we believe in and be in a position to follow through on our commitments, without pressure from special interest groups.

9. We have an extraordinary base of support. Our base of support is made up of: Iowans who believe in property tax reform, those who would like to have an opportunity to profit from Iowa's natural wind resources, citizens who support constitutional principles, supporters of the Second Amendment, proponents of criminal justice reform, entrepreneurs who would like to see a vital and prosperous economy, and every person who believes in restoring our natural resources.

The major parties have no track record to defend in these areas. As we get our message out, these very substantial groups will begin to enthusiastically support our campaign.

10. People are longing for the paradigm shift to freedom. We all love freedom, but for some, that fundamental love of freedom may be locked up deep inside. In the 1700s, Tom Paine articulated the message in way that spoke to the colonial soul. The result was a paradigm shift to liberty culminating in the signing of the Declaration of Independence on July 4, 1776. Our task is to once again make the case for freedom. Do you want to be serfs or do you want to live life to its fullest glory? Do you want to soar like eagles, or die as timid souls who never accomplished great things or tasted the greater possibilities of life?

We believe you want freedom!

What You Can Do Now

To change Iowa we need to do two things: Get Libertarians elected at all levels of government, and set up the local infra-structure for self-sufficiency. Both require your involvement.

> "Never doubt that a small group of commit-
> ted citizens can change the world; indeed it's
> the only thing that ever has."
>
> —Margaret Mead

Saying you are not "into" politics—in this state, at this time—is like a drowning man going down for the third time saying he is not into learning how to swim. We do not have a choice. If we are going to restore our freedoms and our civil society, we must get involved. Clearly, the Republicans and Democrats are not going to save us. It is incumbent on us to elect Libertarians because the Libertarian Party is the only party that understands what is happening to us and that is not beholden to existing institutions.

Locally, you need to run for office, or find candidates for every office, including the school board, city council, county sheriff, and so on. There are over 500 elected Libertarians in this country, far more than any third party in history. Most of those officeholders are local officials; for example, in Colorado, there are towns that have a majority of Libertarians on their city councils.

Seven Steps to Success

At the state level, there are several things you can do to help us win.

1. Understand how important your participation is. This is the most important thing you can do. We can win this election if you and enough people like you believe that we can. Belief is the first step, and that belief will come from reading this book, visiting our web site—www.clevelandforgovernor.org— and continuing to read and learn.

2. Find one other person in your community who supports our programs and our candidacies. Now you have a group.

3. Expand your group. Each of you find one more person who will work to support our campaign.

4. Submit articles to your local paper. Write about the candidates and the issues we are bringing up: property taxes, income taxes, an energy plan, criminal justice, "carry" laws, and the others outlined in this book. Find out what issues are big in your town and start talking to everyone about those issues. Once you have stirred the air, you are ready for the next step.

5. Invite us to come to your town and talk to as many people as possible. William James said, "Act as if what you do makes a difference. It does." He is absolutely correct. Everything we do makes a difference, and if we get enough people to realize that, we will turn this state and country around.

When we visit your town, we prefer to come for a full day. The best way to organize the day is to set up meetings with service clubs, farming groups, high school classes, bridge clubs, and other organizations during the day. In the evening, schedule a meeting at the library or a bank meeting room and advertise that meeting. Prepare a press release and make sure the local paper does an article.

Put posters up a week before the meeting. Tell everyone you know, and all the people who are involved in the campaign, to foster as much word-of-mouth advertising as possible. If you can find some volunteers to call people, that is the best way to increase attendance. We have a copy of an hour-long televised interview with Ed and Clyde, done by a local cable station, that is available to any local cable station in the state. The stations will play it over and over. We can ask them to put information about the local meeting on a tagline before and after they air the tape. The local cable stations also announce community events, and you should make sure the meeting is included.

6. Follow up after the meeting. After the meeting you will have even more people excited and willing to work on this campaign. Remember Helen Keller's statement: "Alone we can do so little; together we can do so much." It is absolutely true. The meeting will result in your being much more powerful, because you will have a local group to work with.

The campaign needs volunteers to go door-to-door, talking to people and handing out literature. We need people to put up yard signs. We need people to do mailings. We need someone in each area willing to be in charge of local campaign efforts, working closely with our state campaign chairman. Elect a leader, and then do everything you can to support that person.

7. Continue to talk to everyone you know and discuss our campaign. The Internet is a fabulous tool for communicating. Use our web site to get information to people and for organizing events. In addition, never stop talking and working with your core group of supporters. We can change Iowa. It is absolutely possible to do this, because our message is based on freedom and truth. This message will resonate with Iowans, but we have to keep talking to everyone about our campaign and our issues.

The Pledge of Allegiance starts with "I" and ends with "all." That is what America is all about: "I" (individual) and "all" (all of us). Jim Rohn said, "When all of us understand how valuable each of us is, that's powerful. And here's what else is powerful: When each of us understands how powerful all of us are."

This is a wonderful statement. The first step is realizing our own individual power. We have the potential to change the world. Each day we decide what we are going to do. Actually, we make those decisions every minute. We decide. We have free will, so we can start anytime we want to begin convincing others to take action in the same direction. When we realize this, we start to understand how powerful we are.

When efforts started by one person reach a critical mass of people, anything is possible.

We are talking about a state of less than 3 million people. We only need 400,000 to win the governorship of this state. There are almost 700,000 people registered as independents! Start realizing your individual power and the power of all of us individuals working together for a bottom-up society based on love and freedom.

Building a Local Infrastructure for Self-sufficiency

To dramatically reduce the size of federal and state government, we must build an infrastructure that would enable us to be self-sufficient locally. There is tremendous power in being self-sufficient and in being in a position to say to federal and state government that we do not need or want their help anymore. When we show by example that social problems are more effectively handled on a local level, we demonstrate to others that delegating these issues to the federal government is a waste of our money.

Our policy proposals outlined in Section Three explain the various elements of a local infrastructure. In addition, the resources listed in the Appendices will help you expand and develop these concepts. We suggest you start in the following areas.

Local currencies. Learning about the Ithaca Hour currency, developed in Ithaca, New York, is a great place to start. We cannot overstate the power of having a currency redeemable for something of value. This is a way for every county in Iowa to revitalize its economy and increase prosperity for everyone. Ithaca is now beginning to develop a local health care plan based on its local currency. For more on the subject, look under "Money, Banking, Currencies" in Appendix 3, as well as read the article by Paul Glover in Appendix 4.

> "The most valuable of all arts will be the art of deriving a comfortable living from the smallest area of soil."
>
> —*Abraham Lincoln*

Local food production. Growing your own food is a key to self-sufficiency. In the Appendix is an article by Dean Goodale, who lives in Jefferson County, Iowa. He explains how every farmer in Iowa could grow all of their own food year-round and net $100,000 a year on less than a quarter of an acre! I know that sounds incredible, but Goodale is making it happen. There is also a piece by Larry Larson, a world expert on heating and cooling with earth tubes. By combining the expertise of these two men, you can create a year-round greenhouse that could provide your family income.

Energy self-sufficiency. The key to energy self-sufficiency is laid out in Chapter 10. Those interested in starting this plan in their community should look at the suggested reading for energy self-sufficiency in the Appendix. The sooner we get a network of individuals in local communities who are knowledgeable in this area, the sooner we can implement our plan. Read the material and contact us now; we don't have to wait until we are elected to start working on these projects.

Community teams. The key to reducing drug abuse and crime is organizing volunteers who are willing to sacrifice time and energy to develop local boards and committees that replace the state systems. The tax base for the communities that develop these programs will be reduced as the number of local citizens in state institutions and on welfare drops. Details of these teams are described in Chapters 15 and 20.

The beginning stages of this reorganization will take different paths in each community. The ancient system of organizing in groups of 10 families who elect a leader, and then every five groups of ten families electing a leader, may be the way for your community to start this process.

Charter schools. Control of education has to be brought back to the local level. If this is your area of interest, you can find out how to lobby for a charter school in your county by pursuing the resources for charter schools in the Appendix. Regaining control of our children's education is a critical area for regaining our freedom.

Constitutional study classes. The constitutional education class that we have participated in over the last three years should be implemented in all of our schools immediately. It is up to you to accomplish this in your area. Evening classes for adults, similar to the program that we set up here in Jefferson County, should be available to every person in Iowa. Be a self-starter and set up the "Evening a Month for America" program in your area. Program information is included in the Appendix under the www.nccs.net web site.

> "Ignore the junk news—work on a worth-
> while project, make a plan, or do something
> to enhance your life."
>
> —*Jeffrey Gitomer*

Our program for Iowa provides the individuals of this state a pathway for growth. Some of our solutions may seem unattainable to you. Everything we propose, however, is based on eternal laws that are as applicable now as they were in the 1770s, or even thousands of years ago. It is simply for us to decide what w,e the people, want. We are in control.

As author Richard Bach said, "Within each of us lies the power of our consent to health and to sickness, to riches and to poverty, to freedom and to slavery. It is we who control these and not another."

Please remember, those who want to have power over us really like the fact that most Americans are content to sit in front of their television sets for six hours a day oblivious to what is going on around them. The average American who relies on the television and newspapers for their news will never have a clue as to what is happening to their money or their vanishing freedoms.

What is necessary is action and that action has to begin now! We want to be a catalyst for changing Iowa. We offer a structure for dynamic positive change in our state. That's what our campaign is about. There is so much joy in starting a movement like this. Being involved in changing this state, bringing it back in tune with the fundamental principles of our republic, will give you immense fulfillment. After you read this book, start immediately on the steps mentioned above. Give copies of the book to your friends. See that everyone you know starts to take action right now.

Talk has value, but it will require more than talk to get the job done! It is one thing to sit around and talk about what is wrong with this state. It is a much different thing to actually take action to change the state. Be a generator of action!

We can only start with ourselves, but as we continue to take action day after day, and gradually add friends and family to our efforts, the action becomes more and more powerful. One of the most inspiring speakers I have ever met is Anthony Robbins. His words of advice are an appropriate conclusion for this book and set an appropriate tone to begin our work of restoring the heart of America.

> "The path to success is to take massive, determined action."
>
> —*Anthony Robbins*

"Actually, what is the political struggle that we witness? It is the instinctive struggle of all people toward liberty. And what is this liberty, whose very name makes the heart beat faster and shakes the world? Is it not the union of all liberties—liberty of conscience, of education, of association, of the press, of travel, of labor, of trade? In short, is not liberty the freedom of every person to make full use of his faculties, so long as he does not harm other persons while doing so? Is not liberty the destruction of all despotism—including, of course, legal despotism? Finally, is not liberty the restricting of the law only to its rational sphere of organizing the right of the individual to lawful self-defense; of punishing injustice?... I invariably reach this one conclusion: The solution to the problems of human relationships is to be found in liberty."

—*Bastiat*

Appendix 1. Vote Libertarian for Iowa

Richard V. Campagna, Candidate for Lieutenant Governor of Iowa

Richard Campagna is a multidisciplinary professional with a long and distinguished record in public and community service. He is an attorney, psychological counselor, college instructor, linguist, and international businessman. After graduating from Brown University in 1972 with a degree in political science, Richard went on to earn degrees from New York University (M.A.), St. John's University (J.D.), Columbia University (M.A.), and the American College of Metaphysical Theology (Ph.D.).

Richard has visited all 50 states on numerous occasions and virtually every country of the world. He has authored books, articles, poems and short stories. Fluent in six languages, Richard has also served as a legal, diplomatic, and medical interpreter. His belief in Libertarian principles and staunch support for our constitution and the common law have never wavered.

Richard was born in New York City and currently resides in Iowa City, Iowa, with his wife of 27 years, Odalys Perez-Medina. Odalys is also an attorney and college instructor. The Campagnas have one son, Robert, a sophomore at Lawrence University in Appleton, Wisconsin. Robert is a football player for Lawrence and is majoring in American history/international relations.

Clyde Cleveland, Candidate for Governor of Iowa

Clyde is a successful entrepreneur with a passion for restoring our natural resources and securing individual freedom. He moved his family, and his venture capital business, to Iowa in 1982. His enterprises have brought more than $27 million of venture capital to Iowa, directly and indirectly creating thousands of jobs.

He was the co-founder of the Fairfield, Iowa, constitutional study group, a successful program dedicated to educating the community on the founding principles of our country. He has been active in the movement to eliminate the federal income tax for over 10 years.

Clyde founded or co-founded seven successful companies, including United Investment Groups Inc. (UIG), for which he served as president and chairman of the board. In conjunction with UIG, Clyde was the general partner of 23 limited partnerships, including real estate, research and development (R&D), and wind energy syndications. The common theme of each R&D partnership was a focus on environmentally friendly companies in the developmental stage of growth. In 1986, Conscious Investors, Ltd. named Clyde the "First Socially Conscious Venture Capitalist" at its international symposium on Conscious Investing in Estes Park, Colorado.

By the age of 34, Clyde had amassed a significant net worth from a successful career in the investment arena. However, in 1986 the so-called Tax Simplification Act was passed which eliminated the tax advantages of Clyde's SEC publicly registered offerings. The inability of his company to market these offerings eventually led to his personal bankruptcy in 1987.

Rising from the ashes, Clyde co-founded an infomercial company in 1990. He was directly responsible for the development of the first two successful golf club infomercials ever produced. "Putt to Win," with Fran Tarkenton and Julius Irving, and "The Longest Drive," with Larry Bird, were considered breakthroughs in the infomercial industry. The industry experts told Clyde that it was impossible to sell a golf club through the infomercial format. These shows had a profound impact on both the infomercial and golf club industries.

Clyde and his wife, Debby, have been married for 32 years. They have four children and have lived in Fairfield, Iowa, since 1981. Clyde's Midwestern ethic was instilled in him during his childhood in Indiana. His father (Clyde) was a World War II Spitfire pilot, and his grandfather (Clyde) started on the family farm in Sullivan, Indiana, eventually becoming a Lake County, Indiana, Superior Court Judge. Clyde has a bachelor's degree in political science from Indiana State University.

Fritz Groszkruger, Candidate for Iowa Secretary of Agriculture

Fritz Groszkruger has attended college in both California and Iowa. He and his wife, Dawn, farm 300 acres in Pocahontas County. They have three adult children.

"I was born to be a libertarian. My dad has always been frustrated by the course our country is taking and he passed that on to me. I heard Ed Clark, the 1980 Libertarian Presidential

Candidate, speak on the "Jan Mickelson Show." After that program, thinking of myself as an anti-war capitalist just didn't seemed to fit anymore. I had a new label. I'm a libertarian." —Fritz Groszkruger

Tim Hird, Candidate for Treasurer of the State of Iowa

Tim Hird served in the Marine Corp from 1967 to 1971, reaching the rank of E5 Sergeant, and then went on to graduate from the University of Wyoming with a Bachelor's of Science degree in electrical engineering in 1976. Now a senior transmission coordinator for MidAmerican Energy, Tim has worked for MidAmerican Energy or its predecessors for the past 26 years. He is the current Treasurer of the Libertarian Party of Iowa.

Kevin Litten, Candidate for Second Congressional District

Kevin Litten is a 1981 graduate of the St. Louis College of Pharmacy. He has been licensed in five Midwestern states and currently practices in a community setting. Kevin is a member of the American Pharmaceutical Association, the Fully Informed Jury Association, the Iowa Sportsmen's Federation, the Izaac Walton League of America, and the National Rifle Association. He is also a member of the United Methodist Church.

A Republican for 20 years, Kevin became disillusioned with that party during 1996. As he explains, "I doubt that my beliefs have ever changed, only my optimism that the

Republicans could actually accomplish any meaningful change related to individual liberties in America. It was hard to switch party affiliation after so many years. I lost friends doing it, but I am happier with myself now and I will never go back until the Republicans adopt our principles and ideals".

Kevin's conversion to the Libertarian Party took place in the summer of 1966, and he was able to vote for Harry Browne for U.S. president that fall. Kevin is currently serving on the executive committee of the state party and is the editor of the party's newsletter, "Libertarians in Action."

"America is a truly blessed and rich nation, but we have fallen into the trap of assuming that only the government can solve our society's ills. America's best destiny lies in increasing our personal liberties and reining in the federal government. If you believe as I do in individual liberty, personal responsibility, and a small, constitutionally limited government, then I hope you will elect me your next congressman in November.

"As P.J. O'Rourke has pointed out, 'Giving money and power to government is like giving whiskey and car keys to teenage boys.' As your congressman, I hope to start sending the money and the power back to the people and the states." —Kevin Litten

Rich Moroney, Candidate for Iowa House District 85 (Northwest Davenport)

Rich Moroney has a Bachelor of Science degree in mathematics from Penn State University and has worked for an insurance company as an actuary for nearly 30 years. Rich has been a Libertarian Party member since 1980.

"I started off a Democrat supporting McGovern in 1972, but figured out that wasn't going to work," he says. "I then went to being a Republican supporting Ford in 1976, but soon figured out that they were no different. I've been Libertarian ever since, keeping my record of never voting for a presidential winner intact.

"The only way we're going to actually slow and then reverse the growth of government is by electing candidates who are independent of the party discipline of the two entrenched parties. Every vote, every issue, every day, no excuses, I'll be in the legislature moving power and responsibility from Des Moines and back to the individuals and communities in Davenport and throughout Iowa."—Rich Moroney

Mark Nelson, Candidate for Iowa Senate District 21

Mark Nelson is the current chairman of the Libertarian Party of Iowa. Under his leadership, the party grew faster than any other state party in America in 2001. He hopes to maintain that growth rate by focusing the party on realistic, tangible activism: supporting candidates and promoting legislation. Before taking the helm of the state party, Mark was mostly involved in issues surrounding education reform.

Edward F. Noyes, J.D., Candidate for Attorney General of Iowa

Ed Noyes was raised on his family's homestead in rural Nebraska. In 1979, he graduated from the University of Nebraska with a Bachelor of Science degree in agriculture and a double major in wildlife biology and agricultural economics.

Ed attended law school at the University of the Pacific and the University of Iowa, graduating in 1985. Since then, he has been in private practice in Fairfield, Iowa, practicing primarily in criminal defense, family law, and civil causes of action. He has also been a commercial and residential real estate developer.

Dedicated to strengthening communities, Ed has had a leadership role in several yearly International Community Service Day events in Jefferson County, Iowa. He is also active in various local youth-mentoring projects, founding the Annual Men and Boys' Canoe Trip for young men without active male role models. In addition, Ed produced one of the first local cable access television programs in Iowa, "Community Empowerment, Rediscovering Our Unlimited Resources," demonstrating how communities can be self-sufficient and successful without depending on federal or state governments.

Ed is a lifelong environmentalist and avid outdoorsman, with a love for camping, canoeing, fishing and motorcycle riding. He works to help maintain a 120-acre wilderness and wildlife preserve, and is a member of the Sierra Club and The Nature Conservancy as well as other environmental organizations.

Ed's other passions include a lifelong study of Native American cultures and the study of the U.S. Constitution. Ed has researched the mechanics of how tribal societies facilitated both the spiritual development of the individual and simultaneous success of the tribe. Over the past three years, he has also completed the "Evening a Month for America" program sponsored by the National Center for Constitutional Studies.

Ed and his wife, Jerrie, live in Fairfield.

Sylvia Olson, Candidate for Iowa Secretary of State

Sylvia Olson helps her husband Ben operate a family farm in Pocahontas County. She also works for the local newspaper. Sylvia and Ben have two sons, one in college and one in high school. As a family, they enjoy sailing, traveling, and learning together.

Sylvia describes herself as a "natural libertarian." "Live and let live, take responsibility for your life, be skeptical of power— these are ideas I was raised with," she says. A member of the Libertarian Party since the 1970s, she has been active in Libertarian politics at the state and local level and has also served as secretary of the Libertarian National Committee.

A love of the natural world and a desire to protect the life of the planet are also important to her. Volunteering is a big part of her life. She has donated time to coaching high school mock trial and youth soccer, raised funds for the local tennis courts, created displays about ecological topics, and helped organize a drug policy symposium, among other projects.

Educated at Harvard/Radcliffe, with a Bachelor of Arts degree in psychology and sociology, she worked as a science teacher and in sales positions before her current career as mother, farmer, and journalist.

"I am running for office to encourage people to get active. If 'just plain folks' don't take an interest in our government, then it gets taken over by professional politicians and the powerful interests that buy the politicians. 'Eternal vigilance is the price of liberty.' That was true in the 18th century, and it is even more true today." —Sylvia Olson

Mei-Ling Shaw, Candidate
for Iowa House District 92

"I was born in Ames, Iowa, in 1979, where I resided until 1998. I moved to Iowa City after high school to attend the University of Iowa. I had intended to study art, but quickly realized I was not moving towards my happiness, rather I was putting myself through an obstacle course. I quit the university, much to the dismay of my loving, worried parents. I worked three jobs for a time, when an unlikely opportunity presented itself. I was fortunate enough to secure an apprenticeship at a very reputable tattoo shop. So, in 1999 I began tattooing. I continued to live and work in Iowa City until the fall of 2000, at which time I moved to Lee County.

"I purchased my building and started my own tattoo shop in 2001. I have long been interested in vintage automobiles and motorcycling. I spend much of my free time reading, writing or drawing. I feel I have a duty to my family and the future to work against the flood of injustice in America. That is why I am running for state representative in the 92nd District.

"My father is a veteran of the Vietnam War. His father is a veteran of World War II. I also have ancestors who fought in the Civil and Revolutionary wars. I plan on continuing my family tradition of remaining vigilant. To see what is right, and not to do it, makes you an accomplice. I see a frightening America on the horizon. There is a rising tide of statism, where people revere the state more than the individual. Many people are already more dependent on the state than on themselves, and our own government puts itself before its citizens. When people hold the state before the individual, individual rights are vanquished, and with them, the individual. History has shown us the rise of fascism stems from fervent nationalism and I cannot consciously be silent when I see this danger. Many know there must be changes made; many feel it, though they cannot see what can be done. So, I will do my best to educate and inform during this campaign. When I win, I will work to restore freedom to protect yourself, freedom to pursue your own happiness, and to stop the state from punishing hardworking people for being productive." —Mei-Ling Shaw

Appendix 2. Recommended Reading

Agriculture

Acres USA This 30-year-old, monthly magazine is a must for any farmer, especially those interested in transitioning to nonchemical intensive agriculture. Subscriptions available by calling 1-800-355-5313 or at www.acresusa.com.

Coleman, Eliot. *The New Organic Grower* (Chelsea Green Publishers, 2nd ed. 1994)

Coleman, Eliot. *Four-Season Harvest* (Chelsea Green Publishers, 1999). These are the primary working texts for organic farming in North America and in the English-speaking world. Coleman is known nationally for his organic farming techniques and is famous for his year-round growing in frigid Maine

Jeavons, John. *How to Grow More Vegetables* (Ten Speed Press, 1995). A classic. Jeavons is internationally known as one of the founders and chief promoters of bio-intensive agriculture. He has shown farmers throughout the world how to farm profitably and sustainably.

Waters, Charles. *A Farmer's Guide to the Bottom Line* (Acres USA, 2002). How to transition to "biological" farming. With case studies as well as practical information, this is an excellent resource for anyone who is interested in starting a farming enterprise of any kind. Available by calling 1-800-355-5313 or at www.acresusa.com.

Drug War

Gray, Jim. *Why the War on Drugs has Failed and What We Can Do About It*. (Temple University Press, 2002). Blockbuster of a book. An expose on the drug war by a judge who deals with it in his courtroom every day.

Gray, Mike. *Drug Crazy: How We Got Into This Mess & How We Can Get Out of It*. (Random House, 1998). An excellent historical background on the problem presented in a readable format, with suggestions for our future.

Masters, William. *Drug War Addiction* (Accurate Press, 2001). A book from the frontlines by a former drug warrior. Sheriff Masters tells the whole truth about this war.

Energy

Flavin, Christopher and Nicholas Lenssen. *Power Surge: A Guide to the Coming Energy Revolution* (W.W. Norton and Co., 1994).

Environment and Business

Anderson, Luke. *Genetic Engineering, Food, and Our Environment* (Chelsea Green Publishing, 1999). An excellent comprehensive view of genetic engineering that can be read in about three hours. To order, contact Chelsea Green, 800-639-4099.

Anderson, Terry L. and Donald R. Leal. *Free Market Environmentalism* (Palgrave, rev. 2001). The authors explore the prospects and pitfalls for improving natural resource allocation and environmental quality through market processes.

They also explain why government policies often exacerbate our environmental problems.

Benyus, Janine M. *Biomimicry* (William Morrow & Co., 1998). Learn how our biggest problems in all fields, from agriculture to construction, are being solved by mimicking natural processes.

Gladwell, Malcolm. *The Tipping Point: How Little Things Can Make a Big Difference* (Little Brown & Co., 2000). Showing how paradigm shifts occur in society, Gladwell examines such examples as the hula hoop fad in the 1950s and the dramatic drop in the New York City crime rate to show how a trend "tips." This is valuable knowledge for anyone who wants to create a rapid transition in behavior.

Hawkin, Paul. *The Ecology of Commerce* (Harperbusiness, 1994). In this ground-breaking book, Hawkin details how restorative justice principles can be applied to all forms of commerce.

Hawkin, Paul. *Natural Capitalism* (Back Bay Books, 2000). A very positive outlook for the future based on the actual experience of entrepreneurs using existing technology to produce superior products with minimal pollution.

Hock, Dee. *Birth of the Chaordic Age* (Berrett-Koehler Publishing, 1999). In this breakthrough book, the founder of one of the largest commercial enterprises on the planet, VISA, tells how he built an incredibly successful organization by focusing totally on fundamental principles of natural law. Within this book lies the secret formula for solving our environmental problems, without top-down, command-and-control, monolithic government.

Schlosser, Eric. *Fast Food Nation* (Houghton Mifflin, 20001). How huge corporations, in cooperation with government, have turned our farmers into serfs.

Guns

The following four books are highly recommended for all gun owners, especially new gun owners.

Ayoob, Massad. *Stressfire* (Police Bookshelf, 1992). How to shoot in a difficult situation.

Ayoob, M. *In the Gravest Extreme: The Role of the Firearm in Personal Protection* (Police Bookshelf, 1980). Everyone with a gun needs to read this book. Twice at least.

Ayoob, M. *The Truth about Self-Protection* (Police Bookshelf, 1983). Examines all the modern urban/suburban defense strategies and devices as alternatives and supplements to guns.

Cooper, J. *Principles of Personal Defense* (Paladin Press, 1989). Prepare your mind to save yourself.

To debunk the myths of government and "gun control," read:

Poe, Richard. *The Seven Myths of Gun Control* (Prima Publishing, 2001). Available at Amazon.com.

Stevens, Richard W. *Dial 911 and Die* (Mazel Freedom Press, 1999). Available from Jews for the Preservation of Firearms Organization, www.jpfo.org/doctors-epidemic.htm.

Stevens, Richard W. and Aaron Zelman. *Death by Gun Control: The Human Cost of Victim Disarmament* (Mazel Freedom Press, 2001). Available at www.jpfo.org/doctors-epidemic.htm.

Wolfe, Claire and Aaron Zelman. *The State vs. the People: The Rise of the American Police State.* (Mazel Freedom Press, 2002). Available at www.jpfo.org/doctors-epidemic.htm.

Health

Balch, Phyllis A. (CNC) and James F. Balch, M.D. *Prescriptions for Nutritional Healing: A practical A to Z reference for drug-free remedies using vitamins, minerals, herbs, and food supplements* (Avery Penguin Putman, 3rd ed. 2000). Every home should have a copy of this book.

Media and Propaganda

Huff, Darrell. *How to Lie with Statistics* (W.W. Norton & Co., 1954).

Rampton, Sheldon and John Stauber. *Trust Us, We're Experts!* (Jeremy P. Tarcher/Putnam, 2001).

Tye, Larry. *Father of Spin: Edward L. Bernays and the Birth of Public Relations* (Crown Publishers, 1999; paperback Owl Books, Fall 2002).

Stevens, Richard W. *Disarming the Data Doctors: How to Debunk the 'Public Health' Basis for 'Gun Control.'* Available at www.jpfo.org/doctors-epidemic.htm.

Money, Banking, Currencies

Glover, Paul. *Hometown Money: How to Enrich Your Community with Local Currency* The founder of Ithaca HOURS explains step-by-step how to start and maintain a local currency system. Since 1991, 95,000 Ithaca Hours, worth $10 each, have been issued and used by thousands of residents, including 480 businesses and 60 community organizations, adding millions of dollars of trading to Ithaca's Grassroots Local Product. Available for $25 from HOURS, Box 365, Ithaca, NY 14851; (607) 272-4330.

Griffin, G. Edward. *Creature from Jekyl Island, A Second Look at the Federal Reserve* (American Media, 3rd ed. 1998). This is a classic history of the Federal Reserve, the people who created it, and the nature of money. It is very well researched and a great read. Griffin has a gift for making complicated concepts easy to understand. Available at www.realityzone.com.

Phillips, Gordon. *Losing Your Illusions* (Self-published, 1998). This book provides a very complete understanding of the relationship between the income tax and the Federal Reserve. It is well documented and a major boundary-breaker. Should be read by every American. Available at www.informamerica.com.

Thoren, Theodore R. *The Truth in Money Book* (Truth in Money, 4th ed., 1994). This book presents an understandable explanation of our current monetary system; it's clearer than any other book on the subject. Unfortunately, it is out of print. Check your library or used book stores.

Politics and Economics

Adams, Charles. *For Good and Evil: The Impact of Taxes on the Course of Civilization* (Madison Books, reprint ed. 1994). An in-depth look at taxation, it covers all major civilizations, including, Egypt, Greece, Rome, Israel, and Spain, with the last chapters dealing specifically with the United States. If you like history, this is a great book to have in your library.

Bastiat, Frederic. *The Law*. (Foundation for Economic Education, 2nd ed., 1998). First published in 1850, this booklet can be found in its entirety at http://bastiat.org/en/the_law.html.

Browne, Harry. *Why Government Doesn't Work* (Liam Works, 1995). Browne does a great job of explaining how and why government programs always follow the same patterns. This is a quick read and a good book to give to friends.

Gross, Martin. *The Tax Racket, Government Extortion from A to Z* (Ballantine Books, 1995). Gross has written several well-researched books. This one will open your eyes about the true nature of our tax system. His books are easy to read and hard to put down. Also recommended is his *A Call for Revolution: How Washington is Strangling America*.

Hazlitt, Henry. *Economics in One Lesson* (Three Rivers Press, 1983). Learn the basic truths of economics in a short amount of time. He cuts through the economic nonsense that pervades our media and educational institutions.

Skousen, Cleon. *The 5,000-Year Leap* (National Center for Constitutional Studies, 1981). This is a great book for understanding the fundamental principles upon which our Constitution and Declaration of Independence are based. Skousen is a highly respected constitutional scholar. In this book, he focuses on the Founders' attempt to create a country based on principles of natural law that would be an example for the world. Available at www.nccs.net.

Skousen, Cleon. *The Majesty of God's Law* (National Center for Constitutional Studies, 1985). This is a classic work on the sources which influenced the Founders. A significant portion of the book is devoted to the Mosaic law and the impact it had on our founding documents. Available at www.nccs.net

Welfare and Poverty

Olasky, Marvin. *Renewing American Compassion* (Regnery Publishing, 1997) Very positive, upbeat, and solution oriented. This is a great book for understanding how private charitable organizations will always outperform government welfare organizations. Olasky gives a clear game plan for how we can wean our nation off government charity and work toward a welfare and poverty program based totally on private institutions. Very well researched and a must-read for anyone who wants to debunk the entire argument for government involvement in providing services. This author understands the true nature of compassion.

Appendix 3. Recommended Web Sites

Agriculture

www.nffc.net

The National Family Farm Coalition (NFFC) was founded in 1986 to serve as a national link for grassroots organizations working on family farm issues. Its membership currently consists of 33 grassroots farm, resource conservation, and rural advocacy groups from 33 states. NFFC brings together farmers and others to organize national projects focused on preserving and strengthening family farms.

www.acresusa.com/original

This is the website for *Acres USA*, which offers the cutting edge in commercial-scale, soil-friendly farming technologies, techniques, markets, news, analysis, and trends. Each oversized monthly issue is packed with practical, hands-on information you can put to work on your farm.

www.ifbf.org/publication/archive/t_search1.asp?number=19120&atype=current

The risk of genetically engineered food is clearly shown in the article "Pseudopregnancies puzzle swine producer." Iowa farmer Jerry Rosman saw his pig farrowing rates drop by 80 percent in less than a year, and he wasn't alone. Four other producers in his area experienced the same decrease. The only common denominator among the five: they all fed their pigs the same corn hybrids.

A follow-up article in the Farm Bureau's publication reported that more Iowa sow herds were experiencing the same problem. See www.ifbf.org/publication/archive/t_search1.asp?number=19212&atype=current.

www.growbiointensive.org

This is an excellent site for those who are interested in getting into farming but have a very small amount of land. It is amazing how much you can grow on a small plot using the methods discussed on this web site.

www.cfra.org/

The Center for Rural Affairs, a private, nonprofit organization, is working to strengthen small businesses, family farms and ranches, and rural communities.

Drug War

www.drugsense.org

This site provides the facts, resources, and latest news about the drug war.

Education

www.edreform.com/charter_schools

This is a comprehensive site on charter schools, that is, independent public schools designed and operated by educators, parents, community leaders, educational entrepreneurs, and others. The schools are sponsored by designated local or state education organizations that monitor their quality and integrity, but allow them to operate free from the traditional bureaucratic and regulatory red tape that hog-ties public schools.

Environment and Business

www.abundance-ecovillage.com/

This is the site of the amazing real estate development in Iowa that incorporates all of the latest technologies for self-sufficient living. This could be a model for how to live in a bottom-up society, with absolute minimal reliance on outside institutions. This self-contained community is self-reliant for its food and energy needs.

www.greenandfree.com/chaordic_age.htm

This is a copy of a speech by Dee Hock. When founding VISA, he structured it by mimicking the fundamental principles of natural systems, providing maximum freedom for participants and maximum growth for the company. It became the largest commercial enterprise on the planet. Hock now devotes his life to restructuring all of our institutions to be in tune with these fundamental principles.

www.chaordic.org

This is the web site for all those interested in creating non-coercive solutions to problems, based on Hock's chaordic model. See what is going on around the world as this new paradigm of structuring our institutions takes hold.

http://www.theatlantic.com/issues/98oct/industry.htm

Learn about the difference between eco-efficiency and eco-effectiveness. Eco-effectiveness is in tune with natural laws and will create prosperity and a restored environment.

www.bio-integrity.org

Visit the Alliance for Bio-integrity web site and see for yourself the internal FDA documents that were turned over in the lawsuit. These documents broke open the FDA's cover-up of its approval of genetically modified organisms.

www.electricemperor.com/enter/eersrch/eersrch.html

Learn how we can provide all of our energy needs without fossil fuels. This is an excellent site about all of the incredible benefits of the hemp plant.

www.chelseagreen.com

A publishing company that specializes in books for sustainable living. Most of the books available from this publisher are relevant to restoring bottom-up government and self-sufficient living.

www.wellnessgoods.com/fl_art_wat_messages.html

This web site contains the amazing photographs from Dr. Emoto's study on water and how it is affected by pollutants as well as sound, and even by our thoughts. This is a breakthrough study showing the link between the human mind and our environment. The power of love, the ultimate solution to our problems, is illustrated vividly.

www.gefoodalert.org

Genetically Engineered Food Alert is a coalition of seven organizations united in their commitment to testing and labeling genetically engineered food.

www.labelgefoods.org

Oregon Concerned Citizens for Safe Foods (a political action committee) was formed specifically to address the issue of labeling genetically engineered foods in Oregon through the initiative process.

www.organicconsumers.org

The Organic Consumers Association is a public interest organization dedicated to building a healthy, safe, and sustainable system of food production and consumption. It is a global clearinghouse for information and grassroots technical assistance.

http://carolmoore.net/greens&libertarians.html

Where Greens and Libertarians meet.

Energy

www.greenandfree.com/energy_independence.htm

More evidence for wind power. If we would work together to end ALL subsidies to ANY energy provider, we would have 90 percent clean, renewable energy in this country in five years. We would have almost no fossil fuel pollution, and we would have created a vibrant new industry in renewable-energy-related enterprises.

Media and Propaganda

www.prwatch.org

Award-winning PR Watch offers investigative reporting on the public relations industry. It helps the public recognize manipulative and misleading PR practices by exposing the activities of secretive, little-known propaganda-for-hire firms that work to control political debates and public opinion.

www.nomorefakenews.com

There are no boundaries on truth at this site. This is the best site I have found for the absolute pure news that the elites running our major media outlets do not want you to hear.

www.greenandfree.com/recognize_skunk.htm

This is an excellent article about Edward Bernays, the so-called father of public relations. The masters of deception have learned their trade well. The authors, Claire Wolfe and Aaron Zelman, explain how we are deceived daily and give practical tips for sifting through the propaganda.

www.thedoctorwithin.com/index33.html

Author Tim O'Shea provides another look at how we are brainwashed daily in many ways through all our major media.

Money, Banking and Currencies

www.nccs.net/store/monetary_reform.html

#1 Recommendation! "The Urgent Need for a Comprehensive Monetary Reform," a report by Dr. W. Cleon Skousen, covers the development of the United States monetary system, how the Federal Reserve System operates and why it has failed, and how to provide the United States with a sound money system.

www.realityzone.com

This is Ed Griffin's web site. He is the author of *The Creature from Jekyl Island: A Second Look at the Federal Reserve*. Griffin's Reality Zone audio tape sets are full of incredible gems, such as Douglas MacArthur's famous farewell speech at West Point, the extraordinary history of the politics of cancer research, how the U.S.'s Korean prisoners of war were brainwashed, and much more.

www.clevelandforgovernor.org/greenspan

This article by Alan Greenspan, long-time chair of the Federal Reserve, was written several years ago when he still told the truth in public. We hope that when you read it, you will be inspired to do further research on the Federal Reserve.

www.netcolony.com/news/hotwire2000/NFAp1.html

The article "Fed up with the Fed" gives a brief history and factual overview of the Federal Reserve.

www.norfed.com

Find out about a currency you can use now that is backed by gold and silver.

www.themoneymasters.com

Learn about how we lost our government to a handful of powerful families.

www.lightlink.com/hours/ithacahours

Learn how Ithaca, New York, turned a dying economy into a thriving economy by developing its own currency.

www.futurenet.org/2Money/Lietaer.html

An excellent discussion regarding local currencies and their value.

Politics and Economics

www.schumachersociety.org/frameset_publication.html

This site contains the most complete listing of resources we have found regarding the restoration of bottom-up government and community-based solutions to problems in every area of life.

www.bomis.com/rings/bastiat/4

Frederic Bastiat gave his incredible presentation, "The Law," to the French Parliament in 1850. It is very likely the clearest expression of the proper role of government ever written. The speech, which you can read here in an hour or two, was later published.

www.nccs.net

The National Center for Constitutional Studies offers many educational resources to help you in your study of the U.S. Constitution and the original intent of the Founding Fathers. It provides a curriculum on American History and the Constitution for all ages that is widely used in home schools as well as charter schools. The "Evening a Month for America," program is explained here and all required resources are available from this site. This site has all of the works by Cleon Skousen, the American scholar famous for his works on the Founders and the Constitution, as well as the classic *The Naked Capitalist*.

www.simpol.org

The International Simultaneous Policy Organization (ISPO) assumes that the destructive effects of competitive corporate globalization can be reversed, and that world opinion can be harnessed to make this happen, by using democratic processes in a completely novel and effective way.

http://spot.colorado.edu/~mcguire/iriquois.htm

Anyone interested in an example of a constitution based on the principles of bottom-up government would find the Iroquois constitution fascinating reading.

www.lexrex.com

Outstanding resources for understanding the fundamental principles of our republic.

www.carolmoore.net/4secretary/positiveplatform.html

The most frequent complaint heard about the Libertarian Party platform is that it is too negative and talks more about what we are against than what we are for. As a solution, Carol Moore offers this draft of a "Positive" Libertarian Party platform.

www.informamerica.com

Look for the video *The Truth about the Income Tax*. This tape will give the viewer a comprehensive alternative view of the income tax, the Federal Reserve, and the Sixteenth Amendment. It is a well-documented and convincing presentation on a subject that affects us all very profoundly.

www.freerepublic.com

Outstanding articles on a wide variety of subjects.

www.realityzone.com

This is Ed Griffin's web site. He is the author of *The Creature from Jekyl Island: A Second Look at the Federal Reserve*. Griffin's Reality Zone audio tape sets are full of incredible gems, such as Douglas MacArthur's famous farewell speech at West Point, the extraordinary history of the politics of cancer research, how the U.S.'s Korean prisoners of war were brainwashed, and much more.

www.glorigraphics.com/constitution/home.cfm

The Fairfield, Iowa, constitutional study group provides a local-chapter model for you to duplicate in your community. This site would be helpful for any community that wants to develop an "Evening a Month for America," program in their area.

www.lp.org/issues

The national Libertarian Party site. This section of the site describes the national party's position on major issues.

www.lpia.org/index.html

The Iowa Libertarian Party web site, including news, issues, and links.

www.whattheheck.com/liberty

Links to 25 other libertarian sites.

http://www.mebbs.com/klitten/ls.htm

This link contains brief Libertarian policy statements on a wide range of issues. This page was designed for Iowa's college students, but it is a good place for anyone to see how Libertarians view the issues of the day.

Appendix 4. 'Must Read' Articles

Of the limitless numbers of articles we could recommend, some of them are so important and relevant to our primary message that we have included them here. We want every person who reads this book to know that there are solutions to all of our problems. Three of the following articles are by individuals in our own community here in Iowa who are making a big difference.

"Earth Tubes" was written by Larry Larson, one of the foremost experts in earth tube technology. This amazing energy-conservation technology is going to have a major impact on our planet. You can use it immediately to retrofit your existing house or in the construction of a new home.

"Applying Earth Tube Technology to Greenhouse Produce" is by Dean Goodale, who is making a very good living in agriculture on less than one acre of land. His story is inspiring and real. In our households, eat food grown by Dean almost daily.

In **"Abundance Eco-village: Care of the Earth, Care of the People, Share the Surplus,"** co-developer Lonnie Gamble describes the Abundance Eco-village in Iowa. This development is completely self-sufficient, and we believe it will be an inspiration for building projects all over the world.

The fourth article is **"Creating Community Economics with Local Currency,"** by Paul Glover. We described this concept in Chapter 19. One of the first local currencies in America, the

Ithaca Hour has significantly increased prosperity for the people of Ithaca, New York. We think local currencies are a very good idea for Iowa counties or any other local community.

The fundamental flaws of our national monetary system still have to be dealt with and that is the subject of the last article, **"Billions for Bankers—Debts for the People."** The author summarizes the nature of fractional reserve banking and its effects on the average citizen. Pastor Sheldon Emry is a Christian minister, and his religious perspective is apparent in some of his observations. But whether you are Jewish, Christian, Moslem, Hindu, Buddhist, atheist, or none of the above is irrelevant. You don't need to agree with his religious convictions to learn from his analysis of the monetary system. It is something that affects us all exactly the same. We chose to include this article because the author takes a seemingly incomprehensible issue and explains it clearly.

Until we resolve the money problem in this country, we will not be able to make the significant changes necessary to restore our prosperity or our freedom.

> "All the perplexities, confusion and distress in America rise, not from defects in their Constitution or Confederation, not from want of honor or virtue, so much as from downright ignorance of the nature of coin, credit, and circulation."
>
> —*John Adams, in a letter to*
> *Thomas Jefferson, 1787*

Earth Tubes

by Larry Larson

> "I know of houses in Michigan that have had continuously operated air tube systems for twenty years with no air quality problems. Their heating and cooling bills were less than $200 per year. Of course, to obtain that level of sustainability, other aspects of the building's construction, design, and engineering have to be considered."
>
> —*Larry Larson*

The "earth-coupled air tube" technology is a low-cost solution to reduce the cost of heating and cooling your home. By using the earth as a heat sink, anyone can heat and cool their house for less. Unlike the ground loop heat pump, air tubes don't require deep wells, compressors, pumps, storage tanks, coils, heat exchangers, or complex plumbing, or have all the problems inherent in a complex equipment/technology intensive heating and cooling system. Properly installed, air tubes don't have any moving parts. They can't break. The only technology required is a fan to move the air through the tubes and into the house. Earth tubes are relatively inexpensive to install and are inexpensive to operate.

In the United States today, many of our biggest problems are related to the high cost of energy, the inefficient use of that energy, and the impact of that energy use on the planet. The old way of solving the problem is to make existing equipment more efficient, more complex, and ultimately more expensive. This solution only delays the inevitable and continues the spiral of wasteful uses of energy.

Often the best solution to a problem is the simplest. The simple solution first requires a shift in how we think about the house we live in and the planet we live on. Only from this change in human consciousness can we hope to change the world we live in. Our home is where we can begin. By using earth coupled air tubes to heat and cool our home, we use the earth as a source of comfort that is in tune with natural law.

In the 1970s and early 1980s, earth air tubes gained a lot of popularity as an aid to conventional air conditioning and heating. They work by simply exposing the air we are drawing through the tubes into the house to the temperature of the soil. As air travels through the tubes, it exchanges temperature with the surrounding soil. The air entering the house will be warmer then the outside air in the winter and cooler than the outside air in the summer.

An earth air tube system uses primarily an open air system. Outdoor air is drawn into the tubes, cooled (in the summer) by the earth, dehumidified, and delivered to the inside of the house. This system provides fresh conditioned air. There are other closed-loop and reverse-direction designs that can be used for special-case situations where additional dehumidification or exit air is required.

For example, if the building is expected to be super tight, then an extra tube or two can be laid that only removes air from the house. If the occupancy and use levels require additional dehumidification, then an extra number of tubes can be laid that loop inside air out underground and back into the building, dehumidifying and re-cooling it. If more makeup air is required, you simply use more tubes or larger diameter tubes.

The best tube material is high-density polyethylene formed into the common black corrugated drainage pipe. This pipe has a corrugated structure which increases the surface area of the pipe allowing for more earth contact and a more efficient heat exchange. It is corrosion resistant, easy to handle, and readily available.

The optimum tube diameter is 8 inches, but pipes of up to 12 inches diameter can be used. The larger-diameter pipes require a longer buried run for optimum performance. The tube has a single slit cut into it along the seam. This is the primary condensate drain for the tube.

The tube trench has to be very carefully constructed to assure proper drainage of groundwater and air-tube condensate. This construction should only be attempted by an experienced installer, as any mistakes can ruin the installation and possibly threaten the health of those living in the house. There are several trench design details that need to be implemented: trench profile, drainage, tube installation, materials used, as well as depth and dimension of the trench according to the diameter of the tubes.

The trench drainage can be a gravity drain to daylight or the trench can direct the water to a sump pump. The danger of using a sump pump is that, if there is ever a loss of power for an extended period of time, the tube and trench drainage system could fill with water. As a result, the interior of the tubes could become plugged beyond repair with silt and sludge.

Condensate drainage in the tubes is very important for maintaining acceptable air quality. The system is designed to assure no soil moisture or organisms ever enter the pipe and possibly pollute the air stream. The preferred method of drainage is a gravity drain to daylight. A sump drain should only be used as a last resort. There are alarms and backup power that can be employed in the case of sump failure or loss of power to the pump.

The tubes in the trench need to be on at least two foot centers for 8-inch pipes. Larger diameter pipes require greater spacing between the pipes. The reason for the spacing is to minimize the chance the tubes will exchange heat with one another rather than with the ground. For 8-inch pipes, the trench will need to be 8 feet deep, 10 feet wide and 100 feet long. For larger diameter pipes, the trench will increase in depth, width, and length. Trenches deeper than 12 feet will be rare and are dangerous, requiring special precautions.

Proper drainage of the trench is of utmost importance if the tube system is going to perform flawlessly for the life of the house. The bottom of the trench must fall consistently and be relatively flat. The bottom of the trench is then filled with 4 to 6 inches of a small diameter (1/2 to 1 inch diameter) pea rock or river rock; washed gravel without the fines is acceptable as a last choice. The pea rock is then covered with a filter cloth so it doesn't get clogged with silt and sediment from the surrounding soil.

The tubes are carefully laid on the filter cloth and staked every 10 feet or so with the drain slit down. All the couplers are taped securely and any cracks or holes are caulked with silicone. The tubes are laid in a serpentine fashion. The ideal is to have the pipes bend at least the diameter of the pipe every 6 feet. This has the effect of preventing the air from flowing in boundary layers inside the pipes. As a result, the air crashes around inside the tubes maximizing the air-to-wall contact for complete heat exchange and, in the summer, removal of excess air moisture.

Once the tubes are secured, the foundation penetration sealed, and the open air intake end of the pipes secured and covered on the surface, the tubes are carefully covered with sand. This locks the tubes into their intended position for the final backfilling with the remaining excavate. Heavy equipment can drive on the trench once it is fully backfilled.

Soil types can cause a wide variance in the tube performance, and in the case of a sugar sand soil type, it can change dramatically the trench profile, eliminating the need for pea rock and filter cloth. Soil temperature is also affected by soil type. The heavy moisture-laden soils have higher heat exchange capacity than do rocky, dry, or sandy soils. In some parts of the country, digging in the ground is nearly impossible. The air tube system will work in nearly all parts of the country where it is possible to dig a trench as described.

The average soil temperature will vary throughout the various parts of the country. The average soil temperature will be within a few degrees of the average air temperature. For instance, in southeast Iowa the average soil temperature is 53 degrees. At a depth of 8 feet, the soil temperature will vary 12 degrees on either side of average. It will drop on an average to 41 degrees in the winter and rise to an average of 65 degrees in the summer. It could temporarily dip below or above those averages if there are extended periods of severe weather. The air tube temperature will follow the soil temperatures. As a result, the air volume flowing through the tubes can be reduced in the winter and increased in the summer.

Once the air tube system is installed, then the interior air handling system has to be installed. The air system inside the house ideally should be some sort of forced air duct system. The design of the forced air system is highly individual, but ideally should feature some sort of exhaust to the outside, high in the common area of the house. The air tubes should be powered 24/7. The fan used to power the tubes should be set on a medium to low velocity. One should not be able to either hear or feel the air flowing. Exposure to constant high-velocity air flow can cause anxiety and nervousness.

The best system for air delivery inside each of the rooms is low delivery and high returns. This matches the natural air flow the house would experience if it were allowed to convect on its own. There should be at least one common air return located as high in the house as possible. This return should be as big as possible within reason. It is important in the winter to capture high heat and return it to the rest of the house. The goal of the air circulation system is to make the people inside the house comfortable. The house doesn't care if it is hot or cold. What matters is that the air be comforting to the people inside. Register location does not necessarily need to be directly next to the load (i.e., under windows and doors).

In the winter, the primary leakage is through the doors and windows. This is by design since the house has to lose air somewhere if any air is expected to come in through the air tubes. So if the primary exit points for the air are the doors and windows, then you would not want to put supply registers directly in front of those areas. Ideally, one wants the air to travel through the room before it exits the room. The duct system design should be left to an installer with air tube design experience.

I know of houses in Michigan that have had continuously operated air tube systems for 20 years with no air quality problems. Their heating and cooling bills were less than $200 a year. Of course, to obtain that level of sustainability, other aspects of the building's construction, design, and engineering have to be considered.

These other design aspects are critical for optimum air tube performance. The walls and ceilings need to be super insulated, preferably with a thermal break built into the wall. A thermal break will reduce the problem of thermal conduction from the outside through the wooden members of the walls. As much as 17 percent of the heat lost through a wall is through conduction. A thermal break reduces the load of the wall, increasing the energy efficiency of the house.

Concrete basements are another big energy drain on the house. Standard portland concrete has virtually no R value. It is actually a conductor and will wick any ground moisture like a sponge. Granted this is done in relative slow motion, but as much as 23 percent of the heat loss of the house can occur through the basement walls. The impact on the earth from cement production nationwide rivals that of the automobile for its contribution to greenhouse gasses. Cement seems so benign when we use it, but its impact on the planet is huge.

Look for other foundation materials. We recommend pressure-treated wood for basements and footings. The wood comes from well-managed forests of southern yellow pine.

The treatment, though it involves the use and distribution of toxic chemicals, is not a petroleum-based material and is relatively low polluting. In addition, it doesn't off-gas or leach into the environment and has been proven to be safe for use in house construction. Wooden foundations are warm, very easy to work with, and easy to insulate.

One of the most important and difficult items to include in your house is a vapor barrier. There are a few simple rules to follow when using a vapor barrier.

1. Always place the vapor barrier on the warm side of the wall, ceiling, or floor.

2. You must construct the wall in such a way as to guarantee that the vapor barrier will never get cold. A cold vapor barrier in the winter could cause a dew point to occur and cause a mold or mildew problem.

3. A vapor barrier is not designed nor should it ever be expected to stop air flow. The wall should be airtight before the vapor barrier is installed.

This brings us to one of the biggest problems in housing construction-breathability. This is a problem which air tubes solve! I have thought a lot about sealed walls versus breathing walls. For me, it comes down to a very simple question. Can I live in a house that is both sustainable and comfortable? Comfort usually comes with a price tag, especially in the weather extremes of Iowa.

The one issue that turned me toward sealed walls is the vapor issue. Do I want to live in a dry house in the winter and a humid house in the summer? What would happen if my house weren't vapor sealed on all walls, floors, and ceilings that are shared with the outside?

My experience has been that, when someone is describing a breathable wall, they are not talking about air breathing; they are talking about how permeable the wall is to vapor. If the impact of vapor loss could be described in dollars and cents, people would start looking for ways to stop its random flow in and out of our houses.

Air tubes certainly do breath. They come in through the wall (or the floor). Air tubes make the house behave more human. We breath through our noses, just like my house breaths through its air tubes. If I asked you to plug your nose and breath through your skin, you would be dead in about 10 minutes. Why should we ask our houses to do the same? Our "human" skin has all kinds of marvelous vapor barriers that can open and close to keep us from drying out or getting too hot. The walls of our house should be designed likewise, to keep us comfortable in the most efficient and sustainable way.

My system works. I have been watching the tube air temperature for two years now and have some data. My lowest tube air temperature this last winter was 38.4 degrees. Last summer the highest temperature was 73.6 degrees. The air tube temperature only reached those extremes when the outside temps were excessive. The average soil temp in this part of the country is 53 degrees, and my air tube temps also averaged out about the same. The deeper in the soil the tubes are buried, the fewer fluctuations in temperature they experience. As I said, at 8 feet deep the soil temp will vary 12 degrees either side of average (41 in the winter to 65 in the summer). The tube air has followed that temperature shift.

So far there is no problem with mold or radon in my system. I tested my system for radon and the results indicated the air tube air was the same as outside air.

As I explained, 90 percent of the air tube design and installation is to insure that the tubes are drained properly. As a result there are no mold problems.

I hope this article has been helpful. It is my intent to arrive at a solution we can all live with for a very long time. If you have any questions or additional information or counter-arguments, please respond to me via email at lsquared@kdsi.net or call me directly at 641-472-4953. I am open-minded and willing to learn more. I am sure there are many things I have to learn. We start by joining the conversation.

Applying Earth Tube Technology to Greenhouse Produce Production in the Midwest

By Dean Goodale, Goodale Family Farms, Jefferson County, Iowa

> "Since greenhouse production is so intensive, a small family farmer could make more on an acre of greenhouse than they could on several hundred acres of row crops."
>
> —Dean Goodale

I have grown organic produce as a market gardener in southeast Iowa for the past five years. Three years ago, I added 4,000 square feet of heated greenhouse space to my operation. I used standard greenhouse heaters that burn propane and had heat and exhaust fans thermostatically automated. I have grown tomatoes, peppers, and various greens throughout the winter months. One crop of tomatoes produced for close to two years. I also grew greenhouse basil, gourmet lettuce mixes, chard, spinach, cut flowers, cilantro, and sugar snap peas.

My best crops could produce up to $1 a square foot per month during peak production. I was able to sell all my produce direct to a retail grocery store. The difference in price I received over my out-of-state competition that sold to wholesalers allowed me enough margin to make a decent profit. Then came the winter of 2000-2001. Our area had very little sun in the fall, followed by a long cold winter and astronomical propane prices. To top it off, Mexican tomatoes flooded the market and held the price at half of what it was in years past.

Even under these conditions, I was still getting by. I wanted to at least double my square footage in order to increase production, but the thought of paying double the amount for heat held me back. So I started looking for alternative methods to heat greenhouses. I found that there are many alternatives. The most effective, least labor-intensive, and lowest-cost method I discovered was an experimental residential home heating technology called "earth tubes." I decided to use this low-tech technology in a greenhouse application.

In residential housing, earth tubes are used for both heating and cooling. The general principle is to bury a 6- or 8-inch drain tile 6 to 8 feet deep in the ground, with an intake 100 feet away from the structure and the output tube inside the structure. The air traveling through the tube over a long enough distance will assume close to the ambient temperature of the ground at a depth of 6 to 8 feet. In Iowa, the temperature at this depth is in the mid-50s. This air is piped into the house and supplemental heating sources are needed only to warm the air from about 55 degrees to the desired indoor temperature. This obviously is much less costly than heating the house from below 0 to the desired temperature. During summer months, the same system is used for cooling.

Greenhouse Application

Using earth tubes to heat and cool a greenhouse generally follows the residential housing model, with one major difference. Rather than placing the intake 100 feet from the structure, the entire system is contained within the greenhouse. The intake stands at one end of the structure with the trench running the length of the greenhouse, and the air outlet initiates from the opposite end from the intake. The air is directed to the growing beds via various ducting designs or allowed to create a general circular airflow inside the greenhouse.

In southeast Iowa, the frost line can go as deep as 30 or more inches in the dead of winter. When trenching across an open field for residential housing applications, the tubes have to be buried at 6 to 8 feet to ensure mid-50s ground temperature. In a greenhouse however, the required depth will be much less. My inflated double-poly greenhouse without heat in the dead of winter never had more than 1 inch of frozen ground. With an earth tube system and an emergency backup heater, the ground will never freeze, and a depth of 3 or 4 feet for the tubes is more than enough for maximum heat in winter.

So what does all this mean for a commercial greenhouse grower? Normal heating costs can be as much as 15 to 30 percent or more of operating costs any given year. If the earth tube technology can allow a grower to eliminate, or substantially reduce that cost, then a competitive advantage is created that could transform the agricultural landscape in cold climates around the world.

There is a working model of a system similar to the one I have described developed by Jerome Osentowski of the Central Rocky Mountain Permaculture Institute outside of Basalt, Colorado. He is located in climate zone 2, and he grows fig trees inside his structures heated by an earth tube system.

My plans are to build a 4,000-square-foot earth tube greenhouse prototype here in Iowa, zone 5, this summer (2002) and see how it does with my regular crops. I am especially interested to see whether the system will grow tomatoes without supplemental heat. If that is the case, there is no reason Iowa could not be competitive with any other part of this country, or Mexico, for winter tomato production or most any other greenhouse crop.

Rather than being the animal food (corn and soy) capital of the world, Iowa agriculture could produce fresh fruits and vegetables year-round for direct human consumption. Since greenhouse production is so intensive, a small family farmer could make more on an acre of greenhouse than they could on several hundred acres of row crops. Imagine reviving the family farm and creating a new agricultural industry while restoring hundreds of thousands of acres to prairie. This would begin the rebuilding of our topsoil, drastically reduce the toxic runoff into our streams and rivers, restore wildlife, stop the contamination of our groundwater and create an eco-tourist attraction like nothing anyone has seen for a hundred years!

Greenhouses require specialized knowledge and skills. The structures need to be built and maintained, irrigation systems need to be designed and run, computerized atmospheric controls need to be designed and managed, etc. Apprenticeship programs could be set up in our high schools, for school credit, to teach all these areas of expertise to students. They would graduate from high school with a greenhouse management certificate and have a highly paid job skill upon graduating. This might also reverse the trend of our population exodus and give our youth not just a reason to stay, but a totally optimistic and bright vision of possibilities for the future. This, in my opinion, is a worthy outlook for the future of agriculture in this great agricultural state of Iowa.

Yes, these ideas are quite a departure from the past, but Iowa's farmers have it tougher and tougher every year and the government's answer is to hand out money. That is not an answer, but an abomination to the dignity of farming, farmers, and taxpayers. Iowa agriculture is not going to improve by continuing to do the same things farmers have done in the past. It is not working economically or ecologically. I personally believe that genetically engineered crops are not the answer either. So far they have hurt farmers economically due to European refusal to buy GM crops. The environment has fared no better with the increased use of Roundup and the cross-contamination of conventional crops. I don't believe that the program I have outlined above is the total answer for the future of farming in Iowa. I do believe it could be a substantial part of the answer.

I believe the other parts of an economical and ecological answer to the future of agriculture in this state are all around us. What is needed more than anything at this point are people in power who are not owned by the existing corporate interests of the past, but leaders with vision who aren't afraid to speak the truth. We need people who will stand up to established institutions when they threaten the well-being of the populace or our natural resources. We especially need leaders who can recognize innovative solutions that are truly in the best interests of all the people in this state and all future generations of Iowans.

Abundance Eco-Village: Care of the Earth, Care of the People, Share the Surplus

By Lawrence A. Gamble, P.E., and Mark Olson, Ph.D.

Abundance Eco-Village is a housing development in Fairfield, Iowa, where energy, waste treatment, water, and food production are provided on site. Energy needs are met by solar and wind; water is supplied by rainwater catchment; wastes and nutrients are recycled and treated as resources; local forests provide building materials; the landscape is full of edible and useful plants; annual vegetable production and perennial fruit production are integrated into the project.

This [article] describes the organization, design, and initial stages of construction of the project. The project is under construction and will eventually consist of 21 single-family homes and three multifamily structures with three units in each.

Introduction

If you have an ethic for living your life that involves care of the earth, what can you do to live in harmony with this ethic in a conventional subdivision in the USA? Well, you can select the right brand of toilet paper, buy recycled paper for your printer, and separate your trash. You can agonize about buying the politically correct laundry and dish soap. And, in most places these days, you can choose paper or plastic. But where does your water come from, where does your electricity come from, where does your food come from, and how is it grown? What happens when you flush the toilet? Where do the building materials come from for the places you inhabit? In conventional subdivisions, the systems that provide these services are often grossly out of tune with an ethic that involves care of the earth.

Electricity is a good example. Despite all the publicity about "green electricity" programs by electric utilities, the fact remains that 95 to 99 percent of most utility energy and capacity requirements are met by fossil fuels (natural gas, coal, oil) or nuclear power.[1] Worse yet, the fuels are used in a thermodynamic cycle, delivered in a transmission system, and used in inefficient appliances that, in the case of electricity delivered to an incandescent light bulb, throws away 95 to 97 percent of the energy in the fuel as waste and delivers only 3 to 5 percent as useful light.[2] The practical choices available for most people in the U.S. mean that perhaps 95 percent of life is lived out-of-tune with an ethic for the earth. In addition, the money spent on these services goes to perpetuate their delivery. Often more money goes to produce undesirable side effects than the desired product or service, as demonstrated in the example for electricity above.

Abundance Eco-Village is an attempt to turn this ratio around and to take the money that people are already spending for energy, water, food, and housing and use it to provide services that are in tune with an ethic of care for the earth and are economic at the same time. (There is a pervasive idea in the USA that fostering the economy and care for the earth must be mutually exclusive goals. This idea is rapidly being shown to be false, and there are now many examples where the opposite is true.[3])

Project Overview and Organization

Abundance Eco-Village is located in Fairfield, Iowa. Fairfield is located in southeast Iowa in Jefferson County. It is located at 41 degrees north latitude, 92 degrees west longitude. Below are some statistics about the climate and site.

- Acres of land: 15 (6 hectares)

- Avg annual rainfall: 35 in (89 cm)

- Ann gal of rainfall: 15,000,000 gal (56,000,000 l)

- Heating degree-days: 6,000 (base 65 deg F)

- Cooling degree-days: 583 (base 65 deg F)

- Avg max summer temp: 84 deg F (28 deg C)

- Avg max summer humidity: 72%

- Avg minimum winter temperature: -13 deg C

- Avg last frost date in spring: May 10

- Avg first frost date in winter: Oct 10

The site is a 15-acre rectangle measuring 600 feet north to south and 1,200 feet east to west. Building lots are 4,900 square feet, with most of the rest of land dedicated to common amenities. Amenities include a common building, common greenhouse and garden space, ponds, orchards, vineyards, and a hostel. We are using Village Homes in Davis, California, as a model for the density, look, and feel of this project.[4]

The project has three individuals as partners, one of whom is a builder (his company is building the houses), one a licensed professional engineer, and the other a biologist. The project is organized as a corporation, which owns all the land and common facilities. Homeowners receive long-term (275 year) leases on their building lots.

Systems Design Overview

Solar- and wind-generated electricity, two qualities of water, and sewer services are provided to each lot. The project is broken down into blocks of six to eight homes, which we call a neighborhood. Each neighborhood has its own solar and wind generation, battery storage, and inverter. Each neighborhood has a 50,000-gallon underground tank for storing water from rooftops. This modular design allows utilities to be built as the project develops, rather than all at the beginning. Sewer and low-grade water systems are provided for the entire project rather than per neighborhood.

Agriculture is an important part of the project. Eighty-give percent of the food eaten in Iowa comes from somewhere else, and we feel that it is important from an environmental, economic, and cultural standpoint to grow food locally.[5] Useful and edible plants are widely planted. There is a common greenhouse space, and we are helping to establish two independent agriculture-related businesses by providing land and greenhouse space and a market for plants and food. The first business is a permaculture plant nursery for the Midwest; the second business is a market garden.

For home design, an integrated, high-performance design approach is being used. All the partners have attended Energy 10 training. All homes are heavily insulated, use the appropriate glazing for each façade, and use earth tubes to temper incoming air in summer and winter. Two houses have been built so far and another is under construction. We have the additional design constraint of Maharishi Sthapatya Ved, which is an ancient system for determining the orientation and placement of buildings that has been recently revived by Maharishi Mahesh Yogi.

Energy Use and Metering

A key element in making utilities affordable is to use energy and water wisely. This does not mean doing without services. Using energy wisely means careful attention to design and the efficiency of systems, technologies and appliances. Each home has a maximum monthly energy budget of 250 kWh, and we are designing each home to use about 100 kWH per month for lighting, refrigeration, electronics, appliances, and HVAC.[6]

The largest energy users are refrigeration, lighting, and HVAC. Energy use guidelines have been developed that help homeowners select appliances and systems for their homes. These guidelines recommend things like daylighting, high-efficiency compact fluorescent and LED lighting, laptop computers, horizontal axis washing machines, earth tube cooling and control of phantom loads. The net result is that the same or better services as used in a conventional home are delivered with one-forth to one-tenth of the energy use. We have also been careful in the design of the common water pumping and sewage systems, using the most efficient pump technology available and gravity feed solutions whenever possible.

Homes have energy and power metering for both the individual home and for each cluster, with a display in a prominent place in each home. In a situation like this, where energy systems are shared and some homeowners may be better educated and careful about energy consumption than others, there is always the possibility that someone will use more than their share of energy. We handle energy sharing like this: If monthly electric usage of each home in a neighborhood is within 10 percent of the other homes, then the costs for backup power (from a biodiesel-powered generator) are shared equally. Otherwise, the largest user pays for fuel that month. It is estimated that biodiesel fuel will cost $4 per gallon. We will also spend a lot of time with new families in the first few months as they learn about energy efficiency and the use of solar- and wind-generated electricity. Our experience with dozens of solar- and wind-powered homes in Fairfield over the last 10 years indicates that the biodiesel backup option will be required less than 3 percent of the year.

Energy Resources

Southeast Iowa has abundant solar and wind power resources, and the complementary nature of the two together provide a reliable power supply. The months that are not sunny are often windy... solar and wind power are complementary on short-term cycles as well. When a front comes through, it gets cloudy, but it also gets windy. At night, when there is never sun, any wind is a bonus. The developers have been involved with the installation of dozens of solar- and wind-powered homes in the area over the last 10 years, and two of us have been living with solar and wind power in Fairfield for nine years. Our experience backs up the data, indicating that a combination of solar and wind power provides a very reliable energy source in this area.

Each neighborhood (six to eight homes) will have a 4 kW PV array, a 7.5 kW, 23-foot-diameter wind generator[7] on a 100-foot tilt down tower, and 100 kWh of lead acid battery storage, a 5600-watt sine wave inverter, and an 8kw biodiesel backup generator.

The Iowa Energy Center has an online modeling program that has a typical year of wind statistics and the energy output profiles of various wind turbines.[8] The Iowa Energy Center also has a program for modeling the energy output of a PV array. Tom Factor, who is located in Fairfield, developed both of these tools. The average annual kWh production per kW of peak PV capacity is 1,534 kWh per square foot (16,567 kWh per square meter). The average annual kWh production per square foot of wind generator blade swept area is 59.4 (641.52 kWh per square meter)[9].

We have also done modeling using the TMY data and data from other sources.

Water

Two sources of pressurized water are delivered to each home. The first comes from the rain catchment tanks and is filtered and treated with UV light. The second is from ponds. The rain catchment water is higher quality and suitable for bathing and washing. The filtered pond water is suitable for uses like flushing toilets and watering plants. Further purification of rain catchment water for human consumption is up to the homeowner and could include filtering, reverse osmosis and further UV treatment.[10] Water is pumped using the highest-efficiency pumps we could find (positive displacement pumps).

Waste and Nutrient Cycling

Black- and greywater are separated at each house. Greywater can be used at the lot or can be sent to a greywater processing system that serves the whole project. Blackwater is sent to a methane digester, which provides a first stage of treatment, reduces the volume of material, and generates biogas (methane). The liquid portion of the material that exits the

digester is fed into a constructed wetland, and the solid portion is dried and buried in a timber tree area every few
months. The methane digester was designed and construction
supervised by Al Rutan, our biogas consultant.

This continuous process digester will process the waste from
the first eight to 10 homes. For optimum gas production, the
digester needs to stay above 90 degrees F year-round. Very little heat leaves the tank, and we only have to supply the losses
from the tank to its environment and any energy required to
heat material coming into the digester. Our design solution is
to use high insulation around the tank, a water bath that is
heated by active solar, and a unique solar building. Rutan has
designed a greenhouse that uses movable insulation and glazing for climate control, utilizing garage door track
technology. We are building a prototype under his direction
to house the digester.

Agriculture

Agriculture and food production are an integral part of
Abundance Eco-Village. For the initial phases of construction, we have installed 4,000 square feet of greenhouse and
have collected several thousand edible and useful plants
from similar climates around the world. We are giving this
collection and greenhouse space to someone as an entice-
ment to start a nursery business at the eco-village. We are
also giving land and greenhouse space to someone to start
an annual vegetable market garden. Our initial collection
will be propagated out to tens of thousands of edible and
useful plants, which will be planted throughout the ecovil-
lage. We have had some of the top permaculture designers
in the U.S. working with us on selecting species, plant guild
establishment strategies, and land water flow and storage

structures (ponds and swales).[11] Our model for the density of planting and the emphasis on edible and useful plants is Village Homes in Davis, California.[12] Iowa has one of the greatest diversities of native fruit and nut trees in North America. We can use the best selections and named varieties of these plants, augmented by seedling varieties, with undesirable seedlings removed in later years.

Space does not permit a complete list as we have over 400 varieties of perennial trees, shrubs, vines, and herbaceous plants, all of which are edible or medicinal, and most of which have beautiful flowers, foliage, and fragrance. See the web site for a complete list (www.abundance-ecovillage.com).

House Design

House design at the eco-village is a team effort made up of the following: the homeowner and his/her designer/architect; the builder (one of the eco-village partners is the builder for the project); the HVAC, plumbing, and electrical contractors; plus other consultants in geothermal, passive solar design, and daylighting. The homes have a maximum monthly electrical energy budget of 250 kwh, about one-fourth the national average, and it is important that the heating and cooling systems do not require lots of electrical energy at the worst times of the year (cold windless nights preceded by a cloudy windless day, for example). Energy 10 software is used to model home performance. We take an integrated approach that starts on the first day of design, as advocated in the Energy 10 design manual.

Cooling provides a special challenge for off-grid homes in our climate. We sometimes get weeks of temperatures with highs near 100 degrees and fairly high humidity. The compressor-driven expansion-type systems we looked at took too much energy (with the exception of very small room-sized units) and for most of the year it is too humid to permit effective use of direct evaporative cooling. We found someone with extensive experience in earth tubes for cooling in humid climates (200 homes in Michigan and Texas) and we have built earth tube systems into the first three homes.[13] The earth tube systems only require a small fan (25 to 50 watts) to provide cooling and dehumidification in summer or fresh air tempering in winter.

[1]   As of 2001, 98 percent of the electricity used in the Midwest is generated from fossil fuels and nuclear power: *Repowering the Midwest*, page 7, Energy Law and Policy Center, 35 East Wacker Drive, Suite 1300, Chicago, IL 60601-2110. www.repowermidwest/org

[2]   The breakdown is as follows: for every 100 units of energy in the fuel delivered to the plant, 60 to 70 units are wasted at the plant because of the third law of thermodynamics, 10 to 15 units are wasted in transmission and distribution to get the energy to its point of use, and, in the case of an incandescent light bulb, 90 percent of the energy delivered to the bulb is turned into waste heat and 10 percent is then delivered as useful light.

[3]   For examples, see Hawken, P, Lovins, A, and Lovins, LH, *Natural Capitalism*, and Bell, Jim *Eco-nomic Security on Spaceship Earth*. www.natcap.org/ and www.jimbell.com/

[4]   Village Homes was designed by Michael and Judy Corbett and built in 1975-1979. See video tour in the film *Global Gardener*, and Corbett, J and Corbett, M, *Designing Sustainable Communities: Learning from Village Homes*, Island Press, 2000. www.context.org/ICLIB/IC35/Browning.htm

[5]   See Wendell Berry, *The Gift of Good Land*, North Point Press, San Francisco, 1981. www.alteich.com/links/berry.htm

[6]   Roughly one-fourth the energy used by a conventional grid connected home.

[7]   Manufactured by Bergey, Model Excel R 7.5 kW, 23-foot rotor diameter. www.bergey.com/

[8]   Derived from Iowa Energy Center we bsite data.

[9]   www.energy.iastate.edu

[10] There are a lot of different opinions on final stage treatment, each having its advocates and detractors. We chose to let the homeowner decide on his/her favorite method and install and maintain it. Most people in Fairfield are already using some type of home water treatment for city water and are familiar with the options.

[11] Douglas Bullock, Jerome Ostentowski, and Bruce Hill. www.permaculture-portal.com and www.crmpi.org/

[12] See films *The Global Gardener* and *Ecological Designers*, and the book, *Designing Sustainable Communities: Lessons Learned From Village Homes*, by Michael and Judy Corbett. www.bullfrogfilms.com/catalog/tgghv.html

[13] Larry Larson, Fairfield, Iowa.

Article excerpts from a presentation at the Solar 2002 Conference by Lawrence Gamble and Mark Olson. Used with permission.

Creating Community Economics with Local Currency

By Paul Glover

Here in Ithaca, New York, we've begun to gain control of the social and environmental effects of commerce by issuing over $85,000 of our own local paper money, to thousands of residents, since 1991. Tens of thousands of purchases and many new friendships have been made with this cash, and millions of dollars value of local trading has been added to the Grassroots National Product.

We printed our own money because we watched federal dollars come to town, shake a few hands, then leave to buy rain-forest lumber and fight wars. Ithaca's HOURS, by contrast, stay in our region and help us hire each other. While dollars make us increasingly dependent on transnational corporations and bankers, HOURS reinforce community trading and expand commerce which is more accountable to our concerns for ecology and social justice.

Here's how it works: the Ithaca HOUR is Ithaca's $10 bill, because 10 dollars per hour is the average of wages/salaries in Tompkins County. These HOUR notes, in five denominations, buy plumbing, carpentry, electrical work, roofing, nursing, chiropractic, child care, car and bike repair, food, eyeglasses, firewood, gifts, and thousands of other goods and services. Our credit union accepts them for mortgage and loan fees. People pay rent with HOURS. The best restaurants in town take them, as do movie theaters, bowling alleys, two large locally owned grocery stores, our local hospital, many garage sales, 55 farmer's market vendors, the Chamber of Commerce, and 300 other businesses. Hundreds more have earned and spent HOURS who are not in the HOUR Town directory.

Ithaca's new HOURly minimum wage lifts the lowest paid up without knocking down higher wages. For example, several of Ithaca's organic farmers are paying the highest common farm labor wages in the world: $10 of spending power per HOUR. These farmers benefit by the HOUR's loyalty to local agriculture. On the other hand, dentists, massage therapists and lawyers charging more than the $10 average per hour are permitted to collect several HOURS hourly.

But we hear increasingly of professional services provided for our equitable wage.

Everyone who agrees to accept HOURS is paid one HOUR ($10) or two HOURS ($20) for being listed in the HOUR Town directory. Every eight months they may apply to be paid an additional HOUR, as a reward for continuing participation. This is how we gradually and carefully increase the per capita supply of our money. Once issued, anyone may earn and spend HOURS, whether signed up or not, and hundreds have done so.

HOUR Town's 1,500 listings, rivaling the Yellow Pages, are a portrait of our community's capability, bringing into the marketplace time and skills not employed by the conventional market. Residents are proud of income gained by doing work they enjoy. We encounter each other as fellow Ithacans, rather than as winners and losers scrambling for dollars.

The Success Stories of 300 participants published so far testify to the acts of generosity and community that our system prompts. We're making a community while making a living.

As we do so, we relieve the social desperation which has led to compulsive shopping and wasted resources.

At the same time Ithaca's locally owned stores, which keep more wealth local, make sales and get spending power they otherwise would not have. And over $10,000 of local currency has been donated to 60 community organizations so far, by the Barter Potluck, our wide-open governing body.

As we discover new ways to provide for each other, we replace dependence on imports. Yet our greater self-reliance, rather than isolating Ithaca, gives us more potential to reach outward with ecological export industry. We can capitalize new businesses with loans of our own cash. HOUR loans are made without interest charges.

We regard Ithaca's HOURS as real money, backed by real people, real time, real skills and tools. Dollars, by contrast, are funny money, backed no longer by gold or silver but by less than nothing—$5.5 trillion of national debt.

Ithaca's money honors the local features we respect, like native flowers, powerful waterfalls, crafts, farms and our children. Our commemorative HOUR is the first paper money in the U.S. to honor an African-American.

Multicolored HOURS—some printed on locally made watermarked cattail (marsh reed) paper, or handmade hemp paper; some with non-Xeroxable thermal ink, all with serial numbers—are harder to counterfeit than dollars.

Local currency is a lot of fun, and it's legal. HOURS are taxable income when traded for professional goods or services.

Local currency is also lots of work and responsibility. To give other communities a boost, we've been providing a Hometown Money Starter Kit.

The Kit explains the step-by-step start-up and maintenance of an HOURS system, and includes forms, laws, articles, procedures, insights, samples of Ithaca's HOURS, and issues of Ithaca Money. We've sent the Kit to over 1,000 communities in 49 states and beyond, and our example has become international.

Ithaca HOUR Fact Sheet

- Since 1991, we've issued over $85,000 of Ithaca HOURS (6,500 HOURS at $10 per HOUR). Five denominations: 2 HRS, 1 HR, 1/2 HR, 1/4 HR, 1/8 HR. Includes a commemorative HOUR, the first paper money in the U.S. to honor an African-American.

- Thousands of people, including 400 businesses, have earned and spent HOURS.

- They have made trades with HOURS valued at millions of dollars, representing hundreds of job-equivalents at $20,000 each.

- HOURS are thus real money—local tender rather than legal tender, backed by real people, real labor, skills and tools.

- Most HOURS have been issued as payments to those who agree to be published backers of HOURS, listed in our bimonthly directory HOUR Town. Every eight months they may send the coupon again to receive a bonus payment—which gradually and carefully increases the HOUR supply.

- 11 percent of HOURS are issued as grants to community organizations. Sixty nonprofits have received grants totaling over 1,000 HOURS ($10,000) since we began.

- 5 percent of HOURS may be issued to the system itself, primarily for paying for printing HOURS.

- Loans of HOURS are made with NO INTEREST CHARGED. These range $50 to $30,000 value.

- HOURS are legal. Professor Lewis Solomon of George Washington University has written a book titled *Rethinking Our Centralized Monetary System: The Case for a System of Local Currencies* (Praeger, 1996) which is an extensive case law study of the legality of local currency. IRS and FED officials have been contacted by media, and repeatedly have said there is no prohibition of local currency, as long as it does not look like dollars, as long as denominations are at least $1 value, and it is regarded as taxable income.

- HOURS are protected against counterfeit. They are multicolored, with serial numbers. The 1995 Quarter HOUR and 1997 Eighth HOUR use thermal ink, invented in Ithaca, which disappears briefly when touched or photocopied. The 1993 Two HOUR note is printed on locally made watermarked 100 percent cattail paper, with matching serial numbers front and back. The 1996 Half HOUR is 100 percent handmade hemp paper. Our District Attorney has declared HOURS a financial instrument, protected by law from counterfeit.

Benefits

- HOURS expand the local money supply

- HOURS promote and expand local shopping, with an endless multiplier

- HOURS double the local minimum wage to $10, benefiting not only workers but businesses as well, who find new and loyal customers.

- HOURS enable shoppers to afford premium prices for locally crafted goods and for locally grown organic food.

- HOURS help start new businesses and jobs

- HOURS reduce dependence on imports and transport fuels

- HOURS make grants to nonprofit community organizations

- HOURS make zero-interest loans

- HOURS stimulate community pride

Long-range Plans

We have started an Ithaca Health Fund: nonprofit, locally controlled health financing, with HOURS as part of premium payment: http://www.lightlink.com/healthfund.

We intend to open a community economic development center called HOUR Town. We'd look forward to being able to provide major funding to community organizations and new business start-ups. We could fund municipal projects like weatherization, transit, and so on. We could purchase land to be retained in farms.

To get the Starter Kit, send $25 (or 2.5 HOURS) or $35 U.S. from abroad (international postal money order), to HOUR Town, Box 6578, Ithaca, NY, 14851.

Our English-language video (17 minutes) is available for $17, or $15 with the Kit ($40 for Kit and video). Spanish-language video (10 minutes) is available with Kit for $12. Credit cards accepted. Call (607) 272-4330 or paglo@lightlink.com. Maximum 1/4 HOUR (any community) accepted.

Reprinted with permission. See www.ithacahours.com for more information.

Billions for Bankers—Debts for the People

by Pastor Sheldon Emry

Introduction

In 1901 the national debt of the United States was less than $1 billion. It stayed at less than $1 billion until we got into World War I. Then it jumped to $25 billion.

The national debt nearly doubled between World War I and World War II, increasing from $25 to $49 billion.

Between 1942 and 1952, the debt zoomed from $72 billion to $265 billion. In 1962 it was $303 billion. By 1970, the debt had increased to $383 billion.

Between 1971 and 1976 it rose from $409 billion to $631 billion. The debt experienced its greatest growth, however, during the 1980s, fueled by an unprecedented peacetime military buildup. In 1998, the outstanding public debt will roar past $5.5 trillion.

The unconstitutional "share" of this debt for every man, woman and child is currently $20,594.86 and will continue to increase an average of $630 million every day, which does not include the $26 trillion in individual credit card debts, mortgages, automobile leases and so on.

U.S. National Debt

The Outstanding Public Debt as of 08/25/98 at 10:28:37 AM PDT is: $5,516,699,306,752.93 The estimated population of the United States is 270,374,697, so each citizen's share of this debt is $20,403.90.

Today, as we stand before the dawn of a New World Order run by internationalist financiers, most of the revenue collected by the federal government in the form of individual income taxes will go straight to paying the interest on the debt alone. At the rate the debt is increasing, eventually we'll reach a point where, even if the government takes every penny of its citizens' income via taxation, it will still not collect enough to keep up with the interest payments.

The government will own nothing, the people will own nothing, and the banks will own everything. The New World Order will foreclose on America.

If the present trend continues, and there is no evidence whatsoever that it will not continue, we can expect the national debt to nearly double again within the next six to eight years. By then, the interest on the debt alone should be in the $400 billion a year range.

Prologue: Three Types of Conquest

History reveals nations can be conquered by the use of one or more of three methods.

The most common is conquest by war. In time, though, this method usually fails, because the captives hate the captors and rise up and drive them out if they can. Much force is needed to maintain control, making it expensive for the conquering nation.

A second method is by religion, where men are convinced they must give their captors part of their earnings as "obedience to God." Such a captivity is vulnerable to philosophical exposure or by overthrow by armed force, since religion by its nature lacks military force to regain control, once its captives become disillusioned.

The third method can be called economic conquest. It takes place when nations are placed under "tribute" without the use of visible force or coercion, so that the victims do not realize they have been conquered.

"Tribute" is collected from them in the form of "legal" debts and taxes, and they believe they are paying it for their own good, for the good of others, or to protect all from some enemy. Their captors become their "benefactors" and "protectors."

Although this is the slowest to impose, it is often quite long-lasting, as the captives do not see any military force arrayed against them, their religion is left more or less intact, they have freedom to speak and travel, and they participate in "elections" for their rulers. Without realizing it, they are conquered, and the instruments of their own society are used to transfer their wealth to their captors and make the conquest complete.

In 1900 the average American worker paid few taxes and had little debt. Last year, payments on debts and taxes took more than half of what he earned. Is it possible a form of conquest has been imposed on America? Read the following pages and decide for yourself. And may God have mercy on this once debt-free and great nation.

The Real Story of Money Control in America

Americans, living in what is called the richest nation on earth, seem always to be short of money. It's impossible for many families to make ends meet unless both parents are in the workforce.

Men and women hope for overtime hours or take part-time jobs evenings and weekends; children look for odd jobs for spending money; the family debt climbs higher.

Psychologists say one of the biggest causes of family quarrels and breakups is "arguing over money." Much of this trouble can be traced to our present "debt-money" system.

Too few Americans realize why the Founders wrote into Article I of the U. S. Constitution: "Congress shall have the power to coin money and regulate the value thereof." (Thomas Jefferson)

They did this, as we will show, in the hope that it would prevent "love of money" from destroying the Republic they had founded. We shall see how subversion of Article I has brought on us the "evil" of which God warns us in 1 Timothy 6:10.

Money is "Created," Not Grown or Built

Economists use the term "create" when speaking of the process by which money comes into existence. "Creation" means making something which did not exist before. Lumber workers make boards from trees, workers build houses from lumber, and factories manufacture automobiles from metal, glass and other materials. But in all these they did not actually "create."

They only changed existing materials into a more usable and, therefore, more valuable form. This is not so with money. Here, and here alone, man actually "creates" something out of nothing. A piece of paper of little value is printed so that it is worth a piece of lumber. With different figures it can buy the automobile or even the house. It's value has been "created" in the truest sense of the word.

"Creating" money is very profitable!

As is seen by the above, money is very cheap to make, and whoever does the "creating" of money in a nation can make a tremendous profit. Builders work hard to make a profit of 5 percent above their cost to build a house.

Auto makers sell their cars for 1 percent to 2 percent above the cost of manufacture and it is considered good business. But money "manufactures" have no limit on their profits, since a few cents will print a $1 bill or a $10,000 bill.

That profit is part of our story, but first let consider another unique characteristic of the thing — money, the love of which is the "root of all evil."

Adequate Money Supply Needed

An adequate supply of money is indispensable to civilized society. We could forgo many other things, but without money industry would grind to a halt, farms would become only self-sustaining units, surplus food would disappear, jobs requiring the work of more than one man or one family would remain undone, shipping and large movement of goods would cease, hungry people would plunder and kill to remain alive, and all government except family or tribe would cease to function.

An overstatement, you say? Not at all. Money is the blood of civilized society, the means of all commercial trade except simple barter. It is the measure and the instrument by which one product is sold and another purchased. Remove money or even reduce the supply below that which is necessary to carry on current levels of trade, and the results are catastrophic.

For an example, we need only look at America's Depression of the early 1930's.

Bankers' Depression of the 1930's

In 1930 America did not lack industrial capacity, fertile farmlands, skilled and willing workers or industrious families. It had an extensive and efficient transportation system in railroads, road networks, and inland and ocean waterways. Communications between regions and localities were the best in the world, utilizing telephone, teletype, radio, and a well-operated government mail system.

No war had ravaged the cities or the countryside, no pestilence weakened the population, nor had famine stalked the land. The United States of America in 1930 lacked only one thing: an adequate supply of money to carry on trade and commerce.

In the early 1930s, bankers, the only source of new money and credit, deliberately refused loans to industries, stores and farms. Payments on existing loans were required however, and money rapidly disappeared from circulation. Goods were available to be purchased, jobs waiting to be done, but the lack of money brought the nation to a standstill.

By this simple ploy America was put in a "depression" and bankers took possession of hundreds of thousands of farms, homes, and business properties. The people were told, "times are hard" and "money is short." Not understanding the system, they were cruelly robbed of their earnings, their savings, and their property.

No Money for Peace, but Plenty for War

World War II ended the "depression." The same Bankers who in the early 1930's had no loans for peacetime houses, food and clothing, suddenly had unlimited billions to lend for army barracks, K-rations and uniforms.

A nation that in 1934 could not produce food for sale, suddenly could produce bombs to send free to Germany and Japan! (More on this riddle later.)

With the sudden increase in money, people were hired, farms sold their produce, factories went to two shifts, mines reopened, and "The Great Depression" was over!

Some politicians were blamed for it and others took credit for ending it. The truth is the lack of money (caused by bankers) brought on the depression, and adequate money ended it. The people were never told that simple truth and in this article we will endeavor to show how these same bankers who control our money and credit have used their control to plunder America and place us in bondage.

Power to Coin and Regulate Money

When we can see the disastrous results of an artificially created shortage of money, we can better understand why our Founding Fathers, who understood both money and God's Laws, insisted on placing the power to "create" money and the power to control it ONLY in the hands of the Federal Congress.

They believed that ALL Citizens should share in the profits of its "creation" and therefore the Federal government must be the only creator of money. They further believed that all citizens, of whatever state, territory or station in life, would benefit by an adequate and stable currency. Therefore, the Federal government must also be, by law, the only controller of the value of money.

Since the Federal Congress was the only legislative body subject to all the citizens at the ballot box, it was, to their minds, the only safe depository of so much profit and so much power. They wrote it out in a simple, but all-inclusive manner: "Congress shall have the power to Coin Money and Regulate the Value Thereof."

How We Lost Control of the Federal Reserve

Instead of the Constitutional method of creating our money and putting it into circulation, we now have an entirely unconstitutional system. This has brought our country to the brink of disaster, as we shall see.

Since our money was handled both legally and illegally before 1913, we shall consider only the years following 1913, since from that year on, all of our money had been created and issued by an illegal method that will eventually destroy the United States if it is not changed. Prior to 1913, America was a prosperous, powerful, and growing nation, at peace with its neighbors and the envy of the world. But in December of 1913, Congress, with many members away for the Christmas Holidays, passed what has since been known as the Federal Reserve Act. (For the full story of how this infamous legislation was forced through our Congress, read *Conquest or Consent*, by W. D. Vennard.)

Omitting the burdensome details, it simply authorized the establishment of a Federal Reserve Corporation, run by a Board of Directors (The Federal Reserve Board). The act divided the United States into 12 Federal Reserve "Districts."

This simple, but terrible, law completely removed from Congress the right to "create" money or to have any control over its "creation," and gave that function to the Federal Reserve Corporation. It was accompanied by the appropriate fanfare. The propaganda claimed that this would "remove money from politics" (they did not say "and therefore from the people's control") and prevent "boom and bust" economic activity from hurting our citizens.

The people were not told then, and most still do not know today, that the Federal Reserve Corporation is a private corporation controlled by bankers and therefore is operated for the financial gain of the bankers over the people rather than for the good of the people. The word "Federal" was used only to deceive the people.

More Disastrous than Pearl Harbor

Since that "day of infamy," more disastrous to us than Pearl Harbor, the small group of "privileged" people who lend us "our" money have accrued to themselves all of the profits of printing our money — and more! Since 1913 they have "created" tens of billions of dollars in money and credit, which, as their own personal property, they can lend to our government and our people at interest (usury).

"The rich get richer and the poor get poorer" had become the secret policy of the federal government. An example of the process of "creation" and its conversion to peoples "debt" will aid our understanding.

Billions in Interest Owed to Private Banks

We shall start with the need for money. The federal government, having spent more than it has taken from its citizens in taxes, needs, for the sake of illustration, $1,000,000,000. Since it does not have the money, and Congress has given away its authority to "create" it, the government must go to the "creators" for the $1 billion.

But, the Federal Reserve, a private corporation, does not just give its money away! The bankers are willing to deliver $1,000,000,000 in money or credit to the federal government in exchange for the government's agreement to pay it back— with interest. So Congress authorizes the Treasury Department to print $1,000,000,000 in U.S. Bonds, which are then delivered to the Federal Reserve bankers.

The Federal Reserve then pays the cost of printing the $1 billion (about $1,000) and makes the exchange. The government then uses the money to pay its obligations. What are the results of this fantastic transaction? Well, $1 billion in government bills are paid all right, but the government has now indebted the people to the bankers for $1 billion on which the people must pay interest!

Tens of thousands of such transactions have taken place since 1913, so that in 1996, the U.S. government is indebted to the bankers for more than $5,000,000,000,000 (trillion). Most of the income taxes that we pay as individuals now goes straight into the hands of the bankers, just to pay off the interest alone, with no hope of ever paying off the principle. Our children will be forced into servitude.

But wait! There's more!

You say, "This is terrible!" Yes, it is, but we have shown only part of the sordid story. Under this unholy system, those United States Bonds have now become "assets" of the banks in the Reserve System which they then use as "reserves" to "create" more "credit" to lend. Current "reserve" requirements allow them to use that $1 billion in bonds to "create" as much as $15 billion in new "credit" to lend to states, municipalities, to individuals and businesses.

Added to the original $1 billion, they could have $16 billion of "created credit" out in loans paying them interest, with their only cost being $1,000 for printing the original $1 billion! Since the U.S. Congress has not issued Constitutional money since 1863 (more than 100 years), in order for the people to have money to carry on trade and commerce they are forced to borrow the "created credit" of the Monopoly bankers and pay them usury-interest!

Manipulating Stocks for Fun and Profit

In addition to almost unlimited usury, the bankers have another method of drawing vast amounts of wealth. The banks who control the money at the top are able to approve or disapprove large loans to large and successful corporations to the extent that refusal of a loan will bring about a reduction in the selling price of the corporation's stock.

After depressing the price, the bankers' agents buy large blocks of the company's stock. Then, if the bank suddenly approves a multimillion dollar loan to the company, the stock rises and is then sold for a profit. In this manner, billions of dollars are made with which to buy more stock. This practice is so refined today that the Federal Reserve Board need only announce to the newspapers an increase or decrease in their "discount rate" to send stocks soaring or crashing at their whim.

Using this method since 1913, the bankers and their agents have purchased secret or open control of almost every large corporation in America. Using this leverage, they then force the corporations to borrow huge sums from their banks so that corporate earnings are siphoned off in the form of interest to the banks. This leaves little as actual "profits" which can be paid as dividends and explains why banks can reap billions in interest from corporate loans even when stock prices are depressed. In effect, the bankers get a huge chunk of the profits, while individual stockholders are left holding the bag.

The millions of working families of America are now indebted to the few thousand banking families for twice the assessed value of the entire United States. And these Banking families obtained that debt against us for the cost of paper, ink, and bookkeeping!

The Interest Amount Is Never Created

The only way new money (which is not true money, but rather credit representing a debt), goes into circulation in

America is when it is borrowed from the bankers. When the State and people borrow large sums, we seem to prosper. However, the bankers "create" only the amount of the principal of each loan, never the extra amount needed to pay the interest. Therefore, the new money never equals the new debt added. The amounts needed to pay the interest on loans is not "created," and therefore does not exist!

Under this system, where new debt always exceeds new money no matter how much or how little is borrowed, the total debt increasingly outstrips the amount of money available to pay the debt. The people can never, ever get out of debt!

The following example will show the viciousness of this interest-debt system via its "built in" shortage of money.

The Tyranny of Compound Interest

When a citizen goes to a banker to borrow $100,000 to purchase a home or a farm, the bank clerk has the borrower agree to pay back the loan plus interest. At 8.25% interest for 30 years, the borrower must agree to pay $751.27 per month for a total of $270,456.00.

The clerk then requires the citizen to assign to the banker the right of ownership of the property if the borrower does not make the required payments. The bank clerk then gives the borrower a $100,000 check or a $100,000 deposit slip, crediting the borrower's checking account with $100,000.

The borrower then writes checks to the builder, subcontractors, etc. who in turn write checks. $100,000 of new "checkbook" money is thereby added to the "money in circulation."

However, this is the fatal flaw in the system: the only new money created and put into circulation is the amount of the loan, $100,000. The money to pay the interest is NOT created, and therefore was NOT added to "money in circulation."

Even so, this borrower (and those who follow him in ownership of the property) must earn and take out of circulation $270,456.00, $170,456.00 more than he put in circulation when he borrowed the original $100,000! (This interest cheats all families out of nicer homes. It is not that they cannot afford them; it is because the bankers' interest forces them to pay for nearly 3 homes to get one!)

Every new loan puts the same process in operation. Each borrower adds a small sum to the total money supply when he borrows, but the payments on the loan (because of interest) then deduct a much larger sum from the total money supply.

There is therefore no way all debtors can pay off the money lenders. As they pay the principle and interest, the money in circulation disappears. All they can do is struggle against each other, borrowing more and more from the money lenders each generation. The money lenders (bankers), who produce nothing of value, gradually gain a death grip on the land, buildings, and present and future earnings of the whole working population. Proverbs 22:7 has come to pass in America. "The rich ruleth over the poor, and the borrower is servant to the lender."

Small Loans Do the Same Thing

If you have not quite grasped the impact of the above, let us consider an auto loan for 5 years at 9.5% interest. Step 1: Citizen borrows $25,000 and pays it into circulation (it goes to the dealer, factory, miner, etc.) and signs a note agreeing to pay the Bankers a total of $31,503 over 5 years. Step 2: Citizen pays $525.05 per month of his earnings to the Banker. In five years, he will remove from circulation $6,503 more than he put in circulation.

Every loan of banker "created" money (credit) causes the same thing to happen. Since this has happened millions of times since 1913 (and continues today), you can see why America has gone from a prosperous, debt-free nation to a debt-ridden nation where practically every home, farm and business is paying usury-tribute to the bankers.

Checking Up On Cash

In the millions of transactions made each year like those just discussed, little actual currency changes hands, nor is it necessary that it do so.

About 95 percent of all "cash" transactions in the U. S. are executed by check. Consider also that banks must only hold 10 percent of their deposits on site in cash at any given time. This means 90 percent of all deposits, though they may actually be held by the bank, are not present in the form of actual cash currency.

That leaves the banker relatively safe to "create" that so-called "loan" by writing the check or deposit slip not against actual money, but against your promise to pay it back! The cost to him is paper, ink and a few dollars of overhead for each transaction. It is "check kiting" on an enormous scale. The profits increase rapidly, year after year.

Our Own Debt is Spiraling into Infinity

In 1910 the U. S. Federal debt was only $1 billion, or $12.40 per citizen. State and local debts were practically non-existent.

By 1920, after only six years of Federal Reserve shenanigans, the Federal debt had jumped to $24 billion, or $228 per person.

In 1960 the Federal debt reached $284 billion, or $1,575 per citizen and state and local debts were mushrooming.

In 1998 the Federal debt passed $5.5 trillion, or $20,403.90 per man, woman and child and is growing exponentially.

State and local debts are increasing as fast Federal debts. However, they are too cunning to take the title to everything at once. They instead leave us with some "illusion of ownership" so you and your children will continue to work and pay the bankers more of your earnings on ever increasing debts. The "establishment" has captured our people with their debt-money system as certainly as if they had marched in with an uniformed army.

Gambling Away the American Dream

To grasp the truth that periodic withdrawal of money through interest payments will inexorably transfer all wealth in the nation to the receiver of interest, imagine yourself in a poker or dice game where everyone must buy the chips (the medium of exchange) from a "banker" who does not risk chips in the game.

He just watches the table and reaches in every hour to take 10 percent to 15 percent of all the chips on the table. As the game goes on, the amount of chips in the possession of each player will fluctuate according to his luck.

However, the total number of chips available to play the game (carry on trade and business) will decrease steadily.

As the game starts getting low on chips, some players will run out. If they want to continue to play, they must buy or borrow more chips from the "banker". The "banker" will sell (lend) them only if the player signs a "mortgage" agreeing to give the "Banker" some real property (car, home, farm, business, etc.) if he cannot make periodic payments to pay back all the chips plus some extra chips (interest). The payments must be made on time, whether he wins (makes a profit) or not.

It is easy to see that no matter how skillfully they play, eventually the "banker" will end up with all of his original chips back, and except for the very best players, the rest, if they stay in long enough, will lose to the "banker" their homes, their farms, their businesses, perhaps even their cars, watches, and the shirts off their backs!

Our real life situation is much worse than any poker game. In a poker game no one is forced into debt, and anyone can quit at any time and keep whatever he still has. But in real life, even if we borrow little ourselves from the "bankers," our local, State and Federal governments borrow billions in our name, squander it, then confiscate our earnings via taxation in order to pay off the bankers with interest.

We are forced to play the game, and none can leave except by death. We pay as long as we live, and our children pay after we die. If we cannot or refuse to pay, the government sends the police to take our property and give it to the bankers. The bankers risk nothing in the game; they just collect their percentage and "win it all." In Las Vegas, all games are rigged to pay the owner a percentage, and they rake in millions. The Federal Reserve bankers' "game" is also rigged, and it pays off in billions!

In recent years, Bankers have added some new cards to their deck: credit cards are promoted as a convenience and a great boon to trade. Actually, they are ingenious devices from the seller and 18% interest from buyers. A real "stacked" deck!

Yes, It's Political Too

Democrat, Republican, and independent voters who have wondered why politicians always spend more tax money than they take in should now see the reason. When they begin to study our money system, they soon realize that these politicians are not the agents of the people but are the agents of the bankers, for whom they plan ways to place the people further in debt.

It takes only a little imagination to see that if Congress had been "creating," spending and issuing into circulation the necessary increase in the money supply, there would be no national debt. Trillions of dollars of other debts would be practically non-existent.

Since there would be no original cost of money except printing, and no continuing costs such as interest, Federal taxes would be almost nil. Money, once in circulation, would remain there and go on serving its purpose as a medium of exchange for generation after generation and century after century, with no payments to the Bankers whatsoever!

Continuing Cycles of Debt and War

But instead of peace and debt-free prosperity, we have ever-mounting debt and cyclical periods of war. We as a people are now ruled by a system of banking influence that has usurped the mantle of government, disguised itself as our legitimate government, and set about to pauperize and control our people.

It is now a centralized, all-powerful political apparatus whose main purposes are promoting war, confiscating the people's money, and propagandizing to perpetuate its power. Our two main political parties have become its servants, the various departments of government have become its spending agencies, and the Internal Revenue Service is its collection agency.

Unknown to the people, it operates in close cooperation with similar apparatuses in other nations, which are also disguised as "governments."

Some, we are told, are friends. Some, we are told, are enemies. "Enemies" are built up through international manipulations and used to frighten the American people into going billions of dollars further into debt to the bankers for "military preparedness," "foreign aid to stop communism," "the drug war," etc.

Citizens, deliberately confused by brainwashing propaganda, watch helplessly while our politicians give food, goods, and money to banker-controlled alien governments under the guise of "better relations" and "easing tensions." Our banker-controlled government takes our finest and bravest sons and sends them into foreign wars where tens of thousands are murdered, and hundreds of thousands are crippled (not to mention collateral damage and casualties among the "enemy" troops.)

When the "war" is over, we have gained nothing, but we are billions of dollars further in debt to the bankers, which was the reason for the "war" in the first place!

And There's More

The profits from these massive debts have been used to erect a complete and, almost hidden, economic colossus, over our nation. They keep telling us they are trying to do us good, when in truth they work to bring harm and injury to our people. These would be despots know, it is easier to control and rob an ill, poorly educated, and confused people, than it is a healthy and intelligent population, so they deliberately prevent real cures for diseases, they degrade our educational systems, and they stir up social and racial unrest. For the same reason, they favor drug use, alcohol, sexual promiscuity, abortion, pornography, and crime. Everything, which debilitates the minds and bodies of the people, is secretly encouraged, as it makes the people less able to oppose them, or, even, to understand what is being done to them.

Family, morals, love of country, the Christian religion, all that is honorable, is being swept away, while they try to build their new, subservient man. Our new "rulers" are trying to change our whole racial, social, religious, and political order, but they will not change the debt-money-economic system, by which they rob and rule. Our people have become tenants and "debt-slaves", to the Bankers, and their agents, in the land our fathers conquered. It is conquest through the most, gigantic fraud and swindle, in the history of mankind. And we remind you again: The key to their wealth and power, over us, is their ability to create "money" out of nothing, and lend it to us, at interest. If they had not been allowed to do that, they would never have gained secret control of our nation. How true Solomon's words are: "The rich ruleth over the poor, and the borrower is servant to the lender "(Proverbs 22:7).

God Almighty warned, in the Bible, that one of the curses, which would come upon His people, for disobeying His laws was: The stranger that is within thee shall get up above thee very high; and thou shall come down very low. He shall lend to thee, and thou shall not lend to him; he shall be the head, and thou shall be the tail. Deut. 28:44-45

Most of the owners of the large banks, in America, are of eastern-European ancestry, and connected with the Rothschild European banks. Has that warning come to fruition in America?

Let us, now, consider the correct method of providing the medium of exchange (money) needed by our people.

Every Citizen Can Be A Stock Holder in America

Under the Constitutional system, no private banks would exist to rob the people. Government banks under the control of the people's representatives would issue and control all money and credit. They would issue not only actual currency, but could lend limited credit at no interest for the purchase of capital goods, such as homes.

A $100,000 loan would require only $100,000 repayment, not $270,456.00 as it is now. Everyone who supplied materials and labor for the home would get paid just as they do today, but the bankers would not get $170,456.00 in interest.

That is why they ridicule and destroy anyone suggesting or proposing an alternative system.

History tells us of debt-free and interest-free money issued by governments.

The American colonies did it through colonial script in the 1700's. Their wealth soon rivaled that of England and brought restrictions from Parliament, which led to the Revolutionary War. Abraham Lincoln did it in 1863 to help finance the Civil War. He was later assassinated by a man many consider to have been an agent of the Rothschild Bank. No debt-free or interest-free money has been issued in America since then.

Several Arab nations issue interest free loans to their citizens today. (Now you can understand what all the commotion in the Middle East is all about, and why the banker-owned press is brainwashing American citizens to think of all Arabs as terrorists). The Saracen Empire forbade interest on money 1,000 years ago and its wealth outshone even Saxon Europe. Mandarin China issued its own money, interest-free and debt-free. Today, historians and art collectors consider those centuries to be China's time of greatest wealth, culture and peace.

Issuing money which does not have to be paid back in interest leaves the money available to use in the exchange of goods and services and its only continuing cost is replacement as the paper wears out. Money is the paperticket by which transfers are made and should always be in sufficient quantity to transfer all possible production of the nation to the ultimate consumers. It is as ridiculous for a nation to say to its citizens, "You must consume less because we are short of money," as it would be for an airline to say, "Our planes are flying, but we cannot take you because we are short of tickets".

Citizen Control of U.S. Currency

Money, issued in such a way, would derive its value in exchange from the fact that it had come from the highest legal source in the nation and would be declared legal to pay all public and private debts.

Issued by a sovereign nation, not in danger of collapse, it would need no gold or silver or other so-called "precious" metals to back it.

As history shows, the stability and responsibility of government issuing it is the deciding factor in the acceptance of that government's currency—not gold, silver, or iron buried in some hole in the ground. Proof is America's currency today. Our gold and silver is practically gone, but our currency is accepted. But if the government was about to collapse our currency would be worthless.

Under the present system, the extra burden of interest forces workers and businesses to demand more money for the work and goods to pay their ever increasing debts and taxes. This increase in prices and wages is called "inflation." Bankers, politicians and "economists" blame it on everything but the real cause, which is the interest levied on money and debt by the Bankers.

This "inflation" benefits the money-lenders, since it wipes out savings of one generation so they can not finance or help the next generation, who must then borrow from the money-lenders and pay a large part of their life's labor to the usurer.

With an adequate supply of interest-free money, little borrowing would be required and prices would be established by people and goods, not by debts and usury.

Citizen Control

If the Congress failed to act, or acted wrongly in the supply of money, the citizens would use the ballot or recall petitions to replace those who prevented correct action with others whom the people believe would pursue a better money policy. Since the creation of money and its issuance in sufficient quantity would be one of the few functions of Congress, the voter could decide on a candidate by his stand on money and other legitimate functions of the Federal government, instead of the diversionary issues which are presented to us today. All other problems, except the nation's defense, would be taken care of in the State, County, or City governments where they are best handled and most easily corrected.

An adequate national defense would be provided by the same citizen- controlled Congress, and there would be no bankers behind the scenes, bribing politicians to spend billions of dollars on overseas military adventures which ultimately serve the schemes of international finance.

Creating a Debt-Free America

With debt-free and interest-free money, there would be no direct confiscatory taxation and our homes would be mortgage-free without approximately $10,000-per-year payments to the bankers. Nor would they get $1000 to $3000 per year from every automobile on our roads.

We would need far fewer financial "help" in the form of "easy payment" plans, "revolving" charge accounts, loans to pay medical or hospital bills, loans to pay taxes, loans to pay for burials, loans to pay loans, nor any of the thousand and one usury bearing loans which now suck the life blood of American families.

Our officials, at all levels of government, would be working for the people instead of devising capers which will place us further in debt to the bankers. We would get out of entangling foreign alliances that have engulfed us in four major wars and scores of minor wars since the Federal Reserve Act was passed.

A debt-free America would leave parents with more time to spend raising their children. The elimination of the interest payments and debt would be the equivalent of a 50 percent raise in the purchasing power of every worker. This cancellation of interest-based private debts would result in the return to the people of $300 billion yearly in property and wealth that currently goes to banks.

Controlling Public Debate and Opinion

We realize that this small, and necessarily incomplete, article on money may be charged with oversimplification. Some may say that if it is that simple the people would have known about it, and it could not have happened.

But this conspiracy is as old as Babylon, and even in America it dates far back before the year 1913.

Actually, 1913 may be considered the year in which their previous plans came to fruition, opening the way for complete economic conquest of our people. The conspiracy is powerful enough in America to place its agents in positions as newspaper publishers, editors, columnists, church ministers, university presidents, professors, textbook writers, labor union leaders, filmmakers, radio and television commentators, politicians ranging from school board members to U.S. presidents, and many others.

These agents control the information available to our people. They manipulate public opinion, elect whomever they want locally and nationally, and never expose the crooked money system. They promote school bonds, expensive and detrimental farm programs, "urban renewal," foreign aid, and many other schemes which place the people more deeply in debt to the bankers.

Thoughtful citizens wonder why billions are spent on one program and billions on another which may duplicate it or even nullify it, such as paying some farmers not to raise crops, while at the same time building dams or canals to irrigate more farm land. Crazy or stupid?

Neither. The goal is more debt. Thousands of government-sponsored methods of wasting money go on continually. Most make no sense, but they are never exposed for what they really are: siphons sucking our Nation's economic lifeblood. Billions for the bankers, debts for the people.

Controlled News and Information

So-called "economic experts" write syndicated columns in hundreds of newspapers, craftily designed to prevent the people from learning the simple truth about our money system.

Sometimes commentators, educators, and politicians blame our financial conundrum on the workers for being wasteful, lazy, or stingy. Other times, they blame workers and consumers for the increase in debts and the inflation of prices, when they know the cause is the debt-money system itself.

Our people are literally drowned in charges and counter-charges designed to confuse them and keep them from understanding the unconstitutional and evil money system that is so efficiently and silently robbing the farmers, the workers, and the businessmen of the fruits of their labor and of their freedoms.

Some, who are especially vocal in their exposure of the treason against the people, are harassed by government agencies such as the EPA, OSHA, the IRS, and others, forcing them into financial strain or bankruptcy. They have been completely successful in preventing most Americans from learning the things you have read in this article.

However, in spite of their control of information, they realize many citizens are learning the truth. (There are several millions of Americans who now know the truth including former congressmen, former revenue agents, ministers, businessmen, and many others).

Therefore, to prevent armed resistance to their plunder of America, they plan to register all firearms and eventually to disarm all citizens, in violation of the 2nd Amendment to the Constitution of the United States of America. A people armed cannot be enslaved. Therefore, they only want guns in the hands of their government police or military forces—hands that are already stained with blood from countless acts of gross negligence and overt homicide, both at home and abroad.

Spread the Word and Do Something to Fix Things.

The "almost hidden" conspirators in politics, religion, education, entertainment, and the news media are working for the banker-owned United States, in a banker-owned World under a banker-owned World Government! (This is what all the talk of a New World Order promoted by Presidents Bush and Clinton is all about.)

Unfair banking policies and taxes will continue to take a larger and larger part of the annual earning of the people and put them into the pockets of the bankers and their political agents. Increasing government regulations will prevent citizen protest and opposition to their control.

It is possible that your grandchildren will own neither home nor car, but will live in "government owned" apartments and ride to work in "government owned" buses (both paying interest to the bankers), and be allowed to keep just enough of their earnings to buy a minimum of food and clothing while their rulers wallow in luxury. In Asia and eastern Europe it is called "communism;" in America it is called "Democracy" and "Capitalism."

America will not shake off her Banker-controlled dictatorship as long as the people are ignorant of the hidden controllers. Banking concerns, which control most of the governments of the nations, and most sources of information, seem to have us completely within their grasp. They are afraid of only one thing: an awakened patriotic citizenry, armed with the truth, and with a trust in God for deliverance. This material has informed you about their iniquitous system. What you do with it is in your hands.

What You Can Do

Pray for America's release from this wicked money control, which is at the root of our debts and wars.

Send copies of this article to officials in your State and Local government, to school board members, principals, teachers, ministers, neighbors, etc. Ask them for their comments..

Write letters to elected or appointed officials. Write "letters- to-the-editor" to newspapers. Most small towns and suburban newspapers are not totally controlled, while most of the big city newspapers are.

Give or mail them out by the hundreds to awaken and educate other Americans to this fantastic plunder of the working people of America. The cost to you is VERY LITTLE compared to the BILLIONS in money and property being STOLEN from our people.

THIS IS NOT COPYRIGHTED, PRINT OUT A COPY AND SHARE IT!

http://www.justiceplus.org/ba